PASTORAL TALKS FOR SPECIAL OCCASIONS

Pastoral Talks for Special Occasions

Harold A. Buetow, PhD JD

ALBA·HOUSE alba house NEW·YORK

SOCIETY OF ST. PAUL, 2187 VICTORY BLVD., STATEN ISLAND, NEW YORK 10314

Library of Congress Cataloging-in-Publication Data

Buetow, Harold A.
  Pastoral talks for special occasions / Harold A. Buetow.
       p.   cm.
     ISBN 0-8189-0700-2
     1. Occasional sermons. 2. Catholic Church — Sermons. 3. Sermons,
  American.   I. Title.
  BX1756.B826P37   1994
  252'.02 — dc20   94-23339
                                                      CIP

Produced and designed in the United States of America by the
Fathers and Brothers of the Society of St. Paul,
2187 Victory Boulevard, Staten Island, New York 10314,
as part of their communications apostolate.

ISBN: 0-8189-0700-2

Printing Information:

Current Printing - first digit   1   2   3   4   5   6   7   8   9   10

Year of Current Printing - first year shown

1994   1995   1996   1997   1998   1999

Table of Contents

Introduction

This volume accompanies three volumes of homilies for the three cycles of the Church year: *God Still Speaks: Listen!* (Cycle A); *All Things Made New* (Cycle B); and *Ode to Joy* (Cycle C). The introductions to those volumes make lengthy observations, some of which may be valuable to the use of this work.

To list those who helped with this work would require a whole volume. They know who they are. To them I gratefully dedicate this book.

Biblical Abbreviations

OLD TESTAMENT

Genesis	Gn	Nehemiah	Ne	Baruch	Ba
Exodus	Ex	Tobit	Tb	Ezekiel	Ezk
Leviticus	Lv	Judith	Jdt	Daniel	Dn
Numbers	Nb	Esther	Est	Hosea	Ho
Deuteronomy	Dt	1 Maccabees	1 M	Joel	Jl
Joshua	Jos	2 Maccabees	2 M	Amos	Am
Judges	Jg	Job	Jb	Obadiah	Ob
Ruth	Rt	Psalms	Ps	Jonah	Jon
1 Samuel	1 S	Proverbs	Pr	Micah	Mi
2 Samuel	2 S	Ecclesiastes	Ec	Nahum	Na
1 Kings	1 K	Song of Songs	Sg	Habakkuk	Hab
2 Kings	2 K	Wisdom	Ws	Zephaniah	Zp
1 Chronicles	1 Ch	Sirach	Si	Haggai	Hg
2 Chronicles	2 Ch	Isaiah	Is	Malachi	Ml
Ezra	Ezr	Jeremiah	Jr	Zechariah	Zc
		Lamentations	Lm		

NEW TESTAMENT

Matthew	Mt	Ephesians	Ep	Hebrews	Heb
Mark	Mk	Philippians	Ph	James	Jm
Luke	Lk	Colossians	Col	1 Peter	1 P
John	Jn	1 Thessalonians	1 Th	2 Peter	2 P
Acts	Ac	2 Thessalonians	2 Th	1 John	1 Jn
Romans	Rm	1 Timothy	1 Tm	2 John	2 Jn
1 Corinthians	1 Cor	2 Timothy	2 Tm	3 John	3 Jn
2 Corinthians	2 Cor	Titus	Tt	Jude	Jude
Galatians	Gal	Philemon	Phm	Revelation	Rv

PASTORAL TALKS FOR SPECIAL OCCASIONS

BAPTISM

Gn 2:7-9; 3:1-7   Rm 5:12-19   Jn 3:1-6

Little Joey came home from school, jumped into his father's lap, and asked: "Where did I come from?" Dad cleared his throat and attempted a simple — but complete — sex answer to his son's question. By the time his dad finished, Joey was slightly fidgeting. "Well," he said, "I just wondered because Jeannie said she came from Detroit."

That misunderstanding was rather like the misunderstanding between Jesus and a leading Jew named Nicodemus. Jesus said that anyone not born from above cannot see the kingdom of God. Naturally, Nicodemus was puzzled. He asked if a grown man could really go back into his mother's womb and be born again. Obviously, that's not possible. The mother goes through great pain to give birth to a baby, and surely doesn't want the process reversed.

The first thing parents do almost without thinking right after their babies are born is to start showing their love for them. They kiss them, hug them, feed them. As they do so, they're helping their child to grow into a mature and loving adult. When parents smile at their baby, in many ways it brings the baby to life: the baby starts to chuckle and to wriggle with happiness. If these signs of love are missing — if a parent starves a baby of love — the child grows up not only unloved but often unlovable.

No child is just its mother's and father's. It's also *God's* child. And he, too, took great pains — even to dying on the cross — to show us how much he loves His children. To show His love, God gave us an ongoing sign. That sign is baptism. God's smile first comes in baptism. It's a sign that we're precious to our heavenly Father. And that's *really* a rebirth.

Although in the early days of the Church most baptisms were of adult converts, the most common form of baptism today is infant baptism. Because infant mortality is no longer a serious concern, there's no need to baptize a few days after birth. In an emergency, of course, anyone can be baptized outside of church by a priest,

1

obstetrician, nurse, friend, or stranger, as long as the person pours clean water on the person, at the same time says, "I baptize you in the name of the Father, and of the Son, and of the Holy Spirit," and has the intention of doing what Jesus and his Church want done.

Inasmuch as baptism is a once-in-a-lifetime event, it can't be repeated. If an emergency baptism has taken place, however, and the baby lives, it's advisable that the parents bring the baby to the church to share in the prayers and blessings which are part of the regular baptismal ceremony (informing the priest of the emergency baptism).

In view of the commitments made at baptism, some ask if people should rather be baptized only when they're old enough to understand what's happening and make up their own mind. But because parents love their children, they want to pass on what they value most. They try to communicate their love of nature or of books, their fondest memories, their hopes and dreams. Parents to whom Catholic faith is important naturally want to give their children a chance to share that faith. Faith can't be forced on anyone, of course, and when their children grow up they will make their own choice — either to live that faith freely or to find some other focus for their lives.

Ordinarily, baptism includes two special persons in addition to the parents: the godparents. In the early days, these were the sponsors who vouched for the faith of the person to be baptized. When infant baptism became the rule, godparents were usually close relatives who promised to take the child into their home and raise him or her in the faith if the parents died — an event that was not uncommon before modern medicine. Today, godparents are usually relatives or friends whose faith can help serve as a good example to the child as he or she is growing up.

Parents and godparents are both important. It's our firm Catholic belief that the sacrament of baptism expresses the wonderful gift of God by which we're "made holy," and become "children of God" and "temples of the Holy Spirit." We must take care, however, not to restrict God's gift to one single moment (the pouring of water) or overlook that part of the sacrament that is our lifelong response to God's gift. It isn't magic!

The ritual of baptism does not bring God's love into being as if that love didn't exist before the ceremony. Baptism is the Church's way of celebrating and enacting the embrace of God who first loved us from the moment of our conception. We have to continue what was begun at baptism, and bring the child up in the faith. That means teaching prayers, talking about Jesus, attending Mass together, and giving good moral training by word and example.

That's why children of non-practicing Catholics or non-Catholics may not be baptized in the Roman Catholic Church. There must be some serious commitment to Catholic education and training. It makes little sense to initiate children into the Roman Catholic Church unless there's a commitment to living the mission of the Church.

The *Rite of Baptism for Children* emphasizes the importance of faithfulness on the part of parents when it says to them that in asking to have their children baptized, "you are accepting the responsibility of training them in the practice of the faith." That word *practice* is crucial. It calls for Christian modeling on the part of parents.

Children first learn to be Christian by *experiencing* Christianity at home. The home prepares children for the local and world Church. It's in the home, the "domestic church," that children first learn the basic trust which is the foundation of faith. Parents, after all, are the primary and principal educators. The way parents love, the way they relate as a couple, and the way they live their beliefs will all contribute to their child's experience of what it means to be a Christian.

The ceremony begins with the minister of the sacrament — priest or deacon — giving a genial greeting and warm welcome on behalf of the Christian community (the Church) to the baby and its family. To invite the faith community to join in the celebration and to participate actively is proper. For one thing, a baby's baptism is a time for joy because the sacrament makes the baby a child of God. For another thing, baptism, being a birth into the Christian community, is by its nature a community event. It's the community, after all, who is journeying with them, providing models for them, supporting them, and nourishing them. Parents should invite, at the very least, relatives, friends, and neighbors to participate in the baptismal liturgy.

When possible, the welcome takes place at the door of the church, because baptism is the entry into the Church. The priest or deacon who is to do the baptizing asks what name the parents have chosen for their baby. Because names are important, the name should be one associated with Christian tradition. (Let's make believe that the minister is a priest, and that he's baptizing a boy named Peter.)

The priest then asks whether the parents accept the responsibility of bringing up their child in the practice of the faith. After their affirmative answer, along with the parents and godparents he traces the sign of the cross on baby Peter's forehead. A sign on something shows its origins or ownership. The sign of the cross is the mark of Christians, for Jesus died on the cross; it's a sign that this child belongs to Christ.

After an appropriate reading from Scripture and a few words of comment on it from the priest, the group offers prayers for Peter and his family to the saints in heaven. The baptism thus becomes a gathering of the entire family of the Church.

The parents and godparents then present Peter for baptism. The priest says a prayer of exorcism and rubs the oil of catechumens on Peter's breast — a reminder of the days when all those who were presented for baptism were *catechumens*, from a Greek word meaning "to be instructed." The oil reinforces the prayer that the baby be delivered from every evil.

Moving to the baptismal font, the priest recites over the water a prayer that reminds everyone present of the significance of water and its relation to baptism. In the entire ceremony, the water is the central symbol. Water brings both death and life. Hurricanes and floods bring death and destruction. Gentle rains and flowing rivers, on the other hand, bring life and rebirth, regenerating the parched earth and giving us refreshment. Water is a symbol of life: without water, there would be no life. Water also makes us clean.

Water is also an important symbol from the Bible. Our initiation process begins with water just as the beginning of creation portrayed in the very first pages of Scripture began with water — chaotic waters that were put into order by the Spirit hovering over them. Consider, too, the flood waters of Noah's day and the saving waters of the Red Sea parted by Moses. Those waters of the Red Sea opened the way for the Israelites to pass from slavery to freedom.

The Hebrews later crossed one more body of water — the river Jordan — to pass into the Promised Land. John the Baptizer baptized in the Jordan River, symbolizing that the baptized were to leave the slavery of sin for the freedom of a new Promised Land. And Jesus began his ministerial journey by being baptized in the Jordan.

Then there are the references to fruitful, life-giving waters offered by the prophets. For example, speaking for Yahweh, Ezekiel announced: "I will sprinkle clean water on you and. . . give you a new heart" (Ezk 37:24ff.), and Isaiah promised, "I will pour out my spirit on your children" (Is 44:3).

As John the Baptist said, Jesus would baptize with water and the Holy Spirit. Spirit is as strong a symbol of baptism as water. To be baptized is to open oneself to the Spirit of Jesus. To be baptized is to have the Spirit help us make order out of the chaos of the sinful world into which we're born. To be baptized is to be welcomed into the Church (the new Promised Land) and to be nourished there as we journey with each other and with Jesus in his ministry.

Before the baptism, however, the baptismal minister reminds the child and the parents and godparents of their baptismal responsibility by asking if they reject sin, the glamor of evil, and Satan, father of sin and prince of darkness. The parents and godparents respond "I do" to each of these questions. After asking again whether the adults want the child to be baptized in the faith they have just professed, the priest performs the essence of the ceremony: he pours water over the child's forehead in the name of the Father and of the Son and of the Holy Spirit. To do anything to someone "in the name of" another is to signify that one belongs to the person or persons named.

Baby Peter is now a Christian. Following an ancient custom, the crown of the baby's head is anointed with the Oil of Chrism. The word "chrism," like the word "Christ," means "the anointed one." Here it signifies one who is given a special work to do. Jesus had the work of uniting us to our heavenly Father; the baptized's special work is to live as a member of Christ's body, the Church.

Chrism's main ingredient is olive oil. Just as athletes used to rub themselves with olive oil to strengthen themselves for the contest ahead, here it's a sign of Christ's strengthening power. Its other ingredient is balsam, a sweet-smelling ointment symbolizing the pleasant odor of holiness. The chrism is a sign of sealing with the gifts of the Holy Spirit. The profession of faith which others make on behalf of the child at baptism will later be affirmed personally by the child in the sacrament of confirmation, when chrism will be used again.

The priest places on the child a small white garment, which is reminiscent of the white baptismal robe that the newly baptized in the early Church received. At the same time he says, "Peter, you have become a new creation, and have clothed yourself in Christ." The clean white clothes are a sign of innocence and the new life of resurrection, and will be referred to again at Peter's burial.

In the early Church, the newly initiated were expected to wear the white garment and keep it unsoiled for the fifty days of Easter. Today, in most cases, it's present only for the duration of the ritual and then is packed away with other family memorabilia. If there is a christening dress in the family, it would be good to use it. If there is none, the parents should consider making or decorating one.

The priest then takes the large Easter candle, which has been burning all during the ceremony, and holds it for one of the adults, saying, "Receive the light of Christ." The candle symbolizes Christ, the light of the world, who will shine on and through the child for life. The adult lights a baptismal candle from it for the child; its coming from the Easter candle reminds us of the flame of faith which comes from Jesus' resurrection. The priest says, "Parents and godparents, this light is entrusted to you to be kept burning brightly. This child of yours has been enlightened by Christ. He is to walk always as a child of the light." The parents might later decorate the candle with baptismal symbols, using acrylic paints or nail polish. If there are other children in the family, they can help.

Lastly, after all present recite the Lord's Prayer, the priest blesses the mother with the child in her arms, then the father and the entire assembly. This concludes the Rite of Baptism for Children.

It would be good if the parents were to keep the white garment, the candle, the prayers, and other symbols of the baptismal ceremony, as well as photos, to share with their child on the child's anniversary of baptism or birth. They serve as powerful reminders of the ongoing importance of the event. As time passes, the baptized might well ask what would be their answer for themselves to the questions answered at their baptism by their parents and godparents.

Most of the real business of baptism comes after the ceremony, with the living up to it. Its effects may be experienced every day: in the way we use our talents to aid and share with others; in the love we extend to family, friends, and — yes — strangers; in the way we live up to the commandments of God and His Church. We've been adopted as children of God. It's now our task to strengthen the bonds that bind Jesus' family in love.

FIRST HOLY COMMUNION

Ph 2:6-11   *Jn 1:1-5, 9-14, 16-18*

A beautiful story is told about a tree that gave and gave until it could give no more (Shel Silverstein, *The Giving Tree* [New York, NY: Harper & Row, 1964]). It goes something like this. Once there was a tree, and she loved a little boy. And every day the boy would come, and he would gather her leaves and make them into crowns and play king of the forest. He would climb up her trunk and swing from her branches and eat her apples. And the boy and the tree would play hide-and-go-seek. And when the boy was tired, he would sleep in her shade. And the boy loved the tree very much. And the tree was happy. But time went by. And the boy grew older. And the tree was often alone.

Then one day the boy came to the tree and the tree said, "Come, Boy, come and climb up my trunk and swing from my branches and eat apples and play in my shade and be happy." "I'm too big to climb and play," said the boy. "I want to buy things and have fun. I want some money. Can you give me some money?" "I'm sorry," said the tree, "but I have no money. I have only leaves and apples. Take my apples, Boy, and sell them in the city. Then you will have money and you will be happy."

And so the boy climbed up the tree and gathered her apples and carried them away to sell. And the tree was happy.

But the boy stayed away for a long time, and the tree was sad. And then one day the boy came back and the tree shook with joy and she said, "Come, Boy, climb up my trunk and swing from my branches and be happy."

"I'm too busy to climb trees," said the boy. "I want a house to keep me warm," he said. "I want a wife and I want children, and so I need a house. Can you give me a house?" "I have no house," said the tree. "The forest is my house, but you may cut off my branches and build a house. Then you will be happy." And so the boy cut off her branches and carried them away to build his house. And the tree was happy.

But the boy stayed away for a long time. And when he came back, the tree was so happy she could hardly speak. "Come, Boy," she whispered, "come and play." "I'm too old and sad to play," said the boy. "I want a boat that will take me far away from here. Can you give me a boat?

"Cut down my trunk and make a boat," said the tree. "Then you can sail away and be happy." And so the boy cut down her trunk and made a boat and sailed away. And the tree was happy — but not really.

And after a long time the boy came back again. "I am sorry, Boy," said the tree, "but I have nothing left to give you. My apples are gone." "My teeth are too weak for apples," said the boy. "My branches are gone," said the tree. "You cannot swing on them —" "I'm too old to swing on branches," said the boy. "My trunk is gone," said the tree. "You cannot climb —" "I'm too tired to climb," said the boy.

"I'm sorry," sighed the tree. "I wish that I could give you something, but I have nothing left. I'm just an old stump. I'm sorry. . . ." "I don't need very much now," said the boy, "just a quiet place to sit and rest. I'm very tired." "Well," said the tree, straightening herself up as much as she could, "well, an old stump *is* good for sitting and resting. Come, Boy, sit down. Sit down and rest." And the boy did. And the tree was happy.

Boys and girls, that tree gave everything she had. And that's the way it is with God and us. God in Jesus gave us everything he had, including his life. To remember him by, he gives us the sacrament called the Eucharist, which is what we receive in Holy Communion.

It's as though Jesus said to his followers, "Remember me, and all that I've said and done in your presence. Remember our times together. Remember my love. And I hope all of you will remember that *I* in turn love *you* so much that I've given all I have, my very life, for you."

The Eucharist is not only a memory, but a living contact with Jesus. His kind of presence here is *new* in the history of all the world. It isn't the physical presence that you sense as you do with your parents and your friends, but a special kind of presence called *sacramental*. He's really here, and he wants to be with us always. He wants to be giving.

He doesn't give us just a nice *taste*, as with a piece of candy or a cookie, but he gives us his presence, his companionship, and a whole way of life that's the best in the world.

In reacting to him, we're not to be like the boy who only took advantage of the tree. As a young boy, he played with her leaves to make believe he was king of the forest, swung from her branches, played hide-and-go-seek, and slept in her shade. The tree was very happy when the boy was there, and very lonely when he wasn't.

When the boy became bigger and wanted money, the tree told him to take her apples and sell them. The boy did, and that made the tree happy. When the boy became still bigger and wanted to get married, the tree gave him permission to cut off her branches, carry them away, and build a house. The boy did, and that, too, made the tree very happy. When the boy wanted a boat, the tree suggested that he cut down her trunk to build it. The boy did, and again that made the tree happy.

And when after a long time the boy came back again, the tree, now just a stump, was very sorry because she had nothing left to give him. But when the boy — now an old man — sat down on her stump to rest, the tree, which by now had given everything she had, was yet again very happy.

That's the way it is with us and God. God is the tree, and we're the little boy. God has given us many things, one of which is His presence in the Eucharist. You know how it is when you're alone and lonely, and you want someone to be there with you: your parents to mind you, your brothers or sisters to play with, or your friends to have fun with. When you come to Jesus in this Sacrament, you're never alone. He's here to be your friend, and to *give* to you.

With the Eucharist, God intends to bring together not only us with God, but us with one another. When as a family we have a meal at home together, we're drawn closer to one another by that sharing more than by anything else. When we provide hospitality to friends by way of a meal — or they for us — we have the chance for closeness that nothing else has. In the Eucharist, God is providing the same chance for us to be close to Him and to each other.

Everybody who receives Communion — those who are like us as well as those who are different, old people and young people, rich and poor — receive the same Lord. When you receive him here in our parish church, you must understand that Holy Communion more than anything else makes our parish one family with ourselves and with the entire human race.

God, through Jesus, is like the "Giving Tree." We shouldn't

be like the boy in the story, but like the tree, which is God, in being giving. This is the beginning of a new close relationship with Jesus. I pray that this friendship will grow stronger each time you receive Holy Communion. Remember that God's love is with you always. All he asks is that you love him in return!

EUCHARISTIC CELEBRATIONS
(Solemn Exposition, for example)
Ac 2:42; 4:32   *Jn 6*

When you get around to writing that first book, to assure its success make it a "how to": "How to Succeed in Marriage without Really Trying," for example, or "How Two Can Live as Cheaply as One," or "How to See Europe on Ten Dollars a Day." Statistics show that the public will make these best sellers.

So this will be a "how to" talk: How to fulfill the ideals, principles, and aspirations (voiced and unvoiced), of your spiritual life. The "how to," *par excellence*, is the Eucharist. This Sacrament so important to God, so excellent, so necessary to people, that God showed His planning over a long period of time. Although to God time is vertical — all time being present to Him at every moment — we think of God in the horizontal time sequence in which we live. For such an important matter as the Eucharist, God shows us in our time-life His great planning. He gives us a well-planned drama in four acts.

Act I, Scene 1 takes place about 1500 B.C. The Jews, long captive in Egypt, want to leave in order to be able to worship freely. Pharaoh Ramses II refuses Moses, so God sends 10 plagues: He changes all the waters into blood, and sends insects, cattle disease, boils, mid-day darkness, frogs, flies, hail, locusts, and lastly, death of the firstborn from the family of the Egyptian King to the lowest beasts. To prevent the death of firstborn Jews, they're instructed to put the blood of a lamb on their doorposts and to have their first meal to be called — in honor of the occasion — "Passover." This meal isn't to be left to chance: They're to fully consume the lamb, none of whose bones are to be broken, and the lamb is to be spotless. With it they're to eat unleavened bread, with wild lettuce.

In Scene 2, shortly later in front of a desert backdrop of sand and sky, we hear the mumblings of almost a half-million Jews for the fleshpots of Egypt. (Tintoretto's painting of this scene tells it all.) Because the Jews didn't have sufficient food for their journey, God had sent what was called manna from heaven, like dew. The people were to gather only enough for each day, except for the sixth day, when they were to gather enough for the seventh day, the Sabbath, as well. For a long time this constituted their only food, and they're now sick and tired of the monotony of its tastelessness.

Act II, Scene 1 takes place roughly 1532 years later. It's another Passover celebration. The Son of God had come about 30 years before at Beth-lehem ("house of bread"), and, like a good Jew, had gone to Jerusalem since his youth to celebrate this feast as the heavenly Father had dictated. Now, past the middle of his public ministry, he has just come from celebrating the Feast of Passover in Jerusalem. Many Passover pilgrims had followed him to Galilee. It's the new Moses, Jesus, with the new Pharaoh, Jewish and Roman officialdom. Jesus teaches them, and then — in the climax of this scene — he takes five loaves of bread and two fish, gives thanks, and distributes them to the people. There are more than 5,000 people, and there are twelve basketsful left over!

In Scene 2, after Jesus and Peter had walked on water (another miracle of *power*), and some miraculous cures at Genesareth, at Capernaum Jesus teaches about the Eucharist. He speaks of the fulfillment of figures that the manna and multiplied loaves had been. Despite the fact that the people were there in the first place because they'd seen the multiplication of the loaves and fish, everybody but Jesus' Apostles ask who could be expected to believe all this, and they all leave.

Act III takes place one year later, at the very next Passover meal, which is to be Jesus' last supper, because it happens right before he died. Among the many things dear to his heart that Jesus says to his Apostles is to tell them how much he had longed to share this paschal meal with them before his passion. At one and the same time he establishes the Sacrifice of the Mass (reminiscent of the sacrifice of the first lamb in Egypt in Act I, Scene 1), and the Sacrament of the Eucharist (the words of which are reminiscent of the same words he had used in the multiplication of the loaves).

Act IV has been taking place ever since. We need this fourth act, because we need Jesus. A poet can peer into the autumn leaves, watch a sunset, listen to a hummingbird and cry out, "It is the Lord!" — but most of us are not poet enough. With all kinds of reverses and pain, we need and want more than his footprints in creation — we want Jesus of Nazareth.

Part of Act IV takes place in Corinth, Greece, about AD 57, when, after Mass, an elderly man reads, "And the bread that we break, is it not the partaking of the body of the Lord? Because the bread is one, we, though many, are one body, all of us who partake of the one bread" (1 Cor 10:17). Another part of this act takes place at Rome in the early twentieth century, when Pope Pius X tells all the faithful that the primary purpose of the Eucharist is not that the honor and reverence due to our Lord may be safeguarded, or that it may serve as a reward of virtue bestowed on the recipients — but that in this great sacrament, Jesus feeds his people and strengthens them in holiness, so that the human family may come to walk in one communion of love. As St. Augustine said, this is a sacrament of personal sanctification, a sign of unity, and a bond of love. And today, not unlike the people in Act II Scene 2, we ask questions about Jesus' presence in the Eucharist.

Jesus' Real Presence in the Eucharist has always been a difficulty. It's contrary to our *senses*, to our *science*, and to our *experience*. Our *senses* indicate that what looks like bread is bread, and what looks like wine is wine. Our *science* discovers only the texture, shape, and composition of material things; there's no way that we can look at a Host under a microscope and find a tiny Jesus. Our *experience* shows us that we know reality by what we sense: There's nothing in the mind which was not somehow first in the senses. Nevertheless, appearances are one thing, reality another.

Jesus is truly present in the Eucharist, because the Son of God told us so. His presence in the Eucharist isn't a "physical" presence, a "moral" presence, or a "spiritual" presence, but a *sacramental* presence.

Why does Jesus become present in the Eucharist *at all*? Well, being in love with us, he wanted to *stay with us*. We can certainly understand that from our sympathy for those who love and are separated. Jesus, too, knew the pain of separation. When, for example, at the little town of Naim he saw a dead man being carried to the cemetery — a young man who was the only child of a widow — his sympathy was enough to bring the young man back to life. He did the same with his beloved Lazarus, for the sake of his sisters. He has a loving sympathy for all of us, too, telling us that all who work and have burdens to bear are to come to him, and he will refresh us (Mt 11:28).

So, being our friend, Jesus wants to *be united with us*. What's more, in a too-forgotten aspect of the Eucharist, he wants to give us the means to *unite us with one another* — that we become companions (from the Latin *cum* and *panis*): literally "bread-sharers." The people of the early Church, putting Jesus' wishes into practice, were of one mind and one heart together (Ac 2:42; 4:32). He hoped that, just as many grains of wheat go into one host, and the juice of many grapes into the wine, so can many people become one in the Eucharist.

Some people ask another question: Why does the Church continue to revere Jesus' presence under the eucharistic species? One answer is that the Church does so to continue the work of salvation: When we pray to our Lord present in the sacramental species, we're praying to the savior who handed over his body and shed his blood in order to save us from our sins. A second answer is that the Eucharist is to continue the work of praise: As God's beloved people, we're expected to give this praise in liturgy, in personal and family prayer, and in our daily lives. With Jesus we praise the Father.

Also, it's in order to call us to personal prayer: Christians need to spend time in private as well as public prayer. Then, too, it's to call us to conversion: the Lord Jesus came to save his people from their sins at all times, and a visit to the Blessed Sacrament provides us with the opportunity of examining our life in the light of God's will.

Still another question that might be asked is: Why does Jesus come to us in *this way*? "This way" is a presence not known anywhere else in the universe: His presence here is sacramental. Many other ways are possible. He could, for example, have come in all his divine glory. But think about that! The only occasion when Jesus revealed the glory of his kingly person was at his Transfiguration, and the Apostle Peter who was there could find no words but foolish ones to express his terror (Mk 9:5). And if Jesus came in pomp and circumstance, he would be making faith and love so easy that there would be no telling our proper motives.

Christ not only *is* in the Eucharist, but *acts* there. Some ways are personal, as in giving a special preserving influence against the fires of passion, and providing spiritual joy and comfort. Others are theological, such as making a soul more pleasing to God, giving sacramental grace, washing us clean of venial sin, removing some of the temporal punishment due to sin, and providing a greater degree of glory for all eternity.

So, the reception of Holy Communion is not *only* a question of *worthiness* — we do pray, "Lord, I am not worthy" — but of *need*. Jesus said, "Blessed are the pure of heart, for they shall see God," because all sin blinds the eyes of faith. So if we want to see God's vision of everything, we recognize the need for *frequent* reception of the Eucharist. Those who looked at the early Christians opined that they would know they are Christians by the way they love. The Eucharist is a community celebration in which, in the words of the song, we come *together* — to celebrate, to remember, to believe.

RELIGIOUS EDUCATION
1 K 3:11-14   Ps 119:9-14   1 Cor 2:1-10   Mt 5:13-16

Imagine that a catastrophe has occurred that's so great that our knowledge of the natural sciences is completely gone: physicists are killed, books destroyed, laboratories sacked. All that's left are fragments, bits and pieces of theories, experimental equipment whose use has been forgotten, half-chapters of books, single pages from articles. Some of the scientific terminology survives, but its meaning is largely lost.

This is what has in fact happened to our understanding of the language of religion. People continue to use many of its key expressions, but have largely, if not entirely, lost their comprehension of many aspects of religion. Charity now typically means patronage of the poor by the well-off. Love means what goes on between movie stars, off and on screen. Service equals unpleasant menial duties. Grace is a girl's name. Redemption is the process by which you get value for your stamps. Gospel is slang for truth. The supernatural is that which has to do with hobgoblins and spooks. Faith is believing what's not so.

This is sad. Good people who are interested in religious education are sometimes tempted to wonder about the value of their work because the current climate of our society has gone from true religion to civil religion to what is a civil exclusion of religion. And the elimination of religion from political discourse reduces God to a sort of hobby.

Religion in personal development is important. Can people be said to have become the best they can be, without religion? If your answer is affirmative, is it sufficient to teach *about* religion, or is *witness* necessary? In our time, the number of those who say we don't need religion is legion. Many of them are suave, polished, and intelligent people. Anyone wishing to oppose them must be similarly educated, polished, and intelligent. And anyone wishing to reach modern youth had better be prepared to defend the presence and advantageousness, if any there be, of religion.

Many academic disciplines give high marks to the advantages of religion in personal formation. Take *Philosophy*, for example, where the leading philosophy of our day, Positivism, is opposed to religious education. Auguste Comte, a Frenchman who is chiefly responsible for Positivism, posited the "Law of the Three Stages."

Comte said that the intellectual advancement of humankind progressed in three stages. This traced the development of the individual as well. The first, and least attractive, is the theological. This stage is wide open to all kinds of superstition. The second stage is the metaphysical, in which the major methodology is philosophical reasoning. The third, last, and best stage is the scientific — or, as Comte called it, *le vie positive*. The resulting predispositions of this philosophy are subjectivism, secularism, materialism, and naturalism.

Greater and greater numbers of modern philosophers see this, and revert to those philosophies which are more realistic in their approach, idealistic in their comprehensiveness, and existential in their purview. There's a great need for religious educators of immense depth here!

The second discipline which proves the need for religion in education is *History*. The history of the peoples of the East — about half of the world's population — shows a dominance of spirituality and mysticism. To fly low over countries like Burma (now Myanmar) is to see religious temple after temple. To visit other countries of the East — Thailand, Japan, China — is to be reverently shown their places of worship.

In the history of the West, religions have made innumerable contributions. The cathedrals, monuments, saints, and the arts, are obvious. But many of religion's contributions to the history of the West are unmeasurable. The spiritual life of many people, not only saints, is evident. Religion has brought about the liberation of many. Religion has provided insights that have carried untold people through difficult times. Religion has resulted in moral transformation that has saved multitudes. And it has provided a vision that has benefited the West.

Despite religion's contributions to the West, religious people have allowed historical nomenclature to get away from them. The tragedy of allowing terminology to get away was perceived by Winston Churchill, who said: "He who defines the terms controls the argument."

The word "Enlightenment," for example, which as a period means everything opposed to a Christian point of view, is an attractive name. We've ceded the term "Dark Ages" (which were in many ways not so dark, and which didn't last for too many ages) to be ascribed to some ages of faith. The Roman Catholic Church used the term "Modernism" to condemn a heresy, at a time when most people want to be called "modern."

A knowledge of the history of the United States makes one proud of religion. Our founding documents and symbols — the Mayflower Compact, the Liberty Bell, the Declaration of Independence, the American Seal, the Northwest Ordinance, declarations of our First President and other presidents, our National Anthem, the motto on our coins, our Constitution — all point to the religious underpinnings of our country.

Shibboleths like "the Separation of Church and State" have attempted to evade these facts but, when these items are understood in context, they support rather than deflect the importance of religion in sustaining democracy in the United States of America. Unfair books, biased texts, and violence against religion have unfortunately been part of the low road of our country.

The Bill of Right's First Amendment to our Constitution opted for the disestablishment of churches, not the separation of the people or their government from religion. No one with any knowledge of history would opt for an established church. And a knowledge of history chooses a wall of separation between church and state, at the same time realizing that this is for the protection of religion from the state and not the other way around, and asking how high the wall and with how many windows and doors.

Anthropology, another modern science, furthers the cause of providing religion in education. When this science was young — toward the end of the nineteenth century — anthropologists who visited pre-literate cultures returned with a glorious picture of happy primitives unhampered by religion. They later learned that their findings were false: In their research questionnaires they used the word "religion," which word the pre-literates didn't have in their vocabulary. The truth was that the pre-literates were *never* without religion. In fact, the pre-literates made no distinction between the secular and the sacred, both being intertwined in their entire living. In truth, the sacred and the secular are *never* completely separate, anywhere, with pre-literates or anyone else.

Another modern science which furthers the cause of providing religion in education is *Sociology*. Sociologists of religion posit two main theories. The first is the Functional Theory, which looks at institutions from the viewpoint of the purpose they serve in society. Religion very definitely serves functions in society, particularly as pertaining to optimal personal development. In what they call the "uncertainty context" — those conditions of life like airplane rides, facing crime, and putting up with obnoxious neighbors — religion is a help. In what they call the "impossibility context" — such unavoidable situations as suffering, death, and hurt — religion serves as a comfort. The Functional Theory finds socialization to be another area helped by religion.

Because no sane person can possibly agree with all that's taking place in society today, Sociology posits another theory, appropriately called the Conflict Theory. This is significant for religion because it deals with such areas as prophetism and class conflict. Prophetism is that area in which some courageous reli- giously-motivated persons — in ancient times called "prophets" — will speak up for God, or what they think is right, against what they perceive is wrong with society. In the class conflict aspect of this theory, sociologists have found the society's lower classes looking to religion for salvation, the upper classes for legitimation, and the middle classes for rational and ethical dimensions to their lives.

A final modern science that has findings about religion is *Psychology*. Many psychological theories are in rapport with the idea that religion furthers the best development of the person. Such are the notions of Gordon Allport, Gabriel Marcel, and others.

Some of the current psychological theories, though, result in the use of what's called the "values clarification" process. The theory means that teachers be careful not to present any values of their own, but only to clarify whatever values come from the students. This often results in what is called "convergence to the mean."

One example of that is to ask the students what they do about premarital sex. As a personification of one extreme of possible answers is Gloves Gladys, who on a date never allows a boy to come too close. The other end of the spectrum is represented by Mattress Millie, who metaphorically carries a mattress wherever she goes and allows whatever comes to happen. Virginal Virginia, a young student contemplating whom to imitate, converges to the mean, which means she winds up somewhere in the middle. This means that, contrary to her initial wishes, she sometimes would allow premarital sex, sometimes not.

These observations from all these sciences enable us to make several conclusions and applications. We should be taking seriously the re-insertion of religion into many areas where they're now absent. One is teacher preparation, in which these highly-important teacher-candidates should be familiarized in greater detail about the place of religion in people's lives. Another is parental obligations. In a time when their children are greatly influenced by media hostile or indifferent to religion, and possibly have companions who can lead them astray, wouldn't parents be motivated by religion to emphasize their children's duties and responsibilities as well as their desire for more and more freedom? In a time when children cry that "everybody else is doing it," wouldn't a firm parental background in religion encourage them to stand firm to solid principles, even if that means going against the tide?

In our current proliferation of crime, could religion help to hold back the statistics, even though admittedly the causes of crime are many? In our current moral vacuousness, with many people showing an alarming lack of conscience, couldn't religious instruction put them straight? If religion has the benefit that all the sciences seem to indicate, don't church-affiliated schools make a contribution to the national interest such that they should be given enough financial assistance to enable them to exist? In government schools, shouldn't more attention be given to religion in their curriculum? Couldn't they at least give some attention to common religious beliefs and codes of ethics?

The truth is that religion and education, or personal development, are essential to each other. By definition, both address the ultimate nature of reality. Both, to be true to themselves, deal with the meaning of the good person, the good life, and the good society. Religious educators, if ever assailed by low morale, should remember the scientific findings of the importance of their work and conduct their classes with assurance, aliveness, and excitement.

RECONCILIATION: CHILDREN

1 Jn 2:1-2   *Lk 15:1-7*

A beautiful story (Teddi Doleski, *The Hurt* [New York: Paulist Press, 1983]) tells of the young boys Justin and Gabriel, who were friends. They played together almost every day. One day Gabriel got mad at Justin. He said, "Justin, you are a pig-faced punk." Justin didn't know what to say. He walked away from Gabriel and went into his own house.

Then a strange thing happened. Hurt entered his room and his life. This Hurt was like a big round stone, all cold and hard. It seemed he could hold it in his hand and feel the hardness.

Justin didn't tell anybody how he felt. Gabriel isn't my friend anymore, he thought. In his room, the Hurt grew bigger. I'll never talk to Gabriel again, he thought. I'll just stay here in my own room by myself. The Hurt grew even bigger.

Justin heard Daddy call him. He was happy that Daddy was home, and ran out to see him. Daddy said, "Justin, I'm very disappointed in you. You tracked mud into the house. Just look at the floor."

Justin went back to his room. Daddy didn't even notice that I put away my hat, he thought. Daddy only notices the bad things I do. The Hurt was huge now. It was bigger than Justin.

Each day after that, Justin saved up all his bad feelings and gave them to the Hurt. The Hurt grew bigger and bigger. Justin didn't really like the Hurt. It wasn't as much fun as Gabriel. But the Hurt was dependable. Justin didn't have to worry that it would be nice one day and mean the next. It was always the same, only bigger.

On Saturdays, Daddy helped Justin clean his room. They put away all the toys and folded the clothes. They dusted and ran the vacuum cleaner and put clean sheets on the bed. But this Saturday, Justin said, "I'll clean my room by myself, Daddy." "OK," said Daddy. "I guess you're getting to be a big boy now. You don't need any help."

Justin didn't feel very big. He felt small. But he didn't want Daddy to come into his room and see the Hurt. It was enormous now. There was hardly even room for Justin. He felt lonely cleaning the room by himself.

That night as Justin slept, he felt the hard cold Hurt pushing against him. When he awoke, he said, "My bed isn't snug anymore. That Hurt is ruining everything. Pretty soon it will be so big that there won't be room for me in here. Then there won't be room for me in the house. Then there won't be room for me in the world. The Hurt will take up all the space." Justin got scared.

"Daddy," Justin said. Daddy was making breakfast in the kitchen. "Daddy, a big Hurt came to live in my room, and it's taking up all the space."

"Where did it come from?" Daddy asked. "It came from Gabriel calling me a bad name." "What name?" asked Daddy. "A pig-faced punk," said Justin. Saying the bad name out loud made him feel better. "I understand why you were hurt," said Daddy. "Did you tell Gabriel how you felt?" "No," said Justin. "I just came home."

Daddy sat down, and Justin climbed into his lap. "Sometimes our friends make us feel very bad," said Daddy. "And other times they make us feel good." "Gabriel made me feel good when I had chicken pox," said Justin. "He drew me a funny picture that made me laugh." "Friends are good to have," said Daddy.

"But what will I do with the Hurt?" asked Justin. "You'll have to let it go," Daddy said. "It's too big to get out of my room now," said Justin. "When you're ready to let it go, it will be small enough."

When Justin went back to his room, the Hurt was a little smaller. "I don't want you here anymore, Hurt," Justin said. "You don't make a very good friend." The Hurt grew even smaller.

Justin went outside to help Daddy wash the car. He said, "Daddy, it hurt my feelings when you saw the mud I tracked in but you didn't see the hat I put away." "I'm sorry," said Daddy. "You are very responsible about putting your things away. Sometimes I forget to tell you I'm proud of you. You're a fine little boy, and I'm glad you're my son."

Justin felt all sunshiny inside. He wanted to make that car glisten. Working with Daddy was fun.

That night at bedtime, Justin opened the window. He pushed the Hurt to the window and left it there. Then he went to bed. The bed felt warm and cozy. In the morning the Hurt was gone. Justin closed the window.

That day Justin went to Gabriel's house. "Do you want to play?" He asked. "OK," said Gabriel. From then on, they played together almost every day. If Gabriel got mad and called Justin a pig-faced punk, Justin called Gabriel a crooked-eyed creep. They both laughed and went back to their playing.

Or sometimes, Justin would say, "Gabriel, I don't like it when you call me names." Gabriel would say, "I'm sorry." And Justin would say, "I forgive you." Then they would play some more. There were times when something bad would happen, and the Hurt would come back. But Justin didn't hide it. And he always let it go before it got big.

And that, boys and girls, is how we ought to act with the hurt that's in us when things aren't right with ourselves, with other people, and with God. We're all sons and daughters of God. God, who loves each and every one of us very much, wants us His children to be like Him by being good to each other, so that we may all live happily together.

But we don't always do what God wants. We say, "I'm going to do as I please." That's what we call sin. When we sin, that hurt puts us further away from God. And sin brings us further and further away from other people, too. God loves us so much that He's made it easy for us to get rid of our hurt by giving us what is called the sacrament of penance, or reconciliation, or confession. There we can say, "I'm sorry."

To find out how big the hurt is, and how much we have to be reconciled, we look into ourselves to see what we may have done wrong. Toward God, have I behaved as a child of His should? Have I given trouble to my parents or teachers? Have I quarreled with others and called them names? Have I been lazy at home or in school? Have I been helpful to my parents, my brothers, and my sisters? Have I thought too much of myself? Have I told lies? Have I used my chances to do good to others?

It's that quiz which prepares us for those familiar words that the priest says in the beginning of Mass: "Dear brothers and sisters, in order to prepare ourselves to celebrate these sacred mysteries (of God's forgiving love) let's call to mind our sins" (that is, let's call to mind the lovelessness for which we must be forgiven).

After finding all our faults, we come to our heavenly Father in confession and say: "Father, I'm sorry for all my sins: for what I have done and for what I have failed to do. I will sincerely try to do better, especially with my worst failings. Please help me to walk by your light."

God our heavenly Father, you see, is always seeking us out when we walk away from the path of goodness. When we've caused hurt, He's always ready to forgive.

Do you remember the story of Jesus, when he was accused of welcoming sinners and eating with them (Lk 15:1-7)? He told the story of shepherds out in the fields. He said that if a good shepherd has a hundred sheep and lost one of them, he leaves the ninety-nine to search for the lost one until he finds it. Then, when he finds it, he puts it on his shoulders, carries it home, and invites his friends and neighbors to rejoice with him. Jesus said that God is like that. He rejoices that much over one sinner who gets himself or herself reconciled.

When we're made clean of the hurt inside ourselves, and the hurt we've caused God and other people, we're so pure that we're happy all over. Do you remember the Bible story of the two disciples walking to the town of Emmaus after Jesus was crucified? They were feeling hurt over all the bad things that had happened to Jesus. Then a stranger joined them and explained that Jesus had to die in order to be able to rise again. When they finally recognized that the stranger was the risen Jesus, they felt good all over. When we don't hurt anymore, we feel good all over, too, and we recognize Jesus wherever he is: in ourselves, in other people, in all the nice things in our life, and in Holy Communion.

RECONCILIATION: ADULTS

Ezk 18:21-23   *Rm 13:8-14*   *Lk 7:36-50*

On a fine summer day in 1911, an unmarried woman of 22 turned her seven-month-old child over to the Hospice for Welfare Children in Paris. The child's name was Jean Genet. Twenty-four hours later he was placed with a foster family. At thirteen he was sent to vocational school. Within ten days he was a runaway, and within two years he was in a boys' penitentiary. At nineteen he joined the army to get out of prison, and when he became a deserter seven years later, he became a beggar, pickpocket, small-time criminal, and male prostitute all across Europe. He also wrote, and one critic pronounced him "rotten with genius." A literary trendsetter, Jean Cocteau, gave him sound advice. "You're a bad thief: You get caught," Cocteau told him. "But you're a good writer."

From then on to his death in 1986, Genet was a novelist, poet, and dramatist, often compared with the greatest, like Proust. Of him it was written that he was an extraordinary mixture of opposites:

thief and philanthropist, convict and poet, self-taught and creative genius, pervert and moralist, prostitute and political activist, agnostic and mystic. Jean-Paul Sartre dubbed him St. Genet, since Genet defined saintliness as putting pain to good use.

Although the contrasts within us are perhaps not as extreme as with Genet, everyone who has ever lived (except the Lord and his mother) contains contrasts between goodness and sin. Pope Pius XII declared that the sin of our century is the loss of the sense of sin. The secularism of our age unfortunately contributes to that loss.

Those who acknowledge the existence of sin throughout history have tried various ways to rid themselves of it. In the Judeo part of our Judeo-Christian tradition, one of the ways of getting rid of sin was the scapegoat — the goat with the people's sins attached to it being driven into the desert. That's not entirely inappropriate: In the goat, with its long face like a carnival devil's mask and its yellow, green-flecked eyes unblinking, they saw the eyes of the evil one. And at the Jewish New Year (Rosh Hashanah) there's a tradition of *tashlich*, going to the nearest shore and hurling one's sins on a piece of paper into the water. This, too, is fitting, considering the breadth and depth of the sea as representing God's mercy.

Jesus was aware of those ways of meeting people's need to get rid of sin. He knew, too, that in the Psalms and in the preaching of the Prophets, the name *merciful* is perhaps the one most often given to God. And when he saw crowds of people he had pity on them. Why pity? That's certainly not what we feel as we look into the faces of a crowd in a football stadium or on Fifth Avenue. Jesus sees something we don't see: the crowd's anxiety and helplessness. Anxious and helpless over what? The story of Zacchaeus (Lk 19) reveals an anxiety over *guilt*. Jesus' resurrection miracles were always a response to an anxiety over *death*. Jesus' experience with the Samaritan woman (Jn 4) revealed a deep-seated anxiety over her inability to quench her thirst for *love*.

Jesus addresses his Good News to all who might ever experience the same anxieties over guilt (of the past), lovelessness (in the present), and death (in the future). Regarding guilt over the past, he says: "Your sins are forgiven" (Mt 9:2, 5); regarding lovelessness in the present: "Whoever drinks of the water I shall give him will never thirst" (Jn 4:14); regarding death in the future: "I will raise you from the dead" (Jn 6:50f., 58).

God is a God of love and mercy, yes, but he's no "patsy." He's a God also of justice and judgment. Jesus cleanses the Temple with a whip to the moneychangers; he leaves Nazareth and can work no miracles there because of its lack of faith; he says it would be better for one who scandalizes a child to be drowned with a millstone around his neck; he issues many "woes" to the wicked; he speaks of the narrow gate to the Kingdom; he gives many parables in which he condemns evil people; he denounces the attitudes and conduct of the Pharisees; he speaks often of the need for repentance.

And in the context of both God's mercy and justice Jesus had a better idea than those that preceded him to get rid of sin. It's a special sacrament (see Jn 20:21-23); the Church has faithfully celebrated this sacrament throughout the centuries — in varying ways, but retaining its essential elements. Depending on which aspect you want to emphasize, it's been variously called the Sacrament of Confession, or of Penance, or of Reconciliation. This sacrament is one of the ways we've effectively been able to work for the creation of what Pope Paul VI called the "civilization of love."

Briefly, what's required to receive this sacrament are three virtues: honesty, persistence, and exultation. With regard to *honesty*, to acknowledge one's sinfulness is the essential first step in returning to God. This was the experience of King David who, having done what was evil in the eyes of the Lord (2 S 11-12), exclaimed that his sin was ever before him (Cf. Ps 50 [51]:3f.).

Concerning *persistence*, we ask out of need and with great expectation, as in Jesus' parables of the resolute friend (Lk 11:5-13) and the unrelenting widow with the unscrupulous judge (Lk 18:1-8). As for *exultation*, it's to persons who are willing to acknowledge their sinful choices that the consoling words of Jesus are addressed: "He who humbles himself will be exalted" (Lk 18:14). What a promise! We *will be* exalted if we will allow ourselves to experience the supreme humiliation of looking at our negative side.

The unregenerate man a priest once met on the street missed these points about reconciliation, and hadn't been to church for quite some time. During their brief conversation, the priest inquired, "Just what do you have against coming to church?" "Plenty," remarked the man. "The first time I went they threw water in my face and the second time they tied me to a woman I've had to support ever since." "I see," said the priest gently, "and the next time they'll throw dirt on you."

The exultation of reconciliation sees its joyful side, and it looks more to the future than to the past. Through reconciliation, God calls us to a new beginning. He helps us to come closer to the true freedom to which we've been called as His sons and daughters. Through this process, God calls us out of self-deception into truth, out of darkness into light, out of death into life.

The penitent woman in St. Luke's gospel is a good example of exultation over the forgiveness of sin. She's in *real life* as eloquent a proclamation of God's love for sinners as is the Prodigal Son in one of the most beautiful *stories* of all time. The *dramatis personae* of this event are the host, his chief guest, the woman, and other guests. The host, Simon the Pharisee, invited Jesus to a festive banquet in his house. The invitation wasn't extended out of altruistic motives. Simon had heard that Jesus was a prophet, which he wanted to investigate for himself, and he knew of Jesus' popularity, from which he wanted to profit.

According to local custom, the host was expected to receive a guest with a kiss; to give water for washing his feet of the dusty roads, a job perhaps relegated to servants; and to anoint the guest's head. The problem for the self-righteous Simon and company was how to appear hospitable to both outsiders: Jesus and the woman whom everyone else there knew to be sinful. Simon's self-righteousness led to little love shown toward Jesus — in fact, not even the minimum courtesies.

The sinful woman, on the other hand, showed a faith in God (v.50) that led her to seek forgiveness. Her knowledgeable faith also told her of her weakness. This is the acknowledgment of weakness of which St. Paul speaks: "When I am weak I am strong" (2 Cor

12:10); and "The Spirit comes to us in our weakness" (Rm 8:26). Christian saints throughout the ages discovered, with Paul, that recognizing our weakness can be the catalyst to new growth. It leads to an emptiness of self that enables God's love to enter. If anyone had told this woman that she was making a fool of herself, she would have wholeheartedly answered, "I don't care. I love him!" If a friend had tried to pull her back, she would have resisted. Because she overwhelmed Jesus with her love, much was forgiven. She gave a powerful lesson on the connection between faith, love and forgiveness.

Whatever her sin, sexual or other, it was well-known. In contrast with the stinginess of the host, her treatment of Jesus was generous. Because she had displayed such acts of love for Jesus, her many sins were forgiven. Jesus drew an acknowledgment of that out of the self-righteous Simon. In allowing the sinner to touch him, he again showed himself to be a friend of sinners.

Our confession of sins must be equally based on the faith, love, humility, acknowledgment of weakness, and openness of the penitent woman. It can't be reduced to a mere attempt at psychological self-liberation, even though it does correspond to the legitimate and natural need, inherent in the human heart, to open oneself to another. It's a liturgical act, solemn in its dramatic nature, yet humble and sober in the grandeur of its meaning. It's a serious striving to perfect the grace of baptism, so that Christ's life may be seen in us ever more clearly. It's an act of courage — again like that of the prodigal son and the sinful woman. It's an act of entrusting oneself, beyond sin, to the mercy that forgives.

The power to "forgive sins" Jesus confers, through the Holy Spirit, upon ordinary men, themselves subject to the snare of sin (Jn 20:22; Mt 18:18). It's undoubtedly the most difficult, sensitive, and demanding ministry of the priest, but also one of the most beautiful and consoling. The sacramental formula "I absolve you" establishes that at this moment the contrite and converted sinner comes into as much contact with the power and mercy of God as the penitent woman.

Knowledge of these qualities of reconciliation prepares us for those familiar words the priest addresses to the congregation at the beginning of every Mass: "Dear brothers and sisters, in order to prepare ourselves for these sacred mysteries (that is, of God's forgiving love) let's call to mind our sins (that is, the lovelessness for which we must be forgiven)."

GOOD FRIDAY

Is 52:13-53:12   *Heb 4:14-16; 5:7-9*   *Jn 18:1-19:42*

We live in one of the most violent centuries in history. We've had two wars that engaged the whole world, the last of which alone killed 50 million people and injured 34 million more. We've endured countless other wars between countries, and internal wars. In fact, more people have been killed in wars in this century than in all the previous wars in history. We've had a Holocaust that tortured and killed six million Jews and at least that many others, and unspeakably violent crimes reported daily in the media.

Why, then, do we come together each year to commemorate the death of one who died almost two thousand years ago, in a faraway land, reports of whose torture seem to be no worse than those we hear of in our day, when tyrants seem to have perfected the science and art of physical and psychological torture?

There are many reasons. Let's consider just two. For one thing, Jesus proved himself to be God, and there's a difference in the nature of what we call "time" between him and us. For us, all time is horizontal. That is to say, two o'clock precedes three o'clock, Tuesday comes after Monday and before Wednesday, April follows March and precedes May, and the year 1995 comes before 1996. It all goes along the same plane.

For God, though, time is vertical. That is to say that in one sense there's no time as we know it in God. In another sense God, being eternal, has all time always present in Himself: All of what we call time, from the first moment of creation until the very end of all things, is always present to Him at every moment.

So if we think that any acutely refined physical or psychological torture devised in our day is worse than what Jesus suffered, we're wrong. Jesus suffered not only the unjust condemnation, abandonment, beating, and crucifixion that we read about in the Gospels and whose nature we know from the history of his period and place; because of the intimacy of His unity with humanity, he suffers all the punishment inflicted on people in all time. He suffers it from all sources — the violence we read about daily in the media as well as our own individual wrongdoings.

We're so confined by our notion of time and by our limited intellects that we're incapable of handling any one concept at any given time. That's why we celebrate the events of the days of Holy Week separately: the Last Supper in the Upper Room on Holy Thursday, Jesus' death at Calvary on Good Friday, His rising from the tomb on Easter Sunday. In truth, however, they're all one. They're called Jesus' Passover. On all these days, we celebrate the one Jesus, once dead and now alive in glory forever. It's the Risen Lord who calls us together on Holy Thursday and Good Friday as well as on Easter Sunday.

That leads us to the second of today's reasons for commemorating Jesus' death today. By his death and resurrection, Jesus conquered sin and death. And God's special Son has invited us to share not only in his sufferings, but also in his victory. Whether we shall really share depends, of course, on how we spend the time he has given us for our lives.

In the Ozark Mountains, old-timers talk about a creature who is as mythical as the Loch Ness Monster in Scotland. This creature is called the Sidehill Hoofer or, as he's also known, the Sidehill Slicker. One leg of this strange creature is shorter than the other. The result is that these creatures are said to run around the Ozark Mountains in only one direction, and can never reach the tops of the mountains.

You don't have to go to the Ozark Mountains to find Sidehill

Slickers: They can be seen in the prairies of the Midwest, in the coastal plains, and in our large cities as well. Indeed, they live throughout the world! They're creatures known for their ability to go down or around — but never up — the hill of Calvary. These Sidehill Slickers find many ways to go in the other direction when they see that the road they're on leads up the hill to any suffering for Jesus.

That shouldn't be us. Although none of us shall probably ever share in an actual crucifixion, in some way every one of us is daily offered a chance to surrender to some kind of death or resurrection — great or small. We suffer a little death every time we refuse to react in anger or self-pity when someone offends us. We feel the kiss of a little death each time we forget about our own needs to address the needs of another. We take on a Good Friday heart whenever we make room in our being for the thousands who are locked in the prison of poverty or who are demoralized because they have lost a job or the family farm.

We also come to little risings. Everyone who has come — by whatever way — to a deeper love of another, every person who has come to accept real grief as being God's will, every human being who has given new life to another by resisting the temptation to manipulate has experienced a little rising.

The celebration of the Lord's Passion on Good Friday confronts every Christian with that one authentic glory of God which has been won for us by an obedience which works unto death. The Easter alleluias are not naive: They're all the more sincere because they ascend from hearts which have gone down into the tomb of baptism.

Have you seen any Sidehill Slickers recently around your part of the country — or perhaps in your bathroom mirror?

CONFIRMATION

Is 61:1-3, 6, 8f.   *1 Cor 12:4-13*   *Mt 25:14-30*

In a recent pre-Christmas season, a newspaper ran a striking photograph of a group of people held at bay by armed guards. The people weren't rioters or protesters; they were Christmas carolers. The town of Vienna, Virginia, had outlawed the singing of religious songs on public property. So these men, women, and children were forced to sing "Silent Night" behind barricades. This country has spent many years now trying to take God out of our society.

At the same time, many criminologists have tried to identify the root causes of our epidemic of violence. According to their preconceived notions, crime should have been rising in the late 1800s because of conditions that caused many people to be out of work. It didn't: It was a time of intense spirituality. It was not until the Roaring Twenties that crime went up. That was the era when Sigmund Freud's views were coming into vogue, saying that people who did wrong were only misguided, or mistreated, or required better environments. Sin? That was only a lot of religious talk.

The crime rate didn't decline again until the Great Depression. The criminologists searched to see if there was a single factor to explain the phenomena. The factor they found was religious faith. Times of need were times of people banding together, times when religion exercised its unique, powerful role in inculcating countless people with a sense of personal responsibility for reshaping their lives.

The scientists concluded that crime was in large part caused by a breakdown of morality, which was in turn caused by a lessening in the practice of religion. Since 1965 the crime rate has steadily risen. In the same period, religious faith has waned. There's never been a case in history in which a society has been able to survive for long without a strong moral code. And there's never been a time when a moral code has not been ensouled by religious truth. So the question is, "Are people likely to be good without God?"

There are, in truth, quite a number of religious people who are abhorrent, and some people who seem good without believing in God. Nevertheless, God is necessary for morality to survive. If there is no God, there is no good and evil; there are only *opinions* about good and evil. Good and evil without God are purely subjective: You think that torturing children is bad, but somebody else thinks that torturing children is good. It's your opinion against theirs. Without a moral source that's above both of you, there's no way to say that your opponent is wrong. You can only say, "I, personally, think that what he did is wrong." Without God, good and evil are only matters of taste, or what a society surmises them to be.

Are we likely to produce people who are good *with* God, or *without* Him? Well, imagine you're walking alone in a bad city neighborhood at midnight. Part of your walk home has to go through a dark alley. At precisely the point of entering the alley, you notice five young men walking toward you. Would you or would you not be relieved to know that they had just attended a Bible class?

If there's no God, morality is what a particular culture says it is. So imagine another situation. Imagine that you're in a very remote part of India whose ancient customs go back a long time. You have great influence in the area and you're informed that the Hindus there are about to engage in Satee. Satee is the ancient Hindu practice of burning a living widow to death with her husband's corpse on his funeral pyre. Would you or would you not try to stop it?

If you say that you would *not* try to stop it, you're implicitly admitting that culture entirely determines morality. Though *you* think widow burning is wrong, the local people think it's right, and who are you to say it's wrong and stop it? But if you *would* try to stop it, then you believe in a universal morality and that morality is not merely a matter of culture; you will therefore use your influence on the local citizens.

Reason alone doesn't bring you to morality. It was *reasonable* to do what the ancient classical Greeks did — leaving deformed children on mountaintops to die. The Greeks only kept healthy, good-looking children alive — after all, that's much more *rational*.

You subconsciously think that's wrong because you're heir to the Judeo-Christian tradition that says that human beings are valuable because, for one thing, we're created in God's image.

Today you've arrived at a new highlight in your progress toward maturity, with new insights, new expectations, a greater conversion of heart, and new responsibilities. To help, you're receiving the sacrament of Confirmation. This sacrament is a validation of your baptism, giving you the opportunity to make, on your own, the commitments that your parents and godparents made for you when you were an infant. And together with baptism, this is a sacrament of initiation. Baptism was your *first* initiation into God's life; Confirmation introduces you to the life of an *adult* Christian, and gives you all the graces you need to face the challenges of adulthood.

In this Sacrament, as you know, you receive the Holy Spirit. In Hebrew, Greek, and Latin, the word for "spirit" is the same as the word for "breath" and for "life." This third person of the Blessed Trinity is on record in many places in the Bible. The first creation account in the Book of Genesis describes the Holy Spirit hovering over the primeval waters. When God created Adam, he took this creature formed from dirt and breathed on him — breath being another word for the Holy Spirit — giving him life (Gn 2:7). Isaiah portrays the Spirit as a guide who would direct the Messiah from within. The Spirit of God rushed upon David on the occasion of his anointing as king (1 S 16:13).

The prophet Elijah recognized the presence of the Spirit not in the rock-shattering earthquake or in the violent storm that he experienced, but in a whispering wind that followed. Among the many other dramatic examples of the Spirit's presence in the Older Covenant was the mystical experience of Ezekiel having a vision of a whole field full of the unburied dry bones of thousands who had fallen in battle. In one of the most unusual and sensational scenes in all literature, the breath of God — which Ezekiel summoned — brought the bones to life and they stood upright, a vast army (Ezk 37:1-14).

With Jesus, the Spirit descended upon him at his baptism and drove him into the desert to be tested. In giving his mission to the Apostles the night before he died to spread the love of God to the world, Jesus *breathed* on them. This may seem a strange procedure to us, but from the Jewish scriptures the Apostles were familiar with God giving his Spirit that way.

And we know the awesome story of the first Christian Pentecost, fifty days after Jesus' resurrection. St. Luke, author of the Acts of the Apostles which tells the story (2:1-13), relates phenomena not unlike those of Mt. Sinai — a rushing wind, smoke, and fire — to initiate this new creation. He introduces the dawning of the age of the Holy Spirit as the dominant reality in the life of the human race. Some people are so spiritless that, had they been alive at the first Pentecost, they would have arrived with fire extinguishers!

The activity of the Spirit is the subject-matter of the rest of the Acts of the Apostles. The Spirit instructs the early missioners, is the driving force in proclaiming the message of salvation, is responsible for conversions to the new faith, gives strength in persecution, is the inspiration for St. Paul's journeys, and is responsible for the inclusion of non-Jews in the early Church. But perhaps the greatest marvel of the Holy Spirit was the fact that weak, timid, and shallow Apostles were changed into bold and wise men who would reach the ends of the earth to proclaim Jesus.

The Spirit of God continues to breathe over the universe. Through his Spirit God makes all things new. The power of Pentecost is in the hands of those who choose to love and forgive and share the peace that is borne from above. God's intervention can shake the world — if we but let it.

Only when we cooperate with the grace of the Holy Spirit which we receive at Confirmation can we have the wonderful experiences of the first Christian Pentecost. Then we may look to enabling better communication between those with wrinkled skin on their bent frames, on the one hand, and disheveled youth with ragged shorts, on the other; between staunch conservatives and radical liberals; and between all other contrasts in society. Then we will dynamically share our faith and our joy. And, if some say we're drunk, as they did of the Apostles on the first Christian Pentecost, we can with St. Peter remind them that it's still early in the morning of our new life in the Spirit.

We need the Holy Spirit of God to arrive at the very best this world can offer! And with this sacrament God is giving him to you!

EARTH DAY

Gn 9:8-17   *Ps 104*   *Rm 8:18-25*   *Mt 6:25-34*

Earth Day takes place in late April. The environment may also be celebrated on the Feast of St. Francis of Assisi (Oct. 4), on the World Day of Peace (Jan. 1), on World Environment Day (early June), and on Arbor Day (which varies by state).

Almost daily we see reports of the tragic condition of what we've come to call the "Third World." Some 1.5 billion people of the world's current 5.5 billion — more than one out of four human beings alive today — are living in "absolute poverty": that is, they don't regularly drink fresh water or eat enough to stay healthy, and they spend most waking hours gathering firewood for fuel, depleting precious forest lands. Diseases transmitted by polluted water kill more than 12 million children worldwide each year.

It's the poor and the powerless who most directly bear the burden of current environmental carelessness. Their lands and neighborhoods are more likely to be polluted or to host toxic waste dumps, their water undrinkable, their children harmed. They suffer acutely from the loss of soil fertility, pollution of rivers and urban streets, and the destruction of forest resources. Overcrowding and unequal land distribution often force them to overwork the soil or migrate to marginal land. People in such places take nothing at all for granted — not health, nor their children's welfare; not food nor survival nor dignity.

What's the picture on the side of developed nations? We're the first generation to see our planet from space — to see so clearly its beauty, limits, and fragility. A space look reveals that, if the earth were the size of an apple, its life-supporting layer would be thinner than its skin — more the thickness of an onion-skin — and very delicate. These factors help us to see more clearly than ever the impact of carelessness, ignorance, greed, neglect, and war on the Earth.

People who have spent time giving themselves to needful societies are shocked to walk back from the developing countries, which now stand, like the child at the candy store window, at the periphery of opportunities, into the developed world which we've made: where consumption of resources remains the single greatest source of global environmental destruction.

The consumer societies in which we live are rapidly becoming shockingly ethics-resistant. We're more prosperous and more wasteful than any in human history. Our planet, with its 10 million kinds of living organisms, is a living system; we forget this at our peril. The Earth is primary. Human beings, while playing a sacred and even special role in God's divine plan, are derivative of the planet: that is, we're derived from chemicals, atoms, the seas, plants, and animals of Mother Earth. We're extinguishing life forms and killing the planet and, as a result, may possibly be on the path to our own extinction as a species.

While we're a minority of the population, we in the industrialized nations employ some 80 percent of the world's economy and use 85 percent of the world's natural resources. We have no more right to exploit and selfishly manipulate the natural world than we have the right to exploit and manipulate other people. Both will retaliate.

Among all the things we should be doing to set our priorities straight, two stand out: to reread our Sacred Scriptures and to reexamine our theology. Our Sacred Writings begin with the biblical vision of God's good Earth in the Hebrew Scriptures. In the beginning, "God looked at everything he had made, and he found it very good" (Gn 1:31) — the heavens and the Earth, the sun and the moon, the Earth and the sea, fish and birds, animals, and humans.

It's no wonder that when God's people were filled with the

spirit of prayer, they invited all creation to join their praise of God's goodness. "Let the earth bless the Lord . . ." (Dn 3:74-81). The Earth, the Hebrew Scriptures remind us, is a gift to all creatures, to "all living beings — all mortal creatures that are on earth" (Gn 9:16f.).

Genesis tells us to subdue the Earth and have dominion over the fish and the birds and every living thing (Gn 1:26, 28); we've interpreted this as making the lower levels of the natural world serve the ends of the higher. This interpretation isn't biblical. We've gotten carried away with the concept of dominion and subjugation and have lost the concept of caring. Humankind isn't the measure of everything: God is!

We're not gods, but stewards of creation. Stewards serve the wishes of the owner in the way they manage the owner's goods. Two fundamental principles guide our moral consideration of stewardship: the integrity of all creation and respect for life.

With regard to the integrity of all creation, we're reminded that ozone depletion, the "greenhouse effect," the unregulated dumping of industrial waste, the burning of fossil fuels, and the unrestricted sacking of the forests, all damage the atmosphere and the environment. The effects of environmental degradation sur- round us: the smog in our cities; chemicals in our water and on our food; eroded topsoil blowing in the wind; oil and wastes on our beaches; the loss of valuable wetlands; radioactive and toxic waste lacking adequate disposal sites; threats to the health of industrial and farm workers; the depletion of the ozone layer; the extinction of species; and global warming.

Environmental problems are not only these massive problems over which the ordinary person has no control except by way of the ballot box. Ride along our city streets and country roads and see the old tires and abandoned cars and refrigerators, the empty cans, the paper and plastic refuse from "fast food" stores, and the omnipres- ent broken glass on sidewalks and streets. All of these assaults on the environment result from personal carelessness and arrogant wastefulness.

Respect for life includes all species: They're all inextricably related to respect for nature. Every creature shares a bit of the divine beauty. Accordingly, it's appropriate that we treat the natural world not just as means to human fulfillment but also as God's creatures.

Also in our Scriptures is the covenant between God and us about our environment. This one, as pertaining to the environment at least, is in some ways more fundamental than the promises God made to Abram, or the pact established on Mt. Sinai, or the new relationship established between God and humankind through Jesus. This covenant is at the very heart of creation. God spoke it to Noah (Gn 9:9-11), who with his family represent the entire human race:

> See, I am now establishing my covenant with you and your descendants after you and with every living creature that was with you: all the birds, and the various tame and wild animals that were with you and came out of the ark. . . .

People are therefore required to live responsibly within the environment, rather than manage it as though we're outside it. We don't merely live within our environment as we live within a building. We're part of it, and it's part of us. Humanity's arrogance and acquisitiveness, however, have led time and again to our growing alienation from nature (see Gn 3f, 6-9, 11ff.). The sins of humankind laid waste the land. Hosea, for example, cries out: "There is no fidelity . . . Therefore, the land mourns, and everything that dwells in it languishes . . ." (Ho 4:1b-3). God sent His prophets to call the people back to their responsibility, but the people hardened their hearts.

In the Gospel message, Jesus came teaching about salvation with a countryman's knowledge of the land. God's grace is like wheat growing in the night (see Mk 4:26-29), divine love like a shepherd seeking a lost sheep (see Lk 15:47), and in the birds of the air and the lilies of the field there are lessons to give up the ceaseless quest for material advantage and to trust in God (see Mt 6:25-33). Jesus' heavenly Father is a vineyard worker, who trims vines so that they may bear more abundant grapes (see Jn 15:18).

The new covenant made in Jesus' blood restores the order of love. Just as in his person Jesus destroyed the hostility that divided people from one another, so he has made it possible to overcome the opposition between humanity and nature. For he's the firstborn of a new creation and gives his Spirit to renew the whole Earth (see Ps 104:30). As his teachings incline us to "serve one another through love" (Gal 5:13), they also dispose us to live carefully on the Earth, with respect for all God's creatures.

Our Christian theology continues to affirm the goodness of the natural world. The ecological crisis challenges us to extend our love of neighbor, which is at the heart of the Christian life, to future generations and to the flourishing of all Earth's creatures. May future generations inherit from us one of their foremost rights: an undamaged Earth!

St. Francis of Assisi is the patron saint of the environmental movement (both in popular usage and by official designation of Pope John Paul II). He invited all creation — animals, plants, natural forces, and Brother Sun and Sister Moon — to give honor and praise to the Lord. We ought to remember that he tamed wolves and preached to the birds and wrote the Canticle of the Sun only after a long period of self-discipline in which he ministered to lepers and other outcasts. A love of the natural world, as St. Francis showed us, can help mightily to preserve and nurture all that God has made.

Further, our theology tells us that all creation is a sacrament. The whole created world reveals God. In our experience of the world, we touch the divine: We discover God. Creation in and of itself, apart from divine revelation, is a "second Bible." In the beginning, the first man and woman walked with God in the cool of the evening. Ever after, people have met the Creator in the loveliness and sublimity of mountaintops, vast deserts, plants and animals, oceans, waterfalls, and gently flowing springs. In storms and earthquakes, they found expressions of divine power. In the cycle of the seasons and the courses of the stars, they have discerned signs of God's fidelity and wisdom.

Our theology teaches us also that, at its core, the environmental crisis is a moral challenge. It calls us to examine how we use and share the goods of the Earth, what we pass on to future generations, and how we live in harmony with God's creation.

Closer examination of our theological tradition shows further dimensions of our ecological responsibility. One is the planetary common good, which shows that some of the gravest environmental problems are clearly global: Poisoned water crosses borders freely; acid rain pours on countries that don't create it; and greenhouse gases and chlorofluorocarbons affect the Earth's atmosphere for many decades, regardless of where they are produced or used.

Another theme is the solidarity of the human race. This involves caring for others (who are companions on the journey) instead of exploiting them. It makes us appreciate God's universal purpose in creating things, whereby he has given the fruit of the Earth to sustain the entire human family without excluding or favoring anyone.

That, in turn, leads us to realize that, embedded in the Gospel and the Church's teaching, is an option for the poor. The goods of the Earth, which in the divine plan should be a common birthright, often risk becoming the monopoly of a few who often spoil it and sometimes destroy it. Unrestrained economic development isn't the answer to improving lives. A mere accumulation of goods and services, even were it for the benefit of the majority, isn't enough for the realization of human happiness. Authentic development supports moderation and even austerity in the use of material resources.

In conclusion, let's remember that the Earth is a generous mother. Sunlight striking the ground in the United States delivers 500 times more energy than we use in a year. An average tree in one year inhales the amount of carbon dioxide from a car that traveled 11,300 miles, and exhales the amount of oxygen needed to keep a family of four breathing for a year.

The Earth will provide in plentiful abundance for all her children, if they will but cultivate her in justice and peace. Because of the great strides in technology and production, we can now wage a winning war on poverty and hunger and misery in the world. Supporting equitable social development (for example, prenatal care, education, good nutrition, and health care) for a better quality of life may well be the best contribution which affluent societies, like the United States, can make to relieving ecological pressures in less developed nations.

The task set before us will require both new attitudes and new actions. Concerning new attitudes, a new sense of the limits and risks of fallible human judgments ought to mark the decisions of policy makers. And in addition to the traditional proven virtues of prudence, humility, and temperance, we must rely on the preeminent Christian virtues of faith, hope, and love.

New actions will consist of various steps. Scientists, environmentalists, economists, and other experts should continue to help with facts. Teachers and educators must emphasize a love for God's creation. Parents should teach their children love of the Earth and delight in nature, and habits of self-control, concern, and care that lie at the heart of environmental morality. Theologians, scripture scholars, and ethicists must help explore, deepen, and advance the insights of our Judeo-Christian tradition.

Business leaders and worker representatives should make the protection of our common environment a central concern for the common good and the protection of the Earth. Church and synagogue members should examine their lifestyles, behaviors, and policies — personal and institutional. Environmental advocates must build bridges between the quest for justice and peace and concern for the Earth. Policy makers and public officials should resist short-term pressures in order to meet our long-term responsibility to future generations.

As citizens, every one of us needs to participate in these discussions and both cleanup and greenup. To clean up means picking up trash, raking, sweeping. To greenup means conserving energy, recycling, and buying and using biodegradable products.

At the heart of a Christian environmental ethic is the virtue of hope. "All things are possible" to those who hope in God (Mk 10:27). Hope gives us the courage, direction, and energy required for this arduous common endeavor. We pray with renewed concern for all God's creation:

Send forth thy Spirit, Lord and renew the face of the earth.

BEGINNING OR ENDING
OF THE SCHOOL YEAR
(OR IN BETWEEN)

Ws 7:7-10, 15f.   Ps 37:3f., 5f., 30f.   1 Cor 2:10-16   Jn 12:44-50

At the end of the school year in the little town of Lenzburg, Switzerland, the entire town is bedecked with flowers to celebrate the Children's Festival (*Jugenfest*). The flowers are everywhere: on cars, out of the windows of homes, in the streets. Both students and teachers carry bouquets. Boys wear flowers in their buttonholes, girls a crown of flowers in their hair. At various locations simultaneously, the town elders call each student to approach and receive a coin and congratulations for completing another school year. The coin is an expression of hope for the future as well as a reward for studying.

At ten o'clock in the morning, the deep church bells ring out for an hour, and the town canon roars every five minutes while students and teachers parade through the winding streets. Several bands accompany them. The joyful crowd consists of parents, families, friends, former students, and townsfolk returning for this happy festival. At night, a fair is held.

All of this celebration is a beautiful tribute to teachers, students, and education.

The one who is in the front line (in more ways than one) of bringing about the proper atmosphere in a school is the teacher. It's a tragedy that many people don't recognize the life and death nature of teaching. Many times the interactions between teachers and pupils bring critical decisions of motivation, reinforcement, reward, ego enhancement, and goal direction. Proper professional decisions enhance life; improper decisions send pupils toward incremental death. Physicians and lawyers probably have neither more nor less to do with life and death than do teachers.

The *best* should teach. Teaching beckons to those with the brightest minds, the finest personalities, and the soundest moral and spiritual commitments. It holds before them a life packed with satisfaction. It appeals to them to put their service to humankind before self. The world seldom notices who teachers are, but civilization depends in many ways on what they do.

There are many terms for the teacher: guide, resource person, change agent, choice presenter, instigator, director, shepherd, role model. For those among us who see knowledge as a discovery — literally, a dis-covery — of truth, the teacher is mostly one who has a priestly role as mediator between the learner and the world of reality. Those who believe in the supreme value of the intellect propound a style of teaching which strives to transmit the best of humankind's heritage and to provide opportunities to challenge a student's intellectual capabilities. Good teachers zealously accept the responsibility of being a role model. All are careful to distinguish legitimate teacher authority from domineering authoritarianism, and emphasize the former.

No matter what the term, Catholics emphasize the teacher — a person who is fully alive and fully human — as a very important person who helps form the young. Their job has gotten tougher and tougher. Over the years, teachers have been asked to identify the top problems in the schools of the United States. In 1940, teachers identified them as talking out of turn, chewing gum, making noise, running in the hall, cutting in line, dress code infractions, and littering. When asked the same question in 1990, teachers identified guns, drug use, alcohol abuse, pregnancy, suicide, rape, robbery, and assault.

Catholics see in teaching a noble vocation that calls for detachment, a commitment that avoids sermonizing, and generosity of spirit. It also requires concern for truth and justice, breadth of vision, an habitual spirit of service, solidarity, and total moral integrity. The standards are high and the demands difficult.

Catholic teachers expect to guide youth toward eternal realities; they know that no one can tell where the teacher's influence ends. They effectuate a union of the school with the local Church. Historically, they are in the tradition of the New Testament: Jesus the teacher, the Apostles' ministry, and St. Paul's inheritance of the Jews' tremendous respect for teaching. They share in the noble tradition of the early Church and the history of Christianity in their love of learning, desire for God, and preservation of culture and civilization.

Good Catholic teachers are ethically sensitive about their obligations to students, parents, and the community. With their students, they strive not only for a meeting of minds, but for a personal relationship. This entails respect, sensitivity, sympathy, concern, some degree of self-revelation, reciprocal dialogue, trust, openness, warmth, and congeniality. Good Catholic teachers encourage opportunities for contact with parents, respect parental rights, supplement the education begun in student's homes, and keep parents informed. They realize their importance to the community, especially the local community of faith. To accomplish all this, they are supportive of colleagues: working together as a team, being active in professional organizations, and being selflessly enthusiastic about continuing education.

To bring about such high-caliber teachers, their formation should be a happy blend of professional training, progress in faith, and personal growth. Professional training will take for granted proficient background in such areas as language, the arts, literature, mathematics, and science, and ability in thinking, reasoning, and understanding. Their development should be in a wide range of cultural, psychological, and pedagogical areas in accord with the discoveries of modern times.

Superadded to all this for the Catholic teacher is the faith dimension. A realization of Catholic identity begins with the awareness that philosophies of life are very much intertwined with schoolwork. Catholic-school teachers must have no doubt about the Catholic school's identity, because confused ideas here make for shaky *ad hoc* decisions all around. The Catholic teacher must have a synthesis of faith, culture, and life, and be alert for opportunities to witness to their faith. Retreats, prayer, sharing, service, and other exercises inculcate habits of reflection and deepening faith.

The personal growth expected of Catholic teachers begins with psychological and spiritual maturity, which recognizes the need for a philosophy of life and of education. Conduct is also important, giving students an example of Christian behavior that includes participation in liturgical and sacramental life. In the face of constant change, good Catholic teachers continuously update themselves. In the thicket of problems with teacher certification and evaluation, Catholic teachers try to develop qualities which leave no doubt of their competence.

The qualities that describe all Catholic-school teachers should apply in an outstanding way to teachers of religion, the subject that is the *raison d'être* of Catholic schools and the heart of their identity. Among these qualities is that they be persons of faith, of a deep personal prayer life and Christian virtue, who correct but don't judge, interpret the world in the light of Christ's revelation, and introduce young people to Jesus. In addition, the religion teacher is informative, evocative, studious, practical, challenging, interesting, addicted to learning, an animator rather than a dictator, caring, trusting, aware of student potential, encouraging, and with good sense, imagination, adaptability, and infectious optimism and enthusiasm.

Religion teachers should have appropriate graduate degrees in the human sciences. Psychological insight into the stages of persons' growth and development — infancy, childhood, pre-adolescence, adolescence, and all the stages of adulthood — is important, because religious growth takes place commensurate with the readiness of each period. Many major psychological theories admit of a beneficial connection between Christianity and the personal formation that is education. Indeed, many personality theories propound the Christian religion as being an important integrative and perfective power for personality.

For greater credibility with students as well as for relief from the strict demands of teaching religion, they should probably teach another subject as well. To alleviate tension and prevent burnout, they should develop a thick-skinned maturity that will fend off criticisms of their not measuring up to the impossible expectations and demands made of them in this irreligious age.

The "master teacher" is the principal. Principals are to be instructional leaders, managers of time and resources, communicators, observers and evaluators of staff, creators of the school's climate, and leaders in goal setting and attainment, school-community relations, discipline, and teacher support. Their qualifications — spiritual, pastoral, professional, and personal — must all be shot through with a Catholic perspective. They must strive to relate well with higher administration as well as with their staff, parents, and student body.

The end, purpose, and center of the Catholic-school enterprise is the student. One of the many ways the Catholic school differs from others is in implementing the time-honored belief that schooling should inculcate virtue in students. Departing from others who talk only about presenting youth with "skills facilitation" and "self-esteem" and about being "comfortable with ourselves," the Catholic school talks about education as the architect of souls.

Since the time of Jesus, who showed a reverence and a solicitude for the human person which nobody has ever exceeded, Catholics see the person, and hence the student, as having a dignity greater than the deserved admiration for all the rest of God's vast creation. In a good Catholic-school setting, students experience their dignity as persons before they know the definition of personhood.

What raises the person to his or her highest dignity is grace, the call to share in God's own nature. Grace acts through nature, and doesn't contradict it. Grace's being of the supernatural order doesn't make it something added to the top of nature like cream on milk; it's the sacred and the natural permeating each other as one organic whole, like water and the grains of sand on the seashore. Because grace brings human nature to perfection, the life of grace is an aspect of the education which Catholic schools provide their students.

All people by virtue of the fact that they are persons have a right to be educated in such a way as to help in the working of divine grace toward full and complete personal formation. This embraces the underprivileged of all faiths and of none. With roots in the Hebrew scriptures, this embrace finds a new expression in Jesus' words and example, and continues today. It includes women, with whom Jesus allowed his radical conduct to become public knowledge. It includes non-Catholic students, before whom the Church allows her teaching to speak for itself.

Because the individual — student or other — doesn't live alone, but coexists with others, there are inevitable individual-community tensions. For the Catholic, how to live this phenomenon is exemplified in Jesus: an individual who takes upon himself the sins of the world, one who is allied with others yet alone. Students, too, must be taught both their individuality and community. They're to come to realize, on the one hand, that they should continually fight the hard battle to be themselves in a world that's often doing its best night and day to turn them into everybody else. At the same time, they're to realize their relationship to the universe, to nature, and to other people.

An area in which we have a right to look for great things in Catholic schools is discipline. The word is from *discipulus*, which has the same root as the word for a follower of Jesus. Discipline means teaching that nothing left loose ever does anything creative. No horse gets anywhere until he's harnessed. No steam or gas ever drives anything until it's focused. No Niagara is ever turned into light and power until it's funneled. No life ever grows until it's disciplined.

The concept of disciples coming to redemption means that Catholic schools look upon their students with higher aspirations than do other schools. In the age-old controversy about the use of fear or love to lead students, Machiavelli and his followers — and they are many, within and outside education — opt for fear. Catholic-school teachers believe that perfect love drives out fear (1 Jn 4:18). They try to choose love — which, of course, includes a demand for appropriate standards — and attempt to help their students understand why.

We celebrate the steps that all of you — teachers, administrators, staff, and students — are taking in the direction of these ideals, and ask God's blessing on your work.

GRADUATION ADDRESS

Ezk 37:1-4   *Ps 19:8-11*   *Ep 4:1-7, 11-13*   *Mk 4:1-9*

On your graduation day, you look back and you look forward. Looking back, you feel sad at having to leave your friends, some of your beloved teachers, the school you've come to love, the learning and other experiences you've had. Looking forward, you face the unknown, but with joy and enthusiasm are eager to get on with life. Each sadness you feel is like a little death, and each joy you have is like a little rising. That's life, which consists of constant little deaths and risings. Through each, we have the opportunity to grow.

That's like the mystical experience of Ezekiel being led into a plain in Babylon and having a vision of a whole field full of unburied dry bones of thousands who had fallen in battle. The bones had long been lifeless. In one of the most unusual and dramatic scenes in all literature, when Ezekiel prophesied in accordance with the directions of God, the breath of God brought the bones to life, and they stood upright, a vast army (Ezk 37:1-4). My graduation wish for you is three bones, of the type Ezekiel saw rising.

The first is a wishbone. You, being young today, surely have all kinds of wishes for the future. Your yearbook shows some of your wishes — to become doctors, or lawyers, or nurses, or teachers, or priests, or other leaders in one field of endeavor or another — and those hopes are what they should be. Aim high, and let the world know you're here.

In the bloom of your youth, you're very optimistic. As long as you're prepared to work hard, too, that's the way you should be. As time goes on, though, and the roses of your wishes become frayed with the dry winds of the world, your wishes may become tarnished. May you always have a wishbone to keep you bright and happy!

The second bone I wish for you is a backbone. You must already know that not everybody sees the world as you do. You must fight for what you see as right — as Jesus did. Ultimately, he faced spies in every crowd, even in far-north Galilee — but he spoke straight from the shoulder. After about only a year of his preaching, the Pharisees threatened to kill him, and *kept* plotting to put him to death. He faced up especially to the *Jerusalem* Pharisees, because of their malice: he firmly resolved to proceed toward Jerusalem to fulfill his mission (Lk 9:51).

You know, of course, that the temptation to be discouraged is common to everyone. Walt Disney was dismissed from a major newspaper and told that he had no talent as an artist; Richard Byrd, the famous pilot who was the first to reach the South Pole, crash-landed the first two times he soloed in a plane, and the third time he flew head on into another plane; Rod Serling, famous author, wrote forty stories before he sold one; Zane Grey, famous writer of Westerns, was fired by five newspapers because he couldn't do the job as a reporter. Ralph Waldo Emerson tells the story of a little boy who, when asked how he learned to skate, replied: "Oh, by getting up every time I fell down." As the poet (Henry Willard Austin) wrote:

> Genius, that power which dazzles mortal eyes,
> Is often perseverance in disguise.

The third bone I wish for you is a funnybone. Unfortunately, to be joyful is often seen as frivolous and to be gloomy as serious. But seriousness isn't necessarily a virtue. The monkey wears an expression of seriousness which would do credit to any college student, but the monkey looks serious because he itches. Solemnity flows out of people naturally, but laughter is a leap.

Remember that, of all the things we wear, our expression is the most important. A few years ago the sales head of one of America's largest corporations assembled his sales force to meet a New York stage director. The stage director was to teach them to smile. Many thought they knew how to smile, but he convinced them that what they thought were smiles turned out to be smirks. The difference, almost infinitesimal, lies in the eyes. In a smile, the eyes also smile. After two weeks' training, the sales people left the smile clinic and in three months increased their sales 15 percent.

We're in the tradition of the wise man who said that the

shortest distance between people is laughter. Life isn't always serious, but some serious matters may be taken care of by laughter. That, in fact, is our whole tradition, beginning with the Jewish Scriptures. Actually Jewish *law* said "You shall rejoice before the Lord your God in all that you undertake" (Dt 15:13). A note of this theme was God's promise to the very old Abraham that he and his wife Sarah would have a son. Because Sarah laughed at the idea, their son when born was named Isaac, a wordplay on the Hebrew verb "to laugh" (Cf. Gn 18:12). Then there was the humorous account of Abraham who, like people in an Eastern bazaar, haggled with God about the number of the just necessary to avoid God's destruction of Sodom (Gn 18:16-22). The Lord was open to Abraham's huckstering: he found that there would be more injustice in the destruction of a few innocent people than in the sparing of many guilty ones.

Even Job, he of so many afflictions, found reasons for laughter, in promising that God will "fill your mouth with laughter, and your lips with rejoicing" (Jb 8:20f.). The Book of Proverbs stated that a glad heart makes a cheerful countenance (Pr 15:13) and that a cheerful heart is a good medicine (Pr 17:22). The psalms give an important place to laughter by saying things like "He who is throned in heaven laughs" (Ps 2:4). And the prophet Zephaniah advised us to shout for joy — the same words used in St. Paul's letter to the Philippians when he told them to rejoice.

And that brings us to the New Testament. Jesus is often depicted as a clown. He was certainly not a circus clown, an entertainer, or a trickster. There are, though, analogies between a clown and Jesus: joy in living, delight in simple things like the lilies of the field, simplicity, the ability through love to transform the ordinary into the sacred, average people sharing a spark of the divine, the vulnerability of a lover, the humility of a servant. And the clown is brother to the sage. Jesus' actions and teaching style were a striking humorous contrast to the serious conventional piety of his time. He wanted to show that religion should be a wedding feast for everybody.

Although there's no record of Jesus laughing outright, there are instances of his humor. It would, for example, be most unusual if he didn't enjoy the wedding ceremony and reception at Cana. Even on the very eve of his crucifixion, he tells us that the reason for our keeping his commandment of love was that his joy might be ours and that our joy might be complete (Jn 15:11).

Even after his resurrection, Jesus continued the theme of life coming out of death, joy out of sadness. When he appeared to the disconsolate disciples at Emmaus, you remember, he brought them joy by explaining the Scriptures to them. Although we would like to know exactly what Scripture passages he referred to, reflection reveals that death and resurrection were constant scriptural themes.

The theme of joy runs through the rest of the New Testament, too. The letter of James tells us that we should consider it all joy when we encounter various trials (1:1). The First Letter of Peter tells us that although you have not seen Jesus you love him; and you rejoice with an indescribable and glorious joy (1:8). One of St. Paul's loveliest letters, his Letter to the Philippians, is called "The Epistle of Joy," even though Paul was in prison while writing it.

Our Christian tradition, even with a cross as its central symbol, continues the principle of joy. Many a good laugh can come from religious themes, like the youth who said, "Lot's wife was a pillar of salt by day, but a ball of fire by night." On the same subject of Lot's wife turning into a pillar of salt, there was little Jimmie, who interrupted the religion teacher to announce triumphantly, "My mother looked back once while she was driving, and *she* turned into a telephone pole!"

The Christian is the laughing adventurer of Christ; a gloomy Christian is a contradiction in terms. St. John Chrysostom described a vision of Christ confronting the devil and laughing at him. St. Francis of Assisi is thought of as everybody's saint because of his jollity. St. Thomas Aquinas, knowing that sadness is a thing of the devil and an enemy of the spiritual life, proposed as a cure a good sleep and a bath. St. Thomas More said, "It is possible to live for the next life and be merry in this." Martin Luther once said: "God is not a God of sadness, but the devil is. Christ is a God of joy." Said John Wesley: "Sour godliness is the devil's religion." Even John Calvin laughed: he wrote, "We are nowhere forbidden to laugh." We Christians realize that we're sinners, but we're at times tempted to forget that we're *redeemed* sinners. That last part is important; it gives us joy and makes our lives complete.

Even though the world be mad, we're born with the gift of laughter; children jingle with laughter as though they had swallowed sleighbells, and their laughter is natural until we take it away from them. To laugh is proper to human beings: to laugh is fitting for us, because hope has a place with us, and our destiny, heaven, must contain an unextinguishable laugh.

Our lives include both comedy and tragedy; we often forget the comedy, and that's a shame. Some who call themselves Christians are unfortunately like the Renaissance genius Botticelli. With great poetic imagination, fantasy, and elegance, he became famous for the softness of his light and his skillful use of perspective. He is famous for many madonnas, an exquisite "Adoration of the Magi," and a solemn "Nativity." But, deeply affected by the dour Savonarola's preaching, he never painted smiling saints.

Modern science confirms that laughter is healing. Some hospitals are taking steps to bring laughter into their patients' lives: setting up humor rooms and closed circuit TV comedy channels. When you laugh, you get fresh air into your lungs and you relax your muscles.

A story is told of the followers of a Guru who sought to learn from their Master the stages he had passed through in his quest for the divine. He said, "God first led me by the hand into the Land of Action, where I dwelt for several years. Then he returned and led me to the Land of Sorrows; there I lived until my heart was purged of every inordinate attachment. That's when I found myself in the Land of Love, whose burning flames consumed whatever was left in me of self. This brought me to the Land of Silence, where the mysteries of life and death were bared before my wondering eyes."

"Was that the final stage of your quest?" they asked.

"No," the Master said. "One day God said, 'Today I shall take you to the innermost sanctuary, the heart of God Himself.' And I was led to the Land of Laughter."

Congratulations on your achievement today, and may God accompany you on your journey with a wishbone, a backbone, and a funnybone!

YOUTH DAY

Is 40:9-11, 29-31   *Ep 4:1-6*   *Mt 5:1-12*

A butter-fingered young man who had been out of work for a long time at last found a job in a chinaware store. He'd been at work only a few days when he smashed a large vase. The boss told him that he would deduct the money from his wages every week until the vase was paid for.

"How much did it cost?" asked the culprit.

"Three hundred dollars," said the boss.

"Oh, that's wonderful," said the young man, "I'm so happy!"

"Why wonderful?" asked the boss.

The young man said, "At last I have a steady job!"

There's no comparison between the young man and youth in general but, if young people want to improve the world, they have a steady job. All over the world, there are problems to be solved. Some reports indicate that three-quarters of today's child population will experience violence before reaching adulthood.

Political discussions have an aversion to spiritual language; criminals don't face sure punishment; lawyers build up successful defenses for those guilty of violent crimes; and the nation seems to be "defining deviancy down," in the memorable phrase of one senator.

Respect for the worth of every person, integrity, responsibility, understanding, compassion, and solidarity toward others are in danger. Instead of morality, civility, and responsibility, our government schools steadfastly refuse to teach right and wrong and are more eager to dispense condoms than moral guidance.

In the media, there's a terrible debasement of music as well as of moral sensitivity. Exports of movies involve such huge amounts of money that it's the United States's second-biggest export after aircraft; their moral values influence the world from stalls in Guangzhou to bazaars in Nairobi. Vigilance about this is work that has yet to be done.

Advertising defines reality for us, educating us away from human personhood by telling us what it means to "be real." Lust replaces chastity, power replaces obedience, and money replaces poverty. Models' faces reflect detachment and self-absorption, their individuality isolated from relationships with others. Advertising advocates that you get what you can while the getting's good, eat in the best restaurants, and patronize the best in entertainment to keep you laughing.

Aside from these signs of decay that are easily visible, there are others that don't easily lend themselves to quantitative analyses. There's a coarseness, a callousness, a cynicism, and a vulgarity in our time and place that are indices of a civilization going rotten. And the worst of it has to do with our youth: Our culture seems almost dedicated to their loss of innocence before their time. The novelist Walker Percy was concerned that the United States, "with all its great strength and beauty, and freedom," might gradually subside into decay from within: "from weariness, boredom, cynicism, greed and in the end helplessness before its great problems."

Complex though the problems be, they're made simpler by the fact that young people are eager to respond by striving for a better world. In their deepest aspirations they ask that society — especially those who control the destinies of peoples — accept them as partners in the construction of a more humane, more just, more compassionate world. Everywhere there are deeply concerned young people particularly sensitive to life's transcendent meaning and ready to give the best of themselves in service to others.

Our being Christian makes the solutions even more simple, at least in the sense that it gives us direction. In seeking solutions, whereas the world works from the outside in, our Lord works from the inside out. The world would take people out of the slums. Christ takes the slums out of people, and then they take themselves out of the slums. The world would mold people by changing their environment. Christ changes people, who then change their environment. The world would shape human behavior, but Christ can change human nature. So the solutions begin with us as individuals.

We often take the fixed stars for granted, because they're always the same at the same time of the year from the same place of observing. Shooting stars and falling stars, however, more easily catch our attention and our awe. So do lightning and thunder. They're out of the usual, and give magnificent displays. We often think of Christ's words as stable stars, and we've seen them and heard them so often that we sometimes take them for granted. We have to stop and think to realize that Christ's words are shooting stars, flashing lightning, and rolling thunder as well, all calling for our attention.

Such is Jesus' Sermon on the Mount. A leading psychiatrist once wrote that if you were to take the sum total of all the articles ever written by the most qualified psychologists and psychiatrists on the subject of mental hygiene, if you were to combine them and refine them, if you were to take the whole of the meat and none of the parsley, and if you were to have these unadulterated bits of pure scientific knowledge concisely expressed by the most capable of living poets, you would have an incomplete summation of the Sermon on the Mount.

The basis of Jesus' whole sermon and the apex of Christian perfection is the Beatitudes. The word Jesus used, which we translate as "blessed," is a very special word that contains elements of joy, happiness, serenity, and loveliness. There's no tense to the beatitudes: Their blessedness exists in the present and continues forever. All the beatitudes speak of *this* world, not of "pie in the sky bye 'n' bye when you die." They contain congratulations on what *is*, and promise a reward that always consists in at least an improved relationship with God. To view our life as blessed doesn't require us to put on a happy face no matter what. It simply demands a more all-embracing vision.

Each of the Beatitudes cuts across the sky of our attention like shooting stars on a clear night. Jesus mentions eight, but there are many more. Each of them goes against the world's wisdom. Jesus' basic thought is that we mustn't place our trust or comfort in this world: Like those who have nothing, we must put all our love and trust in God. According to G.K. Chesterton, a wise man who followed Jesus, Jesus promised his people three things: that they would be absolutely fearless, greatly happy, and in constant trouble. That master of paradox added the thought, "I like getting into hot water — it keeps me clean!"

But, as C.S. Lewis said, to follow the fixed stars that challenge us to love means that we shall be vulnerable. "Love anything," says Lewis, "and your heart will be tugged, and maybe broken. If you want to avoid that, you should give your heart to no one, not even a pet. You shall have to wrap it up with luxuries, avoid entanglements, and lock it up safe in the coffin of your selfishness. But in that coffin — dark, motionless, silent, airless — it will change. It won't be broken; indeed, it will become unbreakable — and impenetrable, and irredeemable. And you'll find that the only place outside heaven where you can be perfectly safe from all the dangers of love is hell."

The First Beatitude strikes the keynote. Jesus is calling "fortunate" not the person who has nothing superfluous, but one who has nothing at all. In the eyes of the world, which pursues such symbols of material success as the right car, the right clothes, and the right neighborhood, such people are of little value. The *anawim*, as Jesus called them in Aramaic, are those who lack material goods; because they're poor, they have no influence; because they have no influence, they're walked over by other people; and because they have no earthly resources, they put their whole trust in God.

Jesus isn't calling material poverty a good thing: It isn't. It isn't good for people to live in slums, not to have enough to eat, and to have their health at risk. And Jesus' words aren't to condemn ambition: In fact, there should be more Christians with ambitions to be in the academic world, the business world, the scientific world, and the technical world. What Jesus condemns is the *inordinate* love of riches, a love that makes impossible meaningful concern for the afflicted.

Though the First Beatitude teaches that it's *always* right to be detached from *things*, the Second Beatitude (v. 4) teaches that it's *never* right to be detached from *people*. Here Jesus speaks of sorrow in the strongest sense: those who have a *passionate* grieving for the loss of one who's loved: for the dead, the vanished, the one who has journeyed away — or for their sins. The mourners' hearts are broken not only for their own losses, but for the sufferings of the whole world.

To those who think falsely that people of strong faith shouldn't have sorrow, Jesus says it's all right, and that mourners will be comforted, because adversity has its uses. An Arab proverb has it that "all sunshine makes a desert." Some delicate flowers are brought forth only by rain, the intense color of others only by cold mountain air; some human growth requires sorrow as its seed.

The Third Beatitude (v. 5) speaks of the meek, or the lowly. By this Jesus means the self-controlled — or, better, the God-controlled. It's the mean between two extremes: excessive anger and lack of care. It's the ability to be angry with the right people about the right things at the right time to the right degree. Anger is the necessary handmaiden of sympathy and fairness, in that the most dedicated must be angry with "society," or "the ruling classes," or "meddling bureaucrats" to be motivated to do something about justice.

Meekness is the quality possessed by Moses, whom Scripture calls by far the meekest man on the face of the earth (Nb 12:3), but who nevertheless was so blazingly angry when he came down from the mountain and found his people worshiping a golden calf that he smashed the idol to smithereens. Meekness is the quality envisioned by the Book of Proverbs (16:32) when it says that he who rules his temper is better than he who takes a city. People can't lead others until they've controlled themselves.

They who hunger and thirst for holiness (v. 6) are those who ardently long for that goodness that is similar to God's. In ancient Palestine, hunger and thirst were real, always threatening, and terrible. It's only when we hunger and thirst as strongly for the kind of holiness that Jesus wants of us, as did the ancients for food and water, and are willing to pay its cost, that we're able spiritually to survive.

The Fifth Beatitude (v. 7) refers to a principle that runs through the New Testament: It's the merciful who shall receive mercy. Mercy isn't a sentimental wave of pity, nor is it indifference to wrongs, but is rather the ability to identify with others, to be willing to suffer with them, and to walk in their shoes. Those who show mercy forgive injuries, go with others through what they're going through, see with others' eyes, think with their thoughts, and feel with their feelings.

The clean of heart of the Sixth Beatitude (v. 8) are those whose inner single-mindedness motivates them to serve God joyfully for His own sake and not primarily out of self-interest. In the midst of the confusion of all the complex sets of values being presented them, they're free of duplicity. Their motives are absolutely pure and single as God is pure and single, and their eyes, thus pure, shall see God even in the small and ordinary events of their lives.

The greatest degree of perfection begins with the Seventh Beatitude's beautiful word "peacemakers" (v. 9). Jesus speaks not of peace*lovers*, but of peace*makers* — those whose lives have a quality that promotes harmony within the human community. Peacemakers contrast with troublemakers and with those who without principle want an easy peace at any price. Those who go out of their way to promote peace make this world a better place to live. Peacemakers will be called children of God because our heavenly Father is a God of peace, and Jesus our brother came to bring peace on earth.

Those who have accomplished all this can arrive at Jesus' Eighth Beatitude (vv. 10-12), which reminds us that fidelity to his precepts is deepened by the test of persecution. Persecution for the early Christians could mean difficulty in getting a job, ostracism in social life, the breakup of family life, and physical torture, as well as death by martyrdom. Those who took Jesus seriously followed his advice in the last beatitude to rejoice and be glad, loving him so much that they were happy to be able to show their love by suffering for him.

For true Christians, some degree of persecution continues to be inevitable. For one thing, true Christians are bound to be the conscience of the world: We must speak up whenever morality is offensive, and we're caught in the perpetual clash between Christ and the world. For another thing, to adhere to Christ's values sometimes means persecution by our own selfish desires.

With all our possibilities of choice out there, do our beatitudes coincide with those of Jesus? The way we can find that out, and the way we can discover all of Jesus' Beatitudes, is through his Church. Bossuet said: "The Church is Jesus Christ prolonged in space and time, and communicated to me." That's what we mean by Christ's Mystical Body. Under her inquisition, Joan of Arc's response to the question, "What if the Church told you to do one thing, Christ another?" was classic. She said: "I always thought they were the same."

The quintessence of Jesus' Mystical Body is shown in the parish, where our unity is symbolized in a church steeple surrounded by the baptistery, confessional, altar, and tabernacle. Besides being the center of our spiritual life, it's also the center of activity of all kinds: civil, social, charitable. Through the Church, the Kingdom of God acts within all of us like leaven in bread.

Through the ages, Catholics have had two interesting tendencies. One is an occasional ghetto mentality: standing aloof, hiding one's head in the sand, and allowing the world to "go to hell if it wants." The second tendency — the youthful one — is to win the world for Jesus. The second is the only way to go. It means that you will always have a steady job

VOCATIONS

1 S 3:1-10   *1 Jn 3:16*   *Jn 1:35-51 [or 35-42]*

There's a plaque in Nazareth that commemorates the greatest event in human history. The plaque reads: "Here the Word was made flesh." It brings to our imagination the young girl of about fourteen years of age who was doing her household chores prayerfully when she was startled by the presence of someone else in the room. This was the angel Gabriel, who six months before had frightened the Jewish priest Zechariah in the gold-plated Temple at Jerusalem. Now he was in this humble cottage to announce that, if she would consent, this young maiden would become the mother of God.

The prayerful young Mary understood some of the difficulties and hardships implied for her in this invitation. She knew from their Mosaic Law that she would be shunned, perhaps even killed. She knew from her Sacred Scriptures that the life of one chosen by God is never an easy one.

All Heaven awaited her answer. She was free: God never takes away this most precious gift when he extends an invitation. If she said no, it might be a very long time before God would extend the invitation to humankind again. But she had all the wonderful qualities of youth. She wanted to do something worthwhile with her life, to contribute something important to the world. She was generous. She wanted to give herself. She had high ideals of heroism and courage. She said yes.

On the instant, she conceived; the Son of God became man. The redemption of humankind had begun. Immediately the good tidings were known in heaven, and little by little they would become known to all the earth. Mary thus acquired the most glorious of her titles, the one from which all others derived: "Mother of God."

In different degrees, all young people share with the young Mary those special qualities that brought about her "yes" to God's request: the desire to do something worthwhile with one's life, and the courageous generosity to give oneself. What's behind the surface meaning of these qualities?

When we look for what's worthwhile, how do we decide? What criteria must be present for our life to be considered important? Must our contribution to society be something material? Ever since the industrial revolution, many people have thought so: Hence in some countries those who haven't contributed something material have had either to change their jobs or starve to death. Or is the importance of our life work to be judged by the amount of money we receive for it? If this is the standard, how explain the psychological depression and even the suicides of people whose jobs have given them all the money they could possibly use?

Deeper thinking reveals that the importance of our work is not judged by standards like these. The dignity of an occupation depends on the degree of life dealt with. Thus, the person who sorts rocks in a chain gang is doing the lowest form of toil, dealing as he does with purely inanimate things. The farmer's task would be higher, because he deals with growing vegetation whose ultimate purpose is to feed people. Next in this ascending scale would be such as the physician, who tries to keep in health a person's body, which is so closely connected with one's soul.

Teachers and poets might have greater dignity, because they function over the rational life of people, upon which the activities of the soul are so dependent. Those who dedicate their lives to the good of the soul through religious profession engage in a work that has a new and higher dignity. Their work has direct consequences in eternity.

Marriage, of course, is also a vocation, as is the single life. The number of single people is increasing, for a variety of reasons: They haven't found a suitable partner, or are caring for a sick relative, or they're selflessly helping a family financially, or their spouse has died, and the like. The single life, to be a true vocation, can't be one motivated by selfishness, but by dedication. Single people can make vital contributions. They generously volunteer their services in many directions: as extraordinary ministers of the Eucharist, religious education teachers, hospital assistants, and in myriad other ways that particular circumstances provide.

Marriage, to Christ, is a sacrament. God consecrates the couple who as an outward sign of the sacrament exchange their consent. The sacrament was instituted by Christ, who showed great interest in marriage and marriage customs, as we see from the marriage at Cana, the story of the ten wise and foolish virgins, and his comparison of the happiness of heaven to a wedding reception. The sacrament gives an increase of sanctifying grace, perfects the natural love a couple has for each other, and gives the right to the actual graces necessary for life together. The unity provided by this sacrament is a shadow of the unity that exists between Christ and his Church; therefore, its chief characteristics are generosity and love.

But we must give attention to *religious* vocation. Of that, Pope Paul VI said: "No other prospect of life offers an ideal more true, more generous, more human, more holy than the humble and faithful vocation to the religious life." In that sense, religious vocation isn't just another profession, even the highest: It isn't something given from below, from humankind, nor does it come solely from one's own inclinations. It's given from above, from God.

Besides wanting to do something worthwhile with her life, there was in Mary's consent to God's request a quality found in all admirable young people: heroic courage. Is the real meaning of courage something connected with fame and headlines? No — and, thanks be to God, there's much more of it on earth than ever comes to the attention of the crowd. Is this courage something that can be developed in a moment? Never — those who have distinguished themselves for courage on the battlefields of life had developed the virtue long before, through the pain of attention to the little details of everyday living.

The only kind of courage of value in the life of anyone is this: to do faithfully what God expects at every moment. Mary, like her son, grew in wisdom and grace by heroically facing troubles and sufferings, recorded and unrecorded, and by doing all that God the Father looked for as the duties of their state in life. One who aspires to the life of a priest, brother, or nun must have Mary's kind of everyday, quiet, prosaic courage.

Do you have a vocation to be a priest, brother, or nun? Only you and your spiritual director, who knows you on an intimate and prolonged basis, can help you take all the necessary details into account. But the final decision must come from you. Therefore you should know the ingredients that go into a religious vocation. In *no* case may we expect that a vocation will come in an extraordinary way, like the message of the angel to Mary. But in *every* case, when all the ingredients are present in the same person at the same time, he or she may have a vocation, and should take it seriously enough to investigate.

Some of the necessary ingredients must be present on the part of the individual, and some on the part of the Church. On the part of the *individual*, there must be at least average fitness in physical health, mental ability, and moral worth. He or she must have a liking for the life of a priest, brother, or nun, and the intention to live up to its demands. While one doesn't have to be perfect, there must be a willingness to seek perfection — especially through poverty, chastity, and obedience.

Poverty, detachment from *things* (2 Cor 6:10: "as poor yet enriching many, as having nothing yet possessing all things"), leaves you completely free to follow Christ. Chastity, which is detachment from *intimate human loves*, yet motivated by love, attaches you to the divine. We can live without sex, but not without love. And obedience detaches you from your own will and gives you to humankind. All the paradoxes of love are present. As with any true love, it's in giving that we receive; so too in giving ourselves to God we are the beneficiaries. The solitariness of the vows of poverty, chastity, and obedience should never motivate one to live a single life of selfish convenience: A religious life is one of service to all.

People with a religious vocation aren't perfect, but bring with them the baggage of all their human qualities. To understand that, we have but to look at the Apostles. Our Lord chose these twelve from among all the people of his time. They'd seen him change water into wine, cure lepers, give paralytics the use of their limbs, heal Peter's mother-in-law, work countless other miracles, and instruct them in a special way. Yet when they sailed into the Lake of Galilee one night and a storm came up, they were afraid because the tired Jesus was asleep in the stern of the boat.

The Apostles were human enough to be frightened when our Lord told them he would send them out as sheep in the midst of wolves. They were human enough to be ill at ease when he gave as a condition of those wanting to be disciples that whoever puts his hand to the plow but keeps looking back is unfit for the reign of God (Lk 9:62). When the mother of James and John interceded that our Lord give a high place in his Kingdom to her sons, there were ten very indignant Apostles — only because they didn't think of it first! And at the Last Supper, after he'd been teaching them intimately for three years, when he entered the room on this his last evening with them on earth, they were fighting over who should sit at the head of the table!

The Church, too, has an essential role to play in vocation. It's from the Church, the Mystical Body of Christ, that the final decision on one's qualifications is given, and also the call to the life. When the fields are whitest for the harvest, and the need for laborers greatest, the Church's call reaches out loudest, farthest, and most insistently.

The need at this particular challenging time is very great. There are vacant confessionals in our churches, vacant teachers' desks in our classrooms, and vacant posts in our hospitals, orphanages, and other institutions of mercy. We need more and more young men and women to turn their backs upon the superficial criteria of the world and think more deeply, arriving at the standards of God.

We can be sure of two things. First of all, the Good Shepherd continues to invite from his sheep those who will share the burden and joy of shepherding. People are being called right now by the Lord to ministerial vocations. Indeed, it is *extremely* likely that there are people here in our assembly of prayer who have sensed within themselves Christ's call.

Secondly, we can be sure that responding to the call isn't easy. Each of us must look deep within ourselves to see how God is calling us: Each must discover our share of the shepherding task. For we are both sheep and shepherds — an exciting mix of graced strength and need. If we live out our Christian vocation and add generous amounts of prayer, we will encourage those called to embrace a Church vocation to acknowledge the sure voice of the Good Shepherd.

We can and must enable the shepherds among us to revel in

handing on to others the life-giving Christ. Yes, the one flock really has one task — to give *life*! Life roots out evil. Life plants the seeds of peace for all people. Life frees us all from sin. Life fills us with joyful hope.

God could have worked people's salvation in any one of countless ways. He could have given a direct revelation of Himself into the life of every person entering this world, a flash of light for everyone to accept or reject. He could have multiplied His presence in a fashion similar to what he does in the Eucharist. He could have acted in many ways that we can't even imagine. But for His plan of salvation he has chosen — ineffable mystery — to need people, as he chose to need Mary. Mary accepted His invitation at the Annunciation. You have no sensible course but to consider what invitation he may be extending to you!

WEDDING — A

Gn 1:26-28, 31a   *1 Cor 12:31 - 13:8a*   *Mt 22:35-40*

Weddings, and their homilies, must be as personalized as possible; in this and the two wedding homilies following, the speaker will have to do this for himself.

The Joy We Feel at a Wedding

Is the pulpit a place for humor? If you judge from most sermons on radio and TV, the answer might be no. Perhaps, however, a wedding is the right occasion for humor and jollity. Although their perspective mightn't be exactly right, even children catch the spirit. That's sometimes not conscious, though, as with Lottie, age 9, who, when asked how her parents met, said: "They were at a dance party. Then they went for a drive, but their car broke down. It was a good thing, because it gave them a chance to find out about their values."

Young girls especially have ideas on how to pick a partner. Sari, age 8, said, "You talk about life while you eat cheeseburgers and make believe that you aren't looking at each other's figures." Angie, 10, was more pessimistic; she said, "Most men are brainless, so you might have to try more than one to find a live one." On the definition of marriage, young Judith, age 9, said, "When you get married you get arranged with a man, and you find a person with rings, and then you hire a flower-child, too."

When asked at what age to marry, Carlos, 10, said: "I would say that 30 years old is a good age, because when you're 30 you've gotten all your excitements out of your system, and you don't mind doing stuff like taking out the garbage." Carolyn, 8, said: "Eighty-four. Because at that age you don't have to work anymore, and you can spend all your time loving each other in your bedroom." Rhonda, 8, thought marriage could take place at any time when you're grown up, and "You're pretty grown up when you know that birds and bees are not just regular creatures."

Perhaps Jesus, too, would favor humor, given the right occasion. He certainly enjoyed life. When, for example, he multiplied the few loaves and fish for over five thousand people, he must have been relying on a sense of humor when he told the apostles to collect the fragments. And when, at the wedding party at Cana, he worked his first miracle by changing water into wine so that the guests of that poor couple could enjoy the traditional long festivities, it must have been with a smile.

All over the world a wedding is a joyous time. Why? Because everyone joins with the father of the bride in being happy to be able to stop paying the bills? No, the answer has to do more with the celebration of love and life. For our part, there's an added reason: in contrast to most of what we see of modern man-woman arrangements, only some of them called "marriage," today's marriage between Nancy and Ken is starting on the right foot.

Some modern marital arrangements — couples living together without any formalities like a ceremony, high divorce rates, spouse beating, child abuse — are awful. Nancy and Ken in arranging this marriage have gone counter to these phenomena. They're having a ceremony, because they realize that their marriage isn't on the same level as buying groceries, contracting for a house, choosing furniture, or getting a pet. They have arranged that their ceremony be in church, because they realize that it takes three, not two, to get married. The three are not, as the comedian suggests, a willing groom, an eager bride, and her anxious mother: The third party is God. Without Him, any arrangement between two people is on a superficial level, and shaky from the start.

Not only do they enter marriage before God; they do it before us, their friends. They do this for two reasons. First, they're proud of this binding of their love, and they want us to share in their joy. Second, they realize that we're all involved in every marriage, because a love relationship always affects society, in one way or another. And they have very actively taken part in arranging the ceremony, especially in choosing the readings. Their choices are very revealing of what they would propose for our consideration as we think about marriage.

Their first reading is a passage from Genesis which tells us that the highest level of God's creation is people. God reached this climax at the conclusion of His work. People are created, the sacred author tells us, in God's image and likeness. He writes not only "image," because of the danger, frequently present in the history of humankind, that people might think that they're in some way gods themselves. No, the author adds, people in God's image are but a *likeness* to Him. The ways of this likeness are too complicated to relate here, but we must see the dignity of this likeness in ourselves, in others, and — especially — in our marriage partners, particularly when all is not as blissful as it is on a wedding day. There might, after all, come a day when, as Anita, age 9, said in answer to the question of what parents have in common: "They both like to argue in the kitchen."

Our likeness to God has other consequences. We must, for example, represent God wherever we are, and in whatever circumstances. Among the ancients, statues representing their kings were placed in those regions of the empire where the king couldn't be present personally. We, by our actions, represent God wherever we are.

Finally, as God is a trinity, humankind is distinguished into two sexes. God's trinity is always active, always creating, always communicating in love. In the human race, sex is for the same purposes. Kissing was not invented, as young Scott, 10, said, "as a way to get a few laughs in the ancient days." Nor is it that, as Robbie, 7, thought when he said, "You have to be married to kiss somebody on the lips. Otherwise you're stuck with their cheeks."

Humankind's sexual activity enables people to communicate in an intimate way not otherwise possible. Genesis distinguishes the divine notion of sex from pagan notions. God's notion is that sex is a special divine blessing to demonstrate love and to accept all its responsibilities. People truly in love look upon sex as the fulfillment of a divine precept and thus something clean. In fact, the usually laconic author of Genesis concludes by telling us that it's all good.

Today's gospel amplifies this theme. In answer to a question from one of the leaders of the people, Jesus says that the greatest capacity of people, and their highest expectation, is love. The first part of Jesus' answer — love of God — is from the Book of Deuteronomy (6:5) in the Jewish scriptures. It's called the *Shema*, the basic and essential belief of Judaism then and now. It's the "summary of the whole Law and the prophets" — that is, of all the Jewish writings. It's the sentence with which every Jewish service still opens, the first text which every Jewish child still commits to memory, and the last words good religious Jews want to utter before they die.

The second part of Jesus' answer — love of neighbor — is from the Book of Leviticus (19:18). Love for God necessarily entails love for people. But love for God must come first, and it's only when we love God that people become fully lovable. When we remove God from our marriages and our lives, we can easily become angry at people. Temptations like these can come even to those who love enough to get married. Love has to be wholehearted.

Love, like other Christian virtues, isn't passive, but active. Not everybody is capable of loving in this way. Pity those who, because of their selfishness, immaturity, phlegmatic nature, or other reason, can never achieve the heights of this wonderful gift.

St. Paul, in one of the most wonderful passages of all Sacred Scripture, the section of his first letter to the Corinthians which Nancy and Ken have chosen as their second reading, amplifies on the nature of love. He reminds us that everybody has gifts, many of them wonderful: the gift of tongues and of prophecy, so that in their speech they're able to sway many to God; great knowledge; passionate faith; and the gift of charity. But unless they're animated by love, they're empty, and worse. The gifts of tongues and prophecy can be tainted by pride, knowledge has the danger of snobbery, those with faith can be cold and aloof, and even those with charity can interpret it as mere almsgiving, which without love can humiliate others.

Paul gives fifteen attributes of the basically indefinable four-letter word "love." We haven't time to go into them in detail, but it's fitting to make the overall observation that, in brief, the lover is other-centered and big-hearted. This summary of how we're to love applies to all followers of Jesus, but especially to those who are married, and most especially at those times when a partner, who isn't perfect, goes against the grain. Never forget to compliment each other; it's the way to stay together.

We're happy that Nancy and Ken have expressed an awareness of the right way to start their marriage. This augurs well for the happiness we all wish them. And it contributes to our happiness in taking part with them in these festivities today. In that spirit, let's all now witness their conferral of the holy Sacrament of Marriage upon each other, and let's enjoy the occasion as true followers of Jesus who enjoyed and made more enjoyable for others the wedding celebration at Cana.

WEDDING — B

Gn 1:26-28, 31   *1 Cor 13:1-8*   *Jn 15:8-12*

Laughter, Dancing, Love, and Marriage

If there is, as Qoheleth said, an appointed time for everything (Ec 3:1-4), today's a time for joy and laughter. People all the world over and in all ages of history have enjoyed marriage as the ultimate consummation of love, as a sign of life, and as the assurance of the continuation of the species. Today we have all those reasons for joy, plus the fact that John and Mary have chosen to celebrate their nuptials before God and us.

It's out of our Judeo-Christian tradition that Mary and John have chosen the scripture readings for today's celebration. The first, from the Book of Genesis, tells us many things that Mary and John must have thought of when they chose it. The climax of creation is reached in humankind; Genesis shows this by pointing out the divine consultation with the heavenly court concerning God's creation of humankind. Humankind is not God, so the word "image" is softened by "likeness," to show that there's only a resemblance between the two.

Genesis also points out that the distinction of the sexes is of divine origin and therefore good. The full meaning of "humankind" is realized only when there is man and woman. This makes possible a special kind of love — a love that is a necessity, not a luxury. It's the only ingredient capable of welding together husband, wife, and children; it's the only cement strong enough to unite into a nation the poor and the rich, the strong and the weak, the employer and the employee. If we don't have love within the home, we won't have it elsewhere: No human relationships will ever be satisfying if not inspired by love that's learned and experienced in the home. In the context of love, our procreative power is the result of a special divine blessing; by using it, we fulfill a divine precept.

The trouble with love today is that people think mostly of

romantic love. There are many humorous aspects of that. For instance, young people think of being head over heels in that kind of love — but head over heels is an uncomfortable position to be in. And it's no coincidence that we celebrate romantic love on the feast day of St. Valentine, a martyr: Who better to be the patron saint of lovers than someone acquainted with pain? Palpitations, sleeplessness, loss of appetite, mood swings, constant sighing, and obsessional thinking are common symptoms of romantic love. Those afflicted are apt to be told, perhaps in the form of a song, "You're not sick; you're just in love." This is meant to comfort them; the same theory holds that a person with severe abdominal pains should be glad to learn it's merely gallstones.

In a more serious vein, it was Jesus' teachings about the mutuality of man and woman that ultimately made possible the modern version of love called the romantic. Romantic love has three faces: intimacy, passion, and commitment. When all three come together in a relationship, one can get complete, or consummate, love. It's the kind toward which many married people strive.

Intimacy is one term for the *emotional* aspect of romantic love. It includes such things as closeness, sharing, communication, and support. Intimacy increases rather steadily at first, then at a slower rate until it eventually levels off and goes beneath the surface. It might be expressed by communicating inner feelings; sharing one's possessions, time, and self; and offering emotional support. *Passion* is the *motivational* side, which leads to physiological arousal and an intense desire to be united with the loved one. Unlike intimacy, it develops quickly — but then married people get used to it. Obviously, it's expressed by kissing, hugging, touching, and making love. *Commitment* is the *cognitive* side. This is both a short-term decision to love another person and a long-term pledge to maintain that love. It can be expressed by fidelity, and by staying with the relationship through the hard times that occur in any relationship.

Among the things that increase in importance as a relationship grows are a willingness to change in response to each other and to tolerate each other's imperfections. In the beginning, some of the other person's flaws mightn't seem important — may even seem kind of cute. But over the long term they may begin to grate. Both parties have to be willing to make some changes to make the relationship work. Almost everything except matching religious beliefs decrease over time.

Why people should be afflicted with love is a mystery. An ancient Greek legend said that humans were originally hermaphroditic, and that no one loved anybody, at least not romantically. Then one day an angry god divided humans in two, creating one half male and one half female. Ever since, people have felt incomplete. When they find their other half, or think they have, they experience the ecstatic torture we've come to call romantic love.

Further along with the humor, some psychologists consider the head-over-heels variety of love a form of addiction. People in love, they note, often display the two principal characteristics of drug abuse: tolerance and withdrawal. At first, lovers are satisfied to be with their partners for short periods, but their tolerance soon builds and they have to increase the dosage. They often put this into expressions like, "I can't get enough of you."

More seriously, it's because Mary and John know that true love is the key to everything that they bring to our attention St. Paul's hymn to love. Love is invisible and immaterial, and yet as real as steel; as elusive as smoke in the wind, yet stronger than death. The essence of Paul's hymn is that love is other-centered and big-hearted. If carefully nurtured, love will, in spite of one's advancing age, continue to expand with the full strength of its beauty.

When Paul tells the characteristics of love, he indicates that, in a well-ordered love life, character and moral training are indispensable. Love is patient — the product of strength, not weakness, and a demonstration of fortitude that sometimes goes to the point of heroic courage. It's kind: many good people, lacking kindness, would have sided with the rulers and not with Jesus if they had had to deal with the woman taken in adultery. The youngest son of a family asked, "What do people say when they get married, Mother?" The mother, uncertain, answered: "They promise to love and be kind to each other." After some consideration, the young boy said: "You're not always married — are you, Mother?"

Love doesn't entertain jealousy, which is a sign of meanness of soul. It doesn't put on airs, but on the contrary is self-effacing: Real lovers don't think they're bestowing a favor by conferring love, but can't get over the wonder that they're loved. Love is never rude: It's gracious, and thus never forgets that courtesy, tact, and politeness are lovely things; it doesn't take the other for granted, or come to use the other — we use things, but we love people, and when we do the reverse, we end in disaster.

Love isn't self-seeking: It tries to give more than it gets. It doesn't brood over injuries: It learns the great lesson of forgetting. It isn't happy about what's wrong, realizing that it's often easier to weep with those who mourn than to rejoice with those who rejoice. It's pleased with the truth, which isn't as easy as it sounds: Sometimes we don't want the truth to come out.

There's no limit to love's forbearance: It can bear any disappointment. It's always ready to trust: It believes the best about other people. It's always ready to hope, reminiscent of Jesus' example and teaching that no human being is hopeless. And it has a power to endure: not only to sit down and passively put up with things, but affirmatively to conquer and change things, to approach with praise. Lastly, love doesn't come to an end: When all the things in which people take pride have passed away, love will still be here.

Because people need an example of how to make all the poetry about love real, Mary and John have chosen a gospel passage from Jesus' Last Supper that reminds us that their love, as everyone's, is tied up with other people. Right before this passage, Jesus had spoken of himself as the vine and all of us as his branches. The vine image was a part of the religious heritage of the Jewish nation. It was the very symbol of Israel: the emblem on the Temple and on the coins of the Maccabees, for example, was the vine. The only thing that can save one from being an empty, non-fruit-bearing branch is a living fellowship with Jesus and his teaching, because he is, as he told us, the vine of God. Abiding in him means meaningful friendship — like the businessman who, when tempted to sharp unethical practice, looks at the picture of his wife and children on his desk and does what's right.

To live in his love, we have to keep his commandments, even as he kept his Father's commandments (v. 10). This is in contrast to the dangerous illusion of some that their love-making ability is innate. Perhaps this illusion is the way the idea has gotten abroad that marriage is somehow inferior to a job, and that a mere wife is a parasite compared to the busy worker. The truths are that married love is a creative enterprise not achieved by instinct or accident, and that marriage is a noble career that requires working at.

Everyone must obey God's commandments as they pertain to one's state in life. Marriage, which symbolizes the close and holy union of Christ and his Church, brings with it many serious obligations — so serious that God gives the grace of a special Sacrament to help fulfill them. Mary and John are going to have to obey the words of God on marriage if they want to make real the fact that their love has just begun. If they do that, their love will in time grow to the point where they will realize that what they feel now for each other is nothing as compared with what will come.

Jesus says that he tells us all this in order that his joy may be ours and our joy may be complete (v. 11). Joy — *complete* joy — is one of the things Jesus lists to which we're called. Though the Christian way may be at times hard, both in the goal and in the traveling, it's a way of joy. The Christian is the laughing adventurer of Christ. A gloomy Christian is a contradiction in terms. We Christians realize that we're sinners, but we're at times tempted to forget that we're *redeemed* sinners. That last part is important: It gives us joy and makes our joy complete.

And we are, all of us, called to *love*. We're in the world not to compete with one another, or to fight with one another, but to love one another. And, lest Jesus be accused of demanding of others what he didn't practice himself, he adds to his commandment that we love one another as he has loved us (v. 12). When we remember that no one has greater love than to lay down one's life for one's friends (v.

13), we're humbled and inspired to greater love, both within and outside of marriage.

The words of an old poem are appropriate not only for Mary and John, but for all of us:

> I want to love you
> without clutching,
> appreciate you
> without judging,
> join you without invading,
> invite you without
> demanding,
>
> leave you without guilt,
> criticize you without blaming,
> and help you
> without insulting.
>
> If I can have the same
> from you
> then we can truly meet
> and enrich each other.

These are some of the thoughts that inspire us as we witness the marriage of Mary and John. If you would be kind enough to stand in witness, they will confer upon each other the holy Sacrament of Marriage.

WEDDING — C

Gn 2:18-24   *Col 3:12-17*   *Mk 10:6-9*

The Importance of Marriage for Happiness and Fulfillment

Before Pope John Paul I was elected Pope, to provide himself some fun, in an article he wrote he quoted Montaigne, who said, "Matrimony is like a prison: those who are outside do everything to enter it, while those who are within do everything to leave it." Several days later, he received a letter from an old teacher of his, who reproved him for quoting Montaigne, and quoted Rostand, who wrote to his spouse: "I love you more every day — today more than yesterday, but much less than tomorrow." Pope John Paul II wrote a book on marriage, translated into English as *Love and Responsibility.* Other popes have written less personally about the subject, the Holy See has written often, and the United States bishops have shown concern about all aspects of marriage.

Why this concern on the part of the Church's leaders about marriage? Because they realize its importance to the happiness of the individual and to the well-being of the human race. The state of modern marriage, as shown in statistics on divorce and unhappiness, provides added reason for their concern. There's an entry, for example, in the Registry of Wills of the District of Columbia, which reads: "I give, devise, and bequeath to my wife thirty pieces of silver, the price Judas received for betraying Christ, as she has betrayed me. The same is to be paid preferably in dimes, but in no case is the amount to exceed $3." Another will in the same registry reads: "I hereby give, devise, and bequeath to my wife nothing but the aggravation and frustration she has caused me all these years." These are but small evidences of the human misery in marriage which people prefer, most times, to keep quiet during their lifetimes.

But marriage is intended to be the salvation, happiness, and progress of those who enter into it, as attested to by the sentiments of Rostand and by all those who have succeeded in it. If one is to succeed, in these times which are against marriage — against sacrifice and commitment, and for self-indulgence — where does one look for the rules?

Human intelligence alone isn't sufficient — as you can readily see, for example, from the mess of today's society in a secularistic world which gives dominance and homage to intelligence and reason. Nor is ordinary authority enough. On the subject of marriage, at least, most authorities are at odds, this being one reason for the ease of the civil licensing of marriage counselors. So we go to the basics — the word of God in Scripture. What one chooses to emphasize in the wealth of possibilities in this area will reveal our own thoughts, too. So we can see the ideas of Marie and Steven here before us through their choices of today's Scripture readings which you've just heard.

Their first reading is from Genesis. It indicates (v. 18) that people are social beings who will find their greatest happiness realizing this and acting upon the way in which God has created them. It contrasts the creation of animals with that of woman (v. 19); animals, named by man, are hence under his control and aren't fit as companions for his total being. Adam giving names to creatures (v. 20) is a way of showing his cooperating with God in creation; to give names to things is a work of creation.

Then comes the more interesting part. Genesis has God cast a deep sleep on the man and take out one of his ribs (v. 21). This, like marriage, is deep, and interior. Then (v. 22) the rib goes from Adam to Eve — so what he's lost he receives back. Referring to the woman, Genesis refers to "this one . . . this one . . . this one" (v. 23) three times. This, then, in contrast with the mere creation of animals, is a special someone. When Adam first sees her, even though he's never seen her before she's familiar. This is a quality of love that all who have experienced it will recognize: There's something familiar about it, but also always something new. The fact that Eve is bone of Adam's bone and flesh of his flesh symbolizes strength and weakness. What Adam's really saying is, "We're one in our strength, and we're one in our weakness. Sharing makes us one." Weakness and need are as much a part of it as strength.

The gospel reading Marie and Steven have chosen from St. Mark starts with the theological conclusion with which the reading from Genesis ended: All the above are the reasons for which people leave their parents and cling to their spouses. This was the beginning of Jesus' answer to the city-slicker Pharisees who met Jesus as he neared Jerusalem and asked him, perhaps in good faith, his views on divorce. Did he agree with the liberal school of Hillel, who said that divorce was legitimate for almost any reason, or with the stricter school of Shammai, who said that divorce was legitimate only for infidelity to one's marriage vows?

Jesus rejected both schools. He indicated a re-creation of marriage as understood in Genesis, in today's first reading. His teaching about marriage and restoring it to its condition at creation is a way of saying that marriage is part of God's method of making a *new* creation. Marriage is a way of contributing to God's re-creating the world.

How this is done by the followers of Jesus, St. Paul tells us in today's second reading. He shows the qualities one must have under the great overriding quality of love. There's no area of life not touched by love; it's all-pervasive. Its ingredients are many. Among them Paul mentions heartfelt mercy — a heart that can be moved by compassion. Very important is kindness — the virtue of the person whose neighbor's good is as dear to him as his own. Goodness by itself can be stern, hard, and cold; kindness is that sort of goodness which Jesus used with the sinning woman who anointed his feet. Humility is the virtue introduced by Christianity. It's Jesus' own invention, and has no room for arrogance.

Another article of the clothing of love is meekness. In our vocabulary, this might better be called gentleness. The very tone of Paul's words here seems to express the gentleness of the follower of Jesus and of the marriage relationship. It's a model for the gentle urging toward progress — in contrast to nagging — that should happen in marriage. It's the happy mean between too much and too little anger. Also important to all love and to married love in particular is patience. Human patience is the reflection of the divine patience which bears with all our sinning and never chases us away;

it includes a realization of the *time* needed for anyone's getting better. Equally important is forgiveness, which never forgets that a forgiven person, as we all are in God's sight, must always himself be forgiving. Finally is doing it all "in the name of the Lord Jesus" — prayerfulness, without which none of all this is possible.

We wish Marie and Steven the fulfillment of all these ideals, with the resulting happiness that will bring. There's a children's story entitled *The Velveteen Rabbit*, which may have something to say to others besides young children. The setting of the story is a children's nursery. Among the toys are a rocking horse and a velveteen rabbit. One day the rabbit begins a conversation with the rocking horse. The rabbit asks, "What is real? Does it mean having things that buzz inside you?" The rocking horse replies, "Real isn't how you're made; it's something that happens to you. When a child loves you, not just to play with, but really loves you, then you become real." "Does it hurt?" asks the rabbit. "Sometimes," replies the rocking horse, because he was always very honest.

"Does it happen all at once or bit by bit?" inquires the rabbit. "It doesn't happen all at once," the rocking horse replies. "It takes a long time. That's why it doesn't happen often to those who break easily or have rough edges, or who have to be carefully kept. Generally by the time you become real, most of your fur has been loved off; you're loose in the joints and shabby. But those things aren't important because when you're real, you can't be ugly except to those who don't understand."

All of this may be but another way of saying that no one has ever stumbled upon a deep human relationship. There's only the painful process of climbing toward it, a process never completed, a process whose outcome is never fully guaranteed. It's the labor of years, often the labor of a lifetime, with much patience, with much sweat, and with some tears. In the words of the rocking horse, "It doesn't happen all at once. It takes a long, long time."

As their time together grows longer, Marie and Steven must look upon marriage as an opportunity for growth. Now, as we witness their exchange of vows which is in the tradition of all this, we ought to let our minds wander: think of marriage in all the world, and of your own marriage. And think of how they can all be made happier. *Deep* happiness, after all, is Christian. Now, and at the reception, let the heartfelt mercy, kindness, humility, meekness, patience, forgiveness, and prayerfulness of which St. Paul speaks pour into our beings. And let the resulting joy pervade. The joy of our religion is never better portrayed than by a wedding party, at one of which Jesus worked his first miracle and stayed around to have fun.

WEDDING ANNIVERSARY
Gn 2:18-24   *Col 3:12-17*   *Mt 19:3-6*

As with the original marriage, this ceremony should be personalized.

What Makes a Marriage Last?

A married couple came to a priest to arrange a wedding anniversary celebration. After the arrangements were completed, the priest sat back and said, "Even after fifty years of marriage, you look very happy. That's quite an achievement these days. Mind telling me how you did it?"

The woman spoke up and said, "It's all because of romance. Twice a week, we have romantic dinners — soft music, candles, soft light. . . ."

The priest interrupted to say, "You mean to say that your success in fifty years of marriage was because of twice-a-week romantic dinners?"

"Yes," the man said, "she goes on Tuesdays, I go on Thursdays."

That couple was not Irene and Bob. Twenty five years ago, Irene and Bob stood before this altar and vowed their love to each other. They must have liked what they did and the years after, because today, some added pounds and several children later, they're back. Considering the number of marriages that end in divorce, people like Irene and Bob who marry "for keeps" are almost an endangered species. What keeps partners like them together in marriages that, in words they used twenty five years ago, are "for better, for worse, for richer, for poorer, in sickness and in health, until death," and that "grow stronger and stronger as the years go on"?

There's no such thing as a perfect marriage, and no spouse has equal strength in every area or always functions well. Lasting unions don't fit any one mold, either. But there are patterns. In some cases, the "glue" is dependency, in which one of the partners may have a recessive personality that allows submergence to the dominant personality of the other. In other cases, it's inertia, whereby it's just too much trouble to go through the hassles involved in breaking up; it's much easier to stay together and pursue separate interests while living under the same roof. In still other cases, it's children and their needs and shared interests, especially when they're young. In all cases, people who celebrate wedding anniversaries have put their partner's wishes very much in the foreground. It includes trust, communication, sharing, and joy. It includes much laughter: As the humorist said, "Angels can fly because they take themselves lightly."

In more cases than one might suspect, the "glue" is religion. That's what, in many cases, builds the foundation of the qualities needed for a successful marriage: such qualities as commitment, for example, and realistic expectations, flexibility, maturity to cope both with the humdrum as well as with crisis, compromise, proper appraisal of sex, and making marriage a priority. In the Jones home, prayer has been a common occurrence, especially in the togetherness of sharing meals, and attendance at Mass regularly is taken for granted. And Irene and Bob chose to celebrate the major aspect of their anniversary by inviting us to share today's liturgy with them. They've also chosen the readings of today's liturgy, which center around the indissolubility of marriage.

That religious tradition of the indissolubility of marriage goes back a long way. The ancient Hebrews had a view of the sacredness of marriage second to none. To remain unmarried after the age of twenty, except to study the Law of Moses, was to break God's commandment to "be fertile and multiply." One who had no children "lessened the image of God upon earth." There were many detailed laws, based upon Mosaic teaching, about marriage.

These laws began as early as the second chapter of the first book of the Bible, Genesis, part of which you heard in today's first reading. The laws aimed very high. Man's "suitable partner" (v. 18), for example, expressed two profound notions: woman complements man, who's a social being by nature, but she isn't a mere service appendage. Animals, named by man (vv. 19f.) and hence under his control, weren't fit companions for his total being. Man's "deep sleep" (vv. 21f.) suggested that God's activity in creating woman was of a mysterious and highly significant nature. The other words — "rib," "bone of my bone and flesh of my flesh," and the naming of "woman" in contrast with "man" (vv. 21-23) — signified the intimate unity of man and woman. Adam repeating "this one" three times (v. 23) indicated that woman, unlike the rest of creation, is special: the "suitable partner" for man that God had spoken of in the first place.

But the ideal and the reality were two different matters. For one, in Jewish custom the woman had come to be only a thing — the possession first of her father and later of her husband. Easy divorce, therefore, was permitted at the pleasure of the man. And the bill of divorce had come to be a one-sentence statement from the husband that he was dismissing his wife. The only drawback for the man was that, unless the woman was a notorious sinner, he had to return her dowry.

Easy divorce had been outlined in the Mosaic enactment that a husband could dismiss his wife if he was "displeased" with her "because he finds in her something indecent" (Dt 24:1). The big question, however, was how that phrase "something indecent" was to be interpreted. The strict school of Rabbi Shammai said it meant adultery, and that alone. The liberal school of Rabbi Hillel interpreted it much more broadly to say it included a wife spoiling her husband's dinner, or going with unbound hair, or talking to men in the streets, or speaking disrespectfully of her husband's parents in his presence, or brawling in a way that her voice could be heard in the next house.

In this controversy, the Pharisees were delighted to pose to Jesus their seeming no-win question in today's gospel. If he went against the whole idea of divorce, he would appear to be setting himself above and against their lawgiver Moses. If he interpreted the "something indecent" either narrowly or broadly, he would be taking sides with either the school of Hillel or Shammai. Jesus' answer took them back to the ideal of the beginning — what we read in today's first reading. Moses's words were only a *concession*: Moses only *permitted* divorce in order to avoid a situation that would otherwise have become chaotic in face of the current promiscuousness. Jesus returned to the *ideal* that God holds forth for marriage.

What is God's ideal? The Jewish term for marriage means *consecration*: a husband consecrated to his wife, and a wife consecrated to her husband. This ideal has consequences. It means, for example, that marriage is a total union of two persons. It means that in marriage two people find the completion of their personhood. It means that the basis of marriage is *togetherness*, and the basis of togetherness in turn is *considerateness*.

In sum, the foundation of a good marriage isn't something complicated or elaborate: It's simply a love which thinks more of the happiness of the other than of oneself, a love which is happy to be of service, a love which is so able to understand as to make it easy to forgive.

The basic meaning of the word "forgive" means to let go, to give up, to cease to harbor grudges. Nowhere does Jesus reveal himself more as a master psychologist than when he speaks about forgiveness. Authentic religion through the ages stresses the need for forgiveness. Now psychology comes along and tells us the same thing — that we achieve inner health through forgiveness, the forgiveness not only of others but also of ourselves.

Without forgiveness there tends to be resentment or guilt. Instead of human connection, there tends to be separate prisons. Forgiveness frees the forgiver as well as the person who accepts forgiveness. Forgiving may be as close as we shall come in the world to fulfilling Jesus' command, "Love one another as I have loved you."

That involves another aspect of what is at times "tough love": listening. Another human being reveals himself and speaks his words in many different kinds of ways: a gesture, a smile, a glance, a groan — ways other than the spoken word. In fact, at times the spoken word is an inadequate way of both speaking and of listening. Someone may say, "I'm no good," when what he means is, "Please prove to me my worth." Someone may say, "I can't stand you," when what is meant is, "You ignored me when I cared about you." Someone may say, "Life has no meaning," when what is meant is, "Give me a reason for hope."

The foundation of a good marriage is, in short, the kind of love that St. Paul's letter to the Colossians speaks of in today's second reading. Every one of the offshoots of love mentioned in that passage has to do with relationships between people. There's no mention of qualities like efficiency or cleverness — not that these qualities are unimportant — but the basic handmaidens of Christian love are the virtues that govern the spirit of human relationships.

As for efficiency, some writers say that the word doesn't belong to the Gospel, that it belongs to our technological society. But those who take a penetrating look *will* find efficiency in the Bible. In the Jewish scriptures, there is, as only one example, the story of Joseph (Gn 39ff.). Efficiency is also in the New Testament, and often. Jesus said that on the day of judgment people will render an account for every careless word they speak (Mt 12:36). In his story of the two sons, he approved the one who got the job done (Mt 21:28). He said we would all be responsible for using our talents (Mt 25:14-30; see also Luke's parable of the gold pieces [19:12-27].)

Others in the New Testament continued the tradition. St. Paul made efficiency a matter of the final judgment when he foretold that at that time the work of each will come to light (1 Cor 3:13), and he wrote that anyone unwilling to work shouldn't eat (2 Th 3:10). And St. James wrote that a doer who acts shall be blessed (Jm 1:25).

But here in his letter to the Colossians, to provide happy solutions to the problem of living together, Paul begins with *compassion*, the ability to feel with others. Sadly, not everyone is capable of that. He includes *kindness*, the virtue of people whose goodness, which when alone can sometimes be harsh, is tempered by considering another's good to be as precious as their own — like the kindness Jesus showed the sinning woman. Paul next mentions *humility*, that tremendous insight introduced to the world by Christianity. Then he mentions *gentleness*, which avoids too much anger because that's disturbing and too little anger because that's a sign of disinterest.

Paul further mentions *patience*, that virtue which never allows despair over the foolishness, insults, and unteachableness of others. And finally there's the *forgiving spirit*, in imitation of the divine. After clothing ourselves in all these virtues, Paul advises (and those in successful marriages have all heeded) that we "put on love" (v. 14). Finally, he advises that we let the word of Christ, rich as it is, dwell in us (v. 16). And, because we inherited from the Jews the fact that we're a singing Church, we're to sing about how lucky we are to have God's directions for happy personal relationships, and to approach this, like everything else, "in the name of the Lord Jesus" (v. 17).

As we've intimated, now and then following the Lord's injunctions that have guided Irene and Bob's marriage involves "tough love." But as the Book of Proverbs reminds us (27:17), as iron sharpens iron, so people sharpen their fellow human beings. And as a result of it all comes happiness. Nathaniel Hawthorne reminded us: "Happiness is a butterfly which, when pursued, is always beyond our grasp, but which, if you sit down quietly, may alight on you. Happiness in the world comes incidentally. Make it the object of pursuit and it leads to a wild-goose chase and is never attained."

We gather today to congratulate Irene and Bob for their having lived these ideals. We also happily join with them in celebration, in thanking God for His many blessings over the years, and in asking

God to continue to bless them and theirs abundantly for many more years to come. We shall now witness the renewal of their marriage vows.

PRIESTHOOD ORDINATION

Is 61:1-3   *Ep 4:1-7, 11-13*   *Lk 4:18*

In the beginning, nothing existed but God. The first evidence we have of anything other than Him is in the first words of the Bible. Because of His goodness, he created the heavens and the earth. Then God said, "Let there be light," and there was light to illumine all this wonder. Then came the land and the seas. God put seed-bearing plants on earth. Then the biblical account mentions the luminaries God gave to contain and distribute the light: the sun, the moon, and the stars. Next, God created life in the waters of earth and, in the air, many birds of all sizes, shapes, and colors. And then he created cattle, beasts, and other animals. Over it all he put people. So excellent were all God's creatures that people have actually worshipped one or the other of them, confusing them with their Creator.

Equally magnificent as this creation of God in the material, natural order, are His creations in the spiritual order. When the Apostles were frightened by Jesus' crucifixion and were without Jesus for the first time in three years, they locked themselves indoors to be safe. After ten days, on what we now call the first Pentecost, the Holy Spirit came upon them, as Jesus had promised he would. He came in the form of tongues of fire, to signify the love and the zeal which would eat up the Apostles in establishing the early Church. A spiritual creation had taken place.

The spiritual creations of God have never ceased. Every time a person is baptized there is a new birth into Christ. Every time a sinner is reconciled, his soul is decorated anew with God's grace. Every time a person receives his Lord in the Eucharist a new beauty is created in his soul.

And every time a bishop extends his hands over a man in ordination to the priesthood, it beautifies the man's soul by making him a partaker of the special priesthood of Jesus Christ, giving him a share in Jesus' office of king, prophet, and witness for God. He will never be the same.

What does a priest do? In a survey of college students, 84 percent identified the priest's principal role as "spiritual leader"; 8 percent said "counselor"; 4 percent said "social reformer." In truth, the role of the priest in the modern world hasn't changed since the beginning, when the author of the Letter to the Hebrews wrote that "every priest taken from among people is appointed for people in the things pertaining to God" (Heb 5:1). Though he may have to perform commendable social works, this isn't his essential role. Though he may have to engage in administrative endeavors, this is insignificant when compared to what he does as a priest. While it may be necessary for him to engage in financial matters, these pale when we remember the meaning of the priesthood.

The priest proclaims the glad tidings, the Word of the Living God. God's Word will heal the broken-hearted, free the oppressed, comfort the sorrowful. The Spirit of God comes upon the priest to carry God's Word everywhere: to believers and non-believers, to the alienated, to the unchurched, to all who long for God. In a pastoral way he visits the homes of the faithful, instructs adults, teaches in the schools. God's Word must be for him the breath of life, the groundwork of his speech, the rationale of his living. He does these things not on his own, but as a priest of the Church. He preaches in the language of authentic Christian doctrine as taught by our Holy Father and by the bishops joined with him.

He serves his brothers and sisters in Christ, making them holy through the sacraments of faith. His service is not like a corporation's obsequious and profitable, "How may we serve you?" but a self-forgetfulness that shows true greatness in genuinely wanting to help others. It's not like that of the worthless servant in the gospel (Mt 24:14-30) who rationalized excuses, but one that takes risks in order to be profitable to the Lord. It's a service like that of St. Peter's mother-in-law who, immediately upon being cured by the Lord, got up to give the Apostles a meal (Mk. 10:45). It's a service like that of John the Baptist, which motivated his giving up his own beloved followers in favor of their going to Jesus. It's like that of St. Paul, who compared his selfless service to that of a nursing mother (2 Th 2:7).

In short, it's a service in the manner of Jesus. He was the "Suffering Servant" of Isaiah, who, though alone, offered himself for all people. Though rich, he emptied himself (Ph 2:6-11) to serve: not in his own way, but in the Father's; and not to exalt himself, but to humble himself. His passion, done in the Father's way, was at the same time a story of servanthood and glory. The priest serves in all these ways, realizing with St. John of the Cross that "the soul of one who serves God always swims in joy."

The love of Christ impels him to the ministry of reconciliation. By the sacrament of penance he reconciles sinners with God and with the fellow members of our Church. As the great French novelist, François Mauriac, said, "He who, at the moment he raises his hands to absolve us, can no longer be distinguished from the Son of Man." When he sits in the confessional, he is judge, physician, and teacher as well as God's own appointed instrument for the forgiveness of sin. Much of the respect, deference, and genuine affection his people show him is linked with his power to forgive sins in the name of Christ. Through this sacrament, the priest accepts the challenge of proclaiming the mercy and love of God.

In baptism he brings men and women to be reborn in Christ, to be adopted sons and daughters of a loving heavenly Father and siblings of God's other people. When he baptizes, he is co-responsible with God for the birth of another child of God and brother or sister of Jesus Christ. By the anointing of the sick he brings healing of soul and body. He prepares couples for Christian marriage, witnessing their covenant in the name of the Church. And on occasion he confers also the sacrament of confirmation, providing God's grace to face the onslaught of the evil one.

Above all, he — in Jesus' name and power — celebrates the Eucharist. Through that wonderful mystery, our Mass, he continues the unique saving Sacrifice of the Cross and the life-giving banquet of his body and blood. St. Vincent Ferrer said: "The Blessed Virgin opened heaven but once; the priest, at every Mass. The Priest's power surpasses even Mary's power."

When he offers the Holy Sacrifice of the Mass, the priest is the envy of the angels. The Mass is the high point of preaching the Gospel; and in this sacred celebration converges all of his work of instruction and, indeed, everything else he does. It's the heart of his mission and the source of his own personal holiness.

The priest is a builder of genuine Christian community. He builds community with his people in the parish, with his brother priests where he lives, and with the presbyterate of his diocese. His brother priests depend on him, he on them. When they joined the bishop in laying their hands on him in the sacred rite of his ordination, it's a sign they welcome him into the fraternity of the priesthood. Like Christ, he's a sign of contradiction, a reminder that this world is not a lasting city, but a place of pilgrimage, getting ready to be with our loving Father in heaven.

All of what the priest does represents a heavy responsibility. Perhaps more than his people realize, he needs their help. He needs them to stand by him in daily prayer. He needs them to challenge him by their faith, their support of his complete commitment to ministry, to purity, to obedience, to the full dedication of his life. He needs them to understand his weaknesses and failings, but never to cater to his weaknesses.

Lastly, the priest is to turn to Mary, to take her as his model of faith, his constant intercessor with her son. Sometimes his priesthood requires the complete trust that Mary showed at her Annunciation. As priest he often encounters the questions Mary felt as she and Joseph fled into Egypt to escape a tyrannical king, or searched for her son in Jerusalem. At times he stands with Mary at the cross of Jesus. His heart, as hers, is pierced with many sorrows. But with Mary he also experiences the joy of the risen Jesus and the strength of the Holy Spirit in the Upper Room. By herself Mary could have accomplished nothing, but in God's plan she became her Lord's mother and mother of the Church. By himself, the priest can do nothing. But with Mary he has an inexhaustible confidence in God's promise and His sustaining love.

The priest is the mediator between God and people. He goes to God in behalf of people — with their aspirations, prayers, sorrows, joys, and offerings. He returns from God to people with God's forgiveness and blessing. But, like the disciples on the road to Emmaus, he experiences disappointments, apparent failures. He experiences some of the confusion that was theirs as they looked for the Lord Jesus. At the same time he remembers that Jesus will always be walking with him on the road of his ministry.

Of so great an honor, no human being is worthy. All good priests are conscious of the words which follow in the passage quoted above: "He is able to have compassion on the ignorant and erring, because he himself also is beset with weakness, and by reason thereof is obliged to offer for sins, as on behalf of the people, so also for himself. And no man takes the honor to himself: he takes it who is called by God" (Heb 5:2ff.).

Before the bishop begins the ceremony of Ordination, he addresses himself to the people present and says, "Dearly beloved brethren, as all on a ship, both the captain and the passengers, have the same reasons for confidence or for fear, they should act together with one mind, seeing that their interests are the same." So it's not only the priest who should rejoice with all of heaven over one sinner who does penance, but every Catholic. It is not only the priest who should feel sorry over evil, but all followers of Christ.

The priesthood doesn't stand alone. It rises or falls with all who are baptized in Christ. All have obligations toward the priesthood. We owe priests respect, keeping in mind all they stand for. We owe it to them, to God, and to ourselves, to consult them. Their experience and training are unique in all this world. As Pope Pius XII said (*Mediator Dei*), "Let all . . . who would live in Christ flock to their priests."

Indeed, why go to the priest? The world provides other possibilities when you need someone: counselors, psychotherapists, psychiatrists, psychologists. How can the priest compete with all that scientific training? For one thing, he provides the much-needed God dimension. This means that he can straighten life into an all-comprehensive dimension for the individual, represent values which alone can save our society, and help swiftly when societal bureaucracy is slow. He can provide that quality we need so much these days: forgiveness. He can objectively and with full confidentiality allay guilt, remorse, regret, and sorrow.

In short, the priest is to help men and women see Jesus — the young, the suffering, the helpless, and the doubters and scoffers, as well as the mature faithful. By his words, by his style of life, by every action, he is to show them Jesus' hands and feet, pierced for love of us, and his side, his open heart. And in that perspective he's to help them to love one another.

All members of a congregation owe it to their priests to work with them, as the command of Christ to go forth and bring all nations to him implies. This cooperation applies no less to the lay person than to the priest. Finally, all owe it to their priests to pray for them: It stands to reason that the devil, knowing priests' tremendous capacity for good, will assail them with vigor.

ANNIVERSARY OF PRIESTLY ORDINATION

Ac 20:17f., 28-32, 36   Ph 4:4-9   Mt 16:13-19

The speaker will have to adapt the particulars of this talk to the special character and work of the celebrant, "Father Jim."

In his youth, as with all young people, Father Jim cast about with questions about what to do with his life. In the midst of the widespread self-centredness of our culture, he came to realize the need for God in our world. He read statements by people like St. John Chrysostom (d. 407), who wrote of priests: "As though already translated to Heaven, as though free from our human passions — so high, to such a dignity, have they been raised!" And Father Jim read stories of heroes like Jean Marie Vianney (1786-1859) who was, for 41 years, the Curè of the little town of Ars in France. When he arrived at Ars in 1818, he set out through personal prayer and penances to convert his 50-family parish. This heavenly patron of all parish priests is most famous, though, for the final years of his life, when 80,000 pilgrims annually flocked to his parish for confession. Among his testimonies on the priesthood was his remark: "How great is the priest! The priest will only be understood in heaven. Were he understood on earth, people would die, not of fear, but of love."

Father Jim heard a voice from the Scriptures that said often, "Come, follow me!" He wanted to join up.

Over the years after ordination, in a world which in many respects is undergoing rapid and continual evolution, Father Jim came to know from personal experience the new obstacles opposing the faith, the sporadic frustration of his work, and priests' occasional loneliness. Changing moral values, most publicly and controversially in the area of the reproductive revolution, has led many Catholics to wonder about the clergy's expertise in areas of moral guidance, and has contributed to the dramatic decline in the use of the sacrament of Penance, with all its ramifications for Father Jim's sense of identity.

Vatican Council II even changed Father Jim's title: Attempting to follow the Scriptures, the Council restricted the word "priest" to Jesus and to the "common priesthood" of the baptized; for ordained men the Council returned to the New Testament expression *presbyter*, or the more modern "ministerial priest." The Council did, however, emphasize that the common priesthood and the ministerial priesthood "differ from one another in essence and not only in degree" (*Lumen Gentium*, 10). In other words, the special priesthood isn't simply a gradation or intensification of the common priesthood: It's essentially different.

The Church is also full of another aspect of Father Jim's definition of himself in calling him "a witness to mystery." This side reflects the unfolding mystery of Jesus Christ. The priest is the one who interprets in all the events of everyday life what Karl Rahner calls "the silent coming of God."

That silent coming is nowhere more evident than in the celebration of the Eucharist. In fact, the Church defines Father Jim as "the celebrant of the Eucharist." From that all else flows. But Father Jim also embodies centuries of involvement by priests in apostolates which have ranged from schools to soup kitchens, from writing books to street preaching — countless evangelical initiatives directed not simply to "the community of faith," but also to heretics, pagans, and public sinners.

The faithful don't celebrate the Eucharist in the same way as the priest. The priest acts in the name of Christ; the faithful offer the sacrifice "through" and "with" the priest. Should the availability of the Eucharist be our first priority? That certainly has a strong scriptural foundation. St. Paul (1 Cor 11:23f.), and each of the synoptic gospels (Mk 14:22f., Mt 26:26f., Lk 22:15f.) records the narrative of Jesus' institution of the Eucharist. And Jesus himself warned that if you don't eat the flesh of the Son of Man and drink his blood, you won't have life in you (Jn 6:53).

The Church has defined Father Jim's priesthood still further. The Church calls him, for example, "the shepherd of the flock." Jesus is the promised good shepherd (cf. Ezk 34), who knows each one of his sheep, who offers his life for them, and who wishes to gather them together as one flock with one shepherd (cf. Jn 10:11-16). Jesus presents himself as "the good shepherd" (Jn 10:11, 14) not only of Israel but of all humanity (cf. Jn 10:16).

Jesus — and good priests like Father Jim — is the shepherd who has come "not to be served but to serve" (Mt 20:28), and who freely offers himself as the "innocent lamb" sacrificed for our redemption (cf. Jn 1:36; Rv 5:6, 12). He feels compassion for the crowds because they were harassed and helpless, like sheep without a shepherd (cf. Mt 18:12-14). He gathers and protects his sheep. He knows them and calls each one by name (cf. Jn 10:3). He leads them to green pastures and still waters (cf. Ps 22-23) and spreads a table for them. Father Jim, like the chief Shepherd, is a loving, caring, guide of his flock, holding them close to his heart.

To be a shepherd also involves authority. In Vatican II, the priest "shares in the authority by which Christ himself builds up, sanctifies, and rules his body" (*Ministry and Life of Priests*, 2). Priests are "so configured to Christ the priest that they can act in the person of Christ the Head" (ibid.). Indeed, "every priest in his own way represents the person of Christ himself" (ibid. 12). He is "father and teacher among the people of God and for them" (ibid. 9). Priests become "living instruments of Christ the eternal priest" (ibid. 12).

Does the "authority" which comes with the priestly office distinguish Father Jim from a non-ordained lay-person who may in fact be doing virtually identical pastoral work? The constant Catholic belief is that ordination confers a sacramental power which permanently distinguishes the priest. What Father Jim does in the Eucharist and in the Sacrament of Reconciliation he does by virtue of that power. The priest doesn't represent the community because the community has elected him. On the contrary, he represents the community because — by virtue of his ordination — he first represents Christ himself, who is the head of the Church.

Increasingly, lay ministers are being installed in public ceremonies very analogous to Father Jim's ordination. There are in addition counselors, psychologists, psychiatrists, secular charitable organizations. With many tasks which were previously reserved to the clergy now seen as being more appropriately the responsibility of the laity, some blurring of the traditionally precise distinctions between clergy and laity has resulted.

Is lay involvement going to force the average pastor to switch from being a "one-man band," who dealt personally with most of his parishioners, into being the "orchestra leader" for a team of specialists? Whereas the definition of the ministerial priest as the one who leads the orchestra can sound extremely flattering, it holds little appeal for countless priests who entered the ministry with the intention of serving the faithful in a personal way — by celebrating the Eucharist, baptizing new Christians, instructing people in the ways of God, hearing confessions, officiating at marriages, and caring for the sick.

A final definition of Father Jim is that he's called to be a "comedian." That is to say, tragedy is the inevitable destruction of the hero. This takes place in the arts as well as in professions like medicine, where the hero inexorably dies. But Father Jim, who sees life's story from a more overarching viewpoint, knows that life is a comedy with even alleged victims sharing in the victory of Jesus' Resurrection.

However we may finally describe Father Jim — as presbyter, or as dispenser of such mysteries as the Eucharist, or as spiritual shepherd, or as comedian — we're always dealing with the fact that there's a mystery which inhabits him as well as his confreres in the priesthood.

Each of the aspects of his ministry has given Father Jim its own unique joy. In presiding over the Eucharist for so many years, he's had the joy of bringing you together not only with God, but with each other. Through baptisms, he's had the exhilaration of making both infants and adults children of God, and thus of making real his conviction of the need of God in the world. Instructing people in the ways of God — in the school, in religious instruction, before baptisms and marriages, in the pulpit, and in casual contacts — has given him the same satisfaction.

Father Jim has been humbled by the great privilege of his position in his people's respect and confidence in hearing confessions, acknowledging the weakness of himself as well as them, and absolving from sin. He's taken delight in being the Church's official representative at marriages and in imitating his Master in the joy of participating in the reception afterwards. He's not only laughed on the happy occasions, but mourned with his people when they were sorrowing.

In all, he's had the tremendous pleasure of sharing the greatest and most intimate times of people's lives. In times of his own discouragement, he's been uplifted by his contact with his people, whose presence — knowingly or not — meant more to him than a football cheering section.

Of course, the key to anyone's understanding of an ordained minister like Father Jim will inevitably lie in one's prior understanding of the nature of the Church. Behind the human exterior of the Church stands the mystery of a more than human reality, in which reformers, sociologists, and organizers have no competence. As a mystery, the Church is essentially related to Jesus Christ. She is his fullness, his body, his spouse. She's the "sign" and living "memorial" of his permanent presence and activity in our midst and on our behalf.

In St. Paul's theology of the Church as the Body of Christ, it's the priest alone who represents Christ as Head to the rest of the Body. That's Father Jim's special vocation to the rest of the faithful who are themselves "the fullness" of Christ (Ep 1:23). Because of the privileged position Father Jim holds, Vatican Council II calls him to be a "father and teacher among the people of God" (*Ministry and Life of Priests*, 9), the "living instrument of Christ the eternal priest" (ibid. 12). He fulfills the role of Christ the Head preeminently "in the mystery of the Eucharistic sacrifice" (ibid. 13).

To see Father Jim as anything less depicts him as being something like baptismal water: ordinary water which has been blessed and set aside for special use — but able to be replaced by any water in emergency situations. Gregory of Nyssa (d. 395) suggests a better image: that there's more in common between the ordained man and the consecrated bread than between him and the baptismal water.

The most important people in the Church ultimately, however, are not the clergy but the saints. Others' call to holiness is in the context of their lives; Father Jim's call is essentially in the form which derives from the sacrament of orders. For him, holiness is intimacy with God; it's the imitation of Christ, who was poor, chaste, and humble; it's unreserved love for people and a giving of himself on their behalf and for their true good. In the celebrated words of St. Augustine: "For you I am a bishop, with you I am a Christian. The former title speaks of a task undertaken, the latter of grace; the former betokens danger, the latter salvation."

For Father Jim, a wonderful model of holiness is present in the Blessed Virgin Mary who, under the guidance of the Holy Spirit, made a total dedication of herself for the mystery of the redemption of the human race. Mary is she who believed that the promise made her by the Lord would be fulfilled (Lk 1:45). Father Jim has always venerated and loved her with a filial devotion, as the Mother of the supreme and eternal Priest, as Queen of the Apostles, and as protectress of his identity in the priesthood.

JUBILEE (OF RELIGIOUS)

Lv 25:8-22   *Ps 33:9*   *2 Cor 6:8-10*   *Lk 4:16-22*

This talk is, on its face, for the anniversary celebration for the profession of a religious sister. It is also intended for the jubilee of any other religious (brothers) or clergy.

For the idea of jubilee which we celebrate today we can thank the ancient Jews, as we see in today's first reading. The word "jubilee" comes from *yobhel*, a ram's-horn trumpet sounded to inaugurate the jubilee year. This "grand sabbatical" marked every fiftieth year, the opening of which was the Day of Atonement. In this year there was no agriculture, all landed property reverted to the original owners or their descendants without payment, and all Hebrews who had by intricate processes become slaves to their own people were set at liberty. This was to remind the Hebrews that not only the land belonged to God, but also the people. In truth, the Jewish scriptures record no historical observance of the jubilee. The key is in a future ideal context. But its spirit of appreciation for personal rights and human dignity synthesizes much of the teaching of the Jewish scriptures.

It remained for Jesus to fulfill the idea of jubilee. Today's gospel tells of the beginning of his preaching, when he came back to his hometown of Nazareth to preach in the little synagogue there. He deliberately opened the scroll to the passage of Isaiah on the Jubilee year (Is 61:1f.). Jesus tells us that he has come to announce a year of favor from the Lord (v. 19). That's the major jubilee for all who believe in Jesus, of which today's (hopefully riotous) celebration is a small part.

What brought us to this point is that more than fifty years ago, Sister Mary felt called to add to any ordinary relationship with Jesus a deeper one. Right from the beginning, she knew from St. Paul that we Christians are nobodies who in fact are well known; dead, yet here we are, alive; sorrowful, though we're always rejoicing; poor, yet we enrich many; seeming to have nothing, yet everything is ours

(2 Cor 6:8-10). She had learned the lesson of St. Peter at a beginning stage of his development when he reminded the Lord that he and the other Apostles had left everything they owned (a few fishing nets and boats!) to follow him, and inquired about the reward. Jesus promised a plentiful return now and life everlasting as well (Lk 18:28-30).

During the intervening years, in the midst of contrary reflections Sister Mary must have thought of those lessons often. Her work with people must have caused her to inquire with Peter about the reward. She must have been astonished with Paul at her abiding joy, her ability to enrich many people who seemed to have more than she, her having everything necessary to bring happiness, and the over-riding joy that comes with giving oneself.

She's kept the lamp of love and faith burning brightly as she served God and His people unceasingly. Like husbands and wives in the growth of their love, she's become aware of how much more deeply and broadly her love relationship with her God is now than it was when she was professed so many years ago. Faith is the way she continued contact with her Lord. In that framework was her human becoming, an allowing process whereby she became who she is.

She has aimed at evangelical perfection and increased the holiness and apostolic zeal of God's Church, and her daily life has enriched the world and borne fruit. The first beginning of the wholeheartedness of her desire to serve God completely by her gift of self has come closer as she came to this day. The solemnizing of the anniversary of this process makes us happy.

There have been many elements of change in her life and the world during the years since her profession; she herself will have to reminisce about those. But the more things change, the more they remain the same. One of the elements of sameness that have sustained her to this day is her commitment to Christ as her center.

That word "commitment" is important. Commitment is a pledge by both intellectual conviction and emotional ties to an involvement which embraces the future as well as the present. Involving loyalty, identification, and participation, commitment is passionate, with plenty of heart as well as head. It goes outside oneself, being related to what one psychologist called a characteristic of psychological maturity. For a religious, commitment reaches out in faith to oneself, to the bettering of one's work, and to all with whom one comes in contact.

In our day, many people — especially youth — ask if it's even possible to *have* commitment. People who "hang loose" and "play it cool" see commitment as especially difficult, if not impossible. That's why some people can't work up the commitment it takes to get married. The philosopher Friedrich Nietzsche said that only those in the category of *Übermensch* ("Superior Man," or "Superman") are capable of commitment. Only Superman has the autonomy that can rise above the herd morality sufficiently to make promises. Nietzsche saw all candidates for vows — baptismal, marital, religious, and those of public office — in this light.

Another philosopher, Jean-Paul Sartre, found commitment to be as contradictory as its source, which is love. Seeing people placed in the uncomfortable position of having to choose between freedom and love, he unhesitatingly said that freedom comes before love and all else. Commitment ties you down, and so it's undesirable.

Sartre's fellow existentialist Gabriel Marcel took the opposite position. He contended that you can get to know yourself and grow only if you commit yourself. He made the very important contribution of showing that human freedom and commitment are not only not contradictory, but are necessarily correlative. Like Nietzsche, he held that all those forces that rob you of humanity — habit, custom, force, mechanization, and the like — deprive you of freedom and hence of the ability to commit yourself. Also like Nietzsche, but with greater sadness, Marcel admitted that many people are actually unable to commit themselves. Sister Mary is in the superior group that's capable of commitment.

Those who hold that it's impossible to *have* commitment argue further that any attempt to *teach* commitment to today's youth demands a response that youth are usually unable to give, and that such a demand infringes drastically on youth's freedom. The attempt to elicit commitment is *sermonizing*, and the leader is to teach, not preach. ("Poppa, don't preach," goes the song.) To the contrary, Sister Mary by her life has not only taught *about* faith, but imparted commitment and provided Christian *witness*. This kind of inclusion is a contribution to the community and the nation.

Sister Mary has held on to all the emphases of the Catholic mind-set: the objective nature of truth, the primacy of the spiritual over the material, the ultimate triumph of good over evil, the realization of the self in the context of a relationship with the Ultimate Being, aliveness to all the anguish and care of existence, passionate concern, full commitment to life, true responsibility, and belief in the greatness as well as the uniqueness of the human being. She became vividly aware of all the problems, conditions, and decisions of human living. From among all the possibilities of life, Sister Mary made a selection and then committed herself. From that she ascended into her own authenticity. In constant self-discovery, successive layers of disguise were stripped away and her "self" was revealed.

Her encounter, dialogue, and involvement are all consonant with the advocacy of social awareness in Catholic theology. That theology today doesn't advocate flight from the world, but commitment to the world's transformation. When you work for the betterment of the world and human society in that way, you're promoting the reign of God.

Dedicated to the Catholic Church's goals of message, community, and service, Sister Mary's religious commitment was an enrichment of her personality. By the nature of her work, her commitment was a moral enterprise dealing with the formation of the "good person," the "good life," and the "good society." Intertwined was her perception of the Church as a loving mother.

God renews the Church in every age by raising up men and women like Sister Mary — "outstanding in holiness, living witnesses of His unchanging love. They inspire us by their heroic lives, and help us by their constant prayers to be the living sign of God's saving power." Jesus consecrated more closely to his service those who leave all things for his sake, and promised that they would find a heavenly treasure. May Sister Mary continue to commit herself and raise her mind and heart to God. May God grant a blessed ending to Sister Mary's journey in following Christ more closely, on which journey she has now accomplished so many wonderful years.

COMMISSIONING OF LAY MINISTERS

Rv 21:5-7   Ps 31   Rm 8:35-39   Mt 28:18-20

The great commissioner of lay ministers is the Lord who, at the end of his life, told us all to make disciples of everybody, baptizing them and instructing them. In accord with that injunction, ministry is "being present to," "paying attention to." Our lay ministers being commissioned today have volunteered their services in a special and concentrated way, consonant with the definition of their task.

They desire not to be served but, like their Lord and Master, to serve their brothers and sisters. To be effective and true to their mission, the Church recommends that they develop a good spiritual life. It's a good spiritual life that can make us worthy to be his ministers.

To be spiritual is to awaken to the light of one's own spirit, whose deepest source is God. When God started His kingdom, he built it not on power, but on spirit. People who have the courage to awaken and inhabit their own interiority become transfigured. To realize this is to turn one's life into a festival. The false burdens of control and power give way to a great sense of acceptance, joy, and celebration. To come into this new way of seeing is to learn to be. As one authority said, "unless you see a thing in the light of love, you do not see at all."

The fact that you've arrived at this point of becoming the Lord's ministers indicates that you realized that you're the salt of the earth, the light of the world. That's a great dignity. If you think of yourself as less, the consequences are no less harmful than the slum child saying "I'm nobody!"

Not unlike St. Paul, through their reflections and their actions our new ministers find that our religion is not a thing, but a person: Jesus Christ. We find that it's easy to see that Jesus Christ is God: His life, miracles, and teachings make that obvious. But for a sound and lasting interior life that befits a special minister of Jesus Christ, it's equally important to see him as a human being, having all the qualities we look for in a person.

Many aspects of the New Testament show the force of his personality. When, for example, he asked Matthew to follow him, this money-minded Jew left his business to comply. His call of John was so momentous that sixty years later, in his gospel, John recorded the exact time of day he met Jesus for the first time. When they tried to kill Jesus at Nazareth, he fled unharmed from their midst. The agents of the Pharisees sent to kill him returned with the stupendous observation that never did anyone speak as this man.

After the people got to know him, they put all their sick out in the street for him to heal them. When the Apostles were impatient with so many people, children as well as adults, who were getting close, he chided them. So enthusiastic was he about going around doing good that even his nights were occupied — for instance, with seekers like Nicodemus.

He had a good sense of humor. When, for example, the Apostles came to him about the crowd of people who had followed him into an inaccessible place without food, before he multiplied the loaves and fish he asked Philip to feed them. At the wedding reception at Cana, he changed water into wine to let the good times roll. When Nicodemus asked him what he had to do to gain eternal life, he answered that he had to be born again, and when Nicodemus took him literally he had to explain his humor. When he and the Apostles were experiencing an unusually severe storm on Lake Galilee, he let them reveal their fright before coming to their rescue.

His qualities of leadership were superb. When he wanted others to join him, he showed that he wouldn't ask them to do anything that he himself wouldn't do. His request was "Come, *follow me.*" He leaves our response to that invitation voluntary: "*If anyone wishes* to follow me, let him take up his cross and follow me." He started the enterprise of his Church with twelve fishermen who showed such little promise that often they couldn't even understand him. The first pope, Peter, was anything but the "rock" that Jesus nicknamed him. But Jesus' leadership was such that even by modern business standards he was a great success.

A quality of his leadership is his fearlessness. When the Pharisees put constant spies in the crowds, he bravely faced them down. When he knew that they were plotting to kill him, he continued on his course. And when it came time for him to go to Jerusalem to knowingly suffer and die, he resolutely set his face to enter the city (Lk 9:51).

His compassion was superhuman. His concern was always for "the little man," no matter what the cost. He often said, "I have compassion on the multitudes." And he showed it with the widow in the little town of Naim, the body of whose only son was being carried to the cemetery; in a dramatic but simple scene, Jesus gave him back to her alive. At the grave of Lazarus, he wept for Lazarus's sisters Martha and Mary. The shortest verse of the Bible tells us that he wept over Jerusalem. His understanding and compassion resulted in a considerateness that was often evident: at the Last Supper, for example, and in Gethsemane, and on the Way of the Cross, and at Calvary.

His appearance was not the sheltered look that some artists give him. He was, in truth, ruddy from being out of doors, muscular from working at carpentry, tough from his fasts, and brawny from being on the road so much of the time.

All these factors may lead to unsuspected insights into Jesus' personality. When you appreciate the personality of Jesus and when you try to develop your own personality to its fullest potential, you can multiply your opportunities for doing good. If in the process of developing your personality for Christ's sake you act in accord with the fundamental principle of theology that grace builds upon nature and doesn't contradict it, your power for doing good will be immeasurable.

Personality is the outcome of a long process of self-integration. When personality is developed sufficiently for grace to work with it most effectively, it has seven marks. First is self-*awareness*, in all its uniqueness and unity. One has one's own uniqueness — and therefore reasonable independence from others. You must have a face of your own to give to Christ, not just the stamp of a crowd. In the beautiful old Black spiritual play *Green Pastures*, when God is trying to get Noah to preach for Him and Noah finally agrees, he says to God, "Ah ain't much, Lord, but ah's all ah's got!"

Self-awareness also demands unity — unity of dignity and humility. This means that you're not divided within yourself; there are no neurotic tendencies in striving for religious perfection. The liberality of Christ is much to be preferred over the rigidity of the Pharisees. We see the unity of dignity and humility also in Christ before Pilate, before Herod, and before the High Priest when he was being sentenced to death.

An over-strong longing for approval makes one extremely sensitive to rejection by anyone, especially authority: for example, there's no venturing into the intellectual realm, no listening to the Holy Spirit — because of the danger of disapproval. There's a spirit of fright instead of the Spirit of the Lord: There's nothing *positive*. Sometimes the need for approval translates into the need of someone like a priest to assume responsibility. There's an expectation of his full attention and a reliance upon this to solve all problems, instead of maturely and lovingly performing one's obligations on one's own.

The second mark of a sufficiently-developed personality is a consciousness of one's own *limitations*. You see evils in isolation, and you recognize that you need other people — to survive, to grow, to make life meaningful. Other people give you a more accurate appraisal of yourself, a chiseling off of rough edges. Even the criticisms of enemies are beneficial — they are, after all, more reliable than the praise of friends. Because you realize your limitations, you realize, ultimately, that you need God.

The third mark of the personality that is sufficiently developed for grace to work most effectively is self-*acceptance*. You accept not only your limitations, but also that your motivations are not all white (which is only for angels), nor all black (which is only for devils, and results in despair). Our motivations are often gray. You accept situations as they arise, and do the best you can. Religion doesn't change people into angels — it's a Church of sinners, not saints.

The fourth mark of the personality that is sufficiently developed to enable grace to work is self-*realization*. Many people with stunted psychological development have *infantile* modes of existence in religious life. To those who haven't developed psychologically, God may be present not as a loving Father, but as a stern Master, because of one's relationship with one's own father. Life is then an attempt to placate God, to be assured you're safe, that God will not "get" you. Sometimes this is used as an escape — like a child who does her homework when she should be doing the dishes, or an adult who prays when he should be working.

No, there must be a development of a *positive, authentic* religious will. With that comes an abiding, *embodying*, phase of an *incarnation* of religious development. This is never-ending. There's a lifelong growth of commitment in thoughts, feelings, desires, and actions. This is strengthened by survival over temptations and trials.

The fifth mark of the personality that is sufficiently developed for grace to work most effectively is the awareness of self-*determination*. The person obeys and wants to, not because of esteem of others, or routine, or custom, but freely. The highest human gift is the gift of self in freedom — not freedom *from*, but freedom *to*.

The sixth mark of the personality that is sufficiently developed for grace to work on you most effectively is *wholeness*. This means that the totality of your personhood is involved, implying *harmony*. In the "religious" personality — that in which a religious mode of existence is the most central — this involves a losing of oneself in order to find oneself, and a finding of oneself in order to lose oneself.

The seventh and last mark of the personality that is sufficiently developed for grace to work on you most effectively is that you be *dynamic*. You realize that you're never a finished product. You can never say, "It's enough — I have stored my full crop in my barn. I can relax, enjoy myself." If you've succumbed to this position, even if you aren't dead in the sense of having stopped breathing, you're dead by default, because there's no real life present.

Fulfillment of all this makes possible *being with others*, both God and people — that is, reciprocity. That puts us into a *communicative* attitude — a gentle play of giving and receiving. Here, the true personality is open to the other.

These facets of the interior life don't take place at once, however, but a little at a time. If an artist were to take his biggest chisel to a block of marble, hit it with his heaviest hammer, with his largest swing, and with his greatest force, he breaks it. Michelangelo's unfinished statuary in Florence shows a different procedure — a very careful one that makes only a little progress from day to day.

It would be good for you who are being commissioned as Jesus' ministers to continue to develop a sound personhood that will enable God's grace to build upon it to the end result of a deep spiritual life and an effective ministry.

We all congratulate you today on your achievement, and we pray both for you and for the people you will serve.

PARISH APPRECIATION DAY

1 P 2:1-7   *Ps 95:3f.*   *Mt 18:15-20*

After World War II, a young American boy married a Japanese girl and settled down in a residential area outside Tokyo. The young couple made many friends and enjoyed entertaining them in their new home. Inevitably, though, at their parties someone would pick up the bugle the young man had kept as a souvenir of the war and go out into the garden to try blowing it.

Amazingly, there were no complaints until one day when an elderly Japanese paid the newlyweds a visit, explaining that he'd come on behalf of the neighbors. They wanted the young couple to know that their presence was esteemed and that they were a valuable asset to the neighborhood. "In fact," the caller concluded, "we want you to know that should you ever need any of us, at any hour, all you have to do is blow your bugle and we'll come running."

Now, that's subtle. We intend to be more direct, like the note which an elderly maiden aunt received from her ten-year-old niece: "Dear Auntie: Thank you for your nice present. I have always wanted a pin cushion, but not very much."

The reason for our wanting to be direct is that we want to express our gratitude and appreciation for all that you've been doing for the parish. This opportunity comes only too rarely. Shakespeare called ingratitude a marble-hearted fiend, and it's been said elsewhere that thanklessness is sharper than a serpent's tooth.

So we want to show that we're sensitive to and grateful for all you've done for the Lord through your parish. As for sensitivity, it's been said that if our world is to be saved, it will be by such virtues as gentleness, kindness, mercy — and sensitivity. If we've been insufficiently sensitive and grateful in the past, we apologize, and hope to make up for it in part by expressing our appreciation now.

We acknowledge Clarence Darrow's answer to a woman who, after he had resolved her legal troubles, said, "How can I ever show my appreciation?" "My dear woman," replied Darrow, "ever since the Phoenicians invented money there has been only one answer to that question." Although we can't practice what he advocated, we do want you to know the depth of our appreciation.

Through time, God chose to need human helpers. To build up his eternal kingdom, he calls people to live and work in the midst of the world and its concerns. He wants the people whom he calls to be effective witnesses to the truth of the gospel and to make his Church a living presence in the midst of that world.

His Church is the sacrament of salvation for everyone. All should feel urgently the call to work in the universal Church through our local parish. In that service, God's initiative comes first. What form, then, should our response take? Perhaps all we contribute is a free and joyful acceptance of the gift. Grace is free, but it's not cheap. Jesus paid dearly for it: It cost him his life.

The Good News that we herald is "ask and you shall receive"

(Mt 7:7; Lk 11:9). It would have been "bad news" if Jesus had said "try and you will succeed." Because we're in a gratuitous order, we've been saved from having to try to "succeed." The rational side of our nature makes us cling to our own autonomy rather than accept this great gift. We were conditioned as children to the idea that you never get anything for nothing; we remain so: "There's no such thing as a free lunch."

That's the attitude that St. Peter had at the Last Supper. His "religious" sense was offended: Instinctively, he felt that Jesus should not be doing something for him, but that he should be doing something for Jesus: "You will never wash my feet" (Jn 13:8). Because Jesus wanted to show the necessity of grasping this new principle of the Kingdom that we are in a gratuitous order, he became stern with Peter: "If I do not wash you, you have no part in me" (Jn 13:8).

We must single out, in no particular order, some who have rendered particular service to our parish and to God. One group are our *readers*. Their main function is to read, in our sacred celebrations, in an *alive* and not phlegmatic fashion, the lessons from sacred Scripture. In behalf of the office they've undertaken, they make every effort to acquire that increasingly warm love and knowledge of Scripture that will make them more perfect disciples of the Lord and carriers of the message of salvation.

Thus with their help men and women come to know God our Father and His son Jesus Christ, whom he sent. In proclaiming God's word to others, in obedience to the Holy Spirit they accept it themselves. In all they say and do they show forth to the world our Savior.

Another group whom we very much appreciate are our *ushers*. They work with no self-glorification or self-promotion, but in quiet, self-sacrificing efficiency to insure proper order. They comprehend that where they serve is not a theater or auditorium, but a unique sacred place called a church. They realize that their task is to inspire a silent reverence that will serve to make prayer easy, help people to recollect themselves out of the busyness of the world, and give proper tribute to God. Ushers are observant to the external needs of individuals, not only at Mass, but as the occasion calls, whether it be in a parking area, an aisle, or a seat. These ministers of hospitality are the very first encounter people have with Jesus when they come to church.

Another group deserving our appreciation is our *altar servers*. The summit and source of the Church's life is the Eucharist, which gives birth to the Christian community and makes it grow. This takes place through the power of the Spirit through the sacred signs of the Church's liturgy, a living memorial of the mystery of redemption. Altar servers are an example to all by their seriousness, their reverence, their attention to detail, and their staying focused on what's going on at the altar. They're faithful in the service of our altar, and seek to understand the deep spiritual meaning of what they do.

Our *musicians* enhance our liturgy through their choral singing as well as their choice of liturgical music. Their purpose is to give glory to God, and they realize that to sing well is to pray twice. In order to sing well, they give time for rehearsals. They direct the singing and the participation of the faithful — those of us whose singing makes the angels wince as well as those who are more gifted. Our cantors particularly deserve our gratitude: They encourage even the shy among us to raise our voices in worship.

Our *deacons* belong to an ancient order in the Church. Explicit testimony of their position of great honor in the early Church is given by St. Paul both in his letter to the Philippians, in which he sends his greetings not only to the bishops but also to the deacons (Ph 1:1), and in a letter to Timothy, in which he highlights the qualities and virtues that deacons must have in order to be proved worthy of their ministry (1 Tm 3:8-13).

The deacon is entrusted with whatever mission local need assigns him: taking the holy Eucharist to the sick confined to their homes, conferring baptism, blessing marriages, preaching the word of God, leading the rites of burial.

As a minister of the Word, of the altar, and of charity, he makes himself a servant of Jesus Christ, who was known among his disciples as the one who served others. He serves God and humankind in love and joy. When his bishop presented him with the book of the gospels, he advised: "Receive the Gospel of Christ, whose herald you now are. Believe what you read, teach what you believe, and practice what you teach." We're fortunate to have our deacons.

Another important group are our *Catholic-school teachers and staff*. The future life of our parish, as well as its present, depends very much on what they do. It's no exaggeration to add that they affect our civilization as well. Priestly mediators between the students and the world of reality, their influence extends into eternity. They're role models who personify to youth the best of Christian living, sharers in the work of Jesus the teacher, representatives to parents of the best that can be offered in the formation of youth, and effectuators of the union of our families with the local as well as the universal Church.

Our *rectory staff* deserves the appreciation of all of us, priests and people together. They make it possible for the priests of the parish to concentrate on the work for which they were ordained. They're in great measure the ones responsible for the efficient running of the parish. They're often the only people to whom callers speak, and their self-sacrificing joy conveys the welcoming parish spirit to one and all.

Our *religious education teachers* of those outside Catholic schools are high on our list of those deserving our appreciation. They spend all kinds of time in many ways to spread the Lord's kingdom. They intensely prepare materials before meeting their charges, giving attention not only to orthodoxy but to speaking eternal truths in today's language for youth to understand. They commit themselves each year to insure their presence at class. Sometimes their presence is appreciated, but often they experience ingratitude from the very students and parents who need them most. As a parish, as well as members of the universal Church, we're in their debt.

Our *lay eucharistic ministers* are another group in the forefront of those meriting our special appreciation. They learn every nuance of taking care of the center of our faith, the Eucharist. They serve the Lord and us by distributing Holy Communion at Masses in church, and also to those unable to come to church because of illness or old age.

Our *sextons* deserve our gratitude for taking care of our sacred precincts. Our parish church is a symbol. When we find it immaculately clean, we're reminded not to soil our soul with the filth of sin. If we see our church to be full of light, we're reminded that God wishes the light of good works to shine in us. Just as we enter this church building, so God wishes to enter our soul.

Equally deserving of special mention are our *sacristans* and those who care for the altar linens and flowers. They act behind the scenes to make sure that all is prepared, and nothing distracting, for the worthy celebration of the sacred rites.

And we extend our appreciation to *all of you*, our church-going parishioners. It's you who constitute the Church — not the pope alone, or the bishops alone, or the clergy alone, but you. You've shown that you appreciate this great dignity by your being here not as strangers or silent spectators, but with devotion and full involvement. By the way you dress for attendance here, you've shown your awareness of laws that go all the way back to the First Testament that before the altar people be properly covered (Gn 3:10f.; Ex 20:26).

By your attendance at Mass and the reverence with which you attend the Eucharist you show your love for the Lord. By the way you've shown sensitivity before the great and holy mysteries you witness here, by your silence as well as your vocal participation in the Church's public prayer, and by your consideration of others' attempts to pray, you've mediated God's presence. And just as every group projects its silent but very real vibes to any sensitive person who appears before them to speak, you have extended your warm and welcoming vibes to support and challenge your priests in a unique way.

Day by day may all of us — those who have served in a special way as well as those who have participated to the best of their ability — live the life of the Gospel and deepen our faith, hope, and love. We pray that we may draw closer to Christ and be his witnesses in the world; that we may share the burdens of others and always listen to the voice of the Holy Spirit; that we will strengthen the faith of our brothers and sisters by word and example, and gather them together around the table of the Eucharist. May our conduct not entail blowing any bugles in our own behalf, but exemplify God's commandments and keep us strong and steadfast in Christ.

CHURCH UNITY

1 Cor 1:10-13   Jn 17:1-11

Can you imagine yourself being present in the scene of today's gospel? It's the night before Jesus died. Aware of his fate on the next day, he prays. He prays both to be heard and to be overheard — heard by his heavenly Father, overheard by his Apostles and us. His prayer is essentially for his Church, asking his Father to complete within it what he had begun. It's also a prayer structured as the Lord's Prayer, and therefore is a model.

Jesus first places his whole being before God. Then he prays that through him God may bestow eternal life on all who accept him. By eternal life Jesus means not the *duration* of life, but the *quality* of life. A life of quality is a life of intimate experience of God. This consists in knowing the true God (Jn 17:3).

In our age of facts, research, and information on every subject imaginable, what does it mean "to *know*"? To know in the Biblical sense denotes *intimate* experience of someone: "Adam knew Eve his wife, and she conceived" (Gn 4:1). What does it mean, especially, to know *God*? Jesus speaks of the God whom he had taught us to call "Father." Jesus had intimately called him "abba" — "daddy." Jesus prays that all who call themselves Christian will come to know himself — with all his compassion, courage, and joy. The person who really knows that God is Father, and recognizes Jesus as the one who reveals Him, enjoys life.

The context in which Jesus speaks shows that by knowing God he means being a part of the community of believers, having a share in the life of God's people. And it means giving glory to God on earth by joining with Jesus in finishing the work that the heavenly Father has given us to do (Jn 17:4). An old poster said, "Be patient with me — God isn't finished with me yet!" And the earth in many places doesn't look like the finished homeland of those who love God and each other, any more than it was when St. Paul wrote to the Corinthians. In that community of these still-immoral people whom Paul had evangelized, rivalries had arisen (v. 11) and Paul was informed that the Christians had formed into several cliques (v. 12).

One clique — probably consisting of the majority — followed Paul. These were mostly non-Jews, who accepted Paul's preaching about the end of the binding force of the Jewish Law and the beginning of the gospel of Christian freedom. Some of them were probably trying to do what some people try to do today: turn freedom into license and do as they please. Other Christians followed Apollos, a Jew from Alexandria, a center of great intellectual activity. Because he was eloquent, intelligent, and learned in the Scriptures, Apollos had made a strong impression on the better-educated minority of the Corinthian Christians; some who wanted to "be somebody" had started to follow him.

Other Jewish Christians, boasting of their attachment to St. Peter, were promoting adherence to the Jewish Law. As with Paul and Apollos, there is no evidence that Peter was personally responsible for this group that rallied around his name.

Paul's reference to a fourth clique, those who grouped around Christ, he probably meant with sarcasm as his personal protest against the other factions. If this group existed, it most likely constituted a small number who self-righteously proclaimed themselves best. Their fault would consist not in their saying that they belonged to Christ, but in their implying that Christ belonged to them alone. Such people still exist.

In this passage, Paul twice calls people who belong to cliques "brothers" (vv. 10f.), showing the kind of love Christians should have for everybody. When he asks that we be united in the same mind and in the same purpose, he's saying many things. He's stating that to be united suggests a mutual adaptation, a readiness to compromise with one another for harmony's sake. He's asserting that disunity among Christians is a disgraceful tear in the expected Christian *koinonia*, or special kind of loving community, and thus a denial of the whole reality of God's saving work in Christ.

Paul's words are a realistic contrast with the idealized picture of the early Church as found in the New Testament's Acts of the Apostles, and thus an antidote to the general picture that there existed a "golden age" of the Church which later broke down. The presence of factions in the Church right from the start reminds us that the perfect condition is something that we Christians must always work towards.

Because people who practice religion, like others, sometimes seek more their own desire for comfort and security than peace and justice, our non-religious brethren criticize religion, humanity's reaching out to God, as being a dangerous source of further disunity and suffering. We who practice our religion should walk, as the greatest people of old walked, with our whole being flooded with joyous light.

Light acquires a transcendental quality. This goes beyond even the light of the bright Mediterranean known to the sacred writers; it's something more, something unfathomable, something holy. This is the light that penetrates directly to the soul, opens the doors and windows of the heart, and makes one effusive and radiant.

Although the search for the unity of *Christians* is of paramount importance for the Church in witnessing effectively to a divided and fragmented Christianity, the building of closer relationships with other faith communities is also important — with the Jews, in view of disturbing signs of renewed anti-Semitism; with religions of the East, representing half of the world's population; with Muslims, who have been an important part of European culture for many centuries and whose fundamentalists are rising to the fore.

We have to remember that we're all in this together. A cartoon shows representatives of the nations of the world as passengers in a small lifeboat, fleeing a sinking ship. As the survivors huddle together, their nightmare worsens as their boat springs a serious leak. One passenger naively remarks, "At least it's not *our* half that's leaking!"

Among the best ways to show what united religions can do was a declaration approved by some 250 religious leaders from around the world on Sept. 4, 1993, in Chicago. They affirmed that a common set of core values is found in the teachings of the world's religions, and that these form the basis of a beneficial global ethic. They declared that each of us human beings depends on the well-being of the entire universe, and so we have respect for the community of all living beings as well as for the preservation of Earth.

They made a commitment to respect life and dignity, and individuality and diversity, so that every person without exception is treated humanely. They considered humankind a family. We must not live for ourselves alone, but should also serve others. No person should ever be considered or treated as a second-class citizen. There should be equal partnership between men and women.

They committed themselves to a culture of nonviolence, respect, justice, and peace. They said we must strive for a just social and economic order, in which all have an equal chance to reach their full potential as human beings. They asserted that a global ethic already exists within the religious teachings of the world that can counter the global distress. While not providing a direct solution for all the immense problems of the world, this global ethic supplies the moral foundation for a better order. Indeed, a global ethic means a fundamental consensus among the world's religions concerns binding values, irrevocable *standards*, and *fundamental moral attitudes*.

Religious and spiritual persons base their lives on an Ultimate Reality, they said, and draw spiritual power and hope therefrom, in trust, in prayer or meditation, in word or silence. We do not consider ourselves better than other women and men, but we trust that the ancient wisdom of our religions can point the way for the future. Humanity has entered a new phase of its history. In our dramatic global situation, humanity needs a vision of peoples living peacefully together. A vision rests on hopes, goals, ideals, standards. It's the communities of faith who bear a responsibility to demonstrate that such hopes, ideals, and standards can be lived.

On the basis of personal experiences and the burdensome history of our planet we have learned that rights without morality cannot long endure, and that *there will be no better global order without a global ethic.*

This doesn't mean glossing over or ignoring the serious differences among the individual religions. But they should not hinder us from proclaiming publicly those things that we already hold in common. Humankind urgently needs spiritual renewal just as urgently as social and ecological reforms. The spiritual power of the religions can offer a fundamental sense of trust, a ground of meaning, ultimate standards, and a spiritual home.

There's a principle that is found and has persisted in many religious and ethical traditions of humankind for thousands of years: *What you do not wish done to yourself, do not do to others.* Or in positive terms: *What you wish done to yourself, do to others!*

Agreement to these fundamental demands results in some irrevocable directives. First among these is a commitment to a culture of nonviolence and respect for life. In the great, ancient religious and ethical traditions of humankind we find the directive: *You shall not kill!* Or in positive terms: *Have respect for life!* A human being is infinitely precious and must be unconditionally protected. To be authentically human, in the spirit of our great religious and ethical traditions, means that in public as well as private life we must be concerned for others and ready to help.

Second among these irrecovable directives is commitment to a culture of solidarity and a just economic order. In the great, ancient religious and ethical traditions of humankind we find the directive: *You shall not steal* — or in positive terms: *Deal honestly and fairly!* Where power and wealth are accumulated ruthlessly, feelings of envy, resentment, and deadly hatred and rebellion inevitably well up in the disadvantaged and marginalized. This leads to a vicious circle of violence and counterviolence. But *there is no global peace without global justice!*

To be authentically human in the spirit of our great religious and ethical traditions means the following: We must utilize economic and political power for service to humanity instead of misusing it in ruthless battles for domination, which involves a spirit of compassion with those who suffer; we must cultivate mutual respect and consideration; we must value a sense of moderation and modesty, instead of an unquenchable greed for money, prestige, and consumption; and we need mutual concern, tolerance, readiness for reconciliation, and love.

The third irrevocable directive is commitment to a culture of tolerance and a life of truthfulness. In the great, ancient religious and ethical traditions of humankind we find the directive: *You shall not lie!* Or in positive terms: *Speak and act truthfully!* This is especially true for those who work in the mass media (who are duty-bound to objectivity, fairness, and the preservation of human dignity); for artists, writers, and scientists; for the leaders of countries, politicians, and political parties, to whom we entrust our freedoms; and finally, for representatives of religion.

The fourth irrevocable directive is a commitment to a culture of equal rights and a partnership between men and women. In the great, ancient religious and ethical traditions of humankind we find the directive: *You shall not commit sexual immorality!* Or in positive terms: *Respect and love one another!* No one has the right to degrade others to mere sex objects. Sexual exploitation and sexual discrimination must be condemned as one of the worst forms of human degradation. The social institution of marriage, despite all its cultural and religious variety, is characterized by love, loyalty, and permanence.

Abiding by these principles and directives should result in a transformation of human consciousness. Toward this end, keeping a sense of responsibility alive is the special task of religions. So the religious leaders urged, first, that, although a universal consensus on many disputed ethical questions may be difficult to attain, we should look for suitable solutions in the spirit of the fundamental religious principles. Secondly, as many professions as possible, such as physicians, scientists, business people, journalists, educators, and politicians, should develop up-to-date codes of ethics.

Lastly, and above all, the various communities of faith should formulate their very specific ethics: about, for example, the meaning of life and death, the enduring of suffering, the forgiveness of guilt, selfless sacrifice, the necessity of renunciation, compassion, and joy.

With the love of Christ and the vision of St. Paul, let's try to cooperate in bringing about church unity for the sake of the contributions to the world that only religion can make. And let's have that action begin in our local community through cooperation with other church communities, through joint community projects, and by helping one another along our respective paths to God.

WORLD PEACE (VETERANS DAY, ETC.)

Is 32:15-20   Jm 3:13-18   Ps 72   Jn 14:23-29

Anyone who visits a military cemetery understands that those who are buried in these rows upon rows of graves are heroes: They fought for their way of life, were committed to their ideals, dedicated to duty, treading through evening mud and morning mist under a heavy backpack, moving courageously toward the enemy. At the same time, the visitor sees, paradoxically, that wars are failures. The ends they achieved could have been accomplished much better by peaceful means. No such speculation detracts, however, from the tremendous debt we owe our veterans for all they gave — in too many cases their very lives, all that they had to give — in obedience to their country's call.

To put peace into perspective, believers rightly look to our sacred Scriptures. There, the term "peace" has been understood in different ways at various times and in various contexts, our Scriptures having been written over a long period of time and in many varied historical situations. On the whole, the ancient Hebrews believed in peace as being tied to their fidelity to their covenant with God. The first response God wants from hearts that seek peace, according to Isaiah, is that we do what we can for the liberation of His poor. Jeremiah said that what it means to know God is to defend the cause of the poor and needy (Jr 22:15f.). This is repeated many times in the Bible.

In the traditions of Jesus' covenant, while the characteristics of the *shalom* of the Jewish Scriptures are present, all discussion of war and peace must be seen within the context of the unique revelation of God that is Jesus Christ and of the reign of God which Jesus inaugurated. To bring about God's reign, Jesus calls for a new way of life which fulfills and goes beyond the law. One of the most striking characteristics of this new way of peace on earth is forgiveness — the forgiveness of God for people, and of people for one another.

In all of his life and ministry, Jesus refused to defend himself with violence. He endured cruelty so that God's love might be fully manifest. Even at his death, Jesus cried out for forgiveness for those who were his executioners. Only in light of this can Jesus' gift of peace — a peace which the world cannot give (Jn 14:27) — be understood. So intense was that gift and so abiding was its power that the remembrance of it and the daily living of it became the hallmark of the community of faith.

Even this brief examination of peace in the scriptures makes it clear that they don't provide us with detailed answers to the specifics of the questions which we face today — nuclear weapons, for example. The sacred texts do, however, provide today's concrete realities with urgent direction.

Peace must be understood in positive terms. In the words of Pope John Paul II in 1982 at Coventry, England, whose cathedral was destroyed in World War II, "Peace is not just the absence of war. Like a cathedral, peace must be constructed patiently and with unshakable faith." Mother Teresa said that peace starts with a smile.

Moreover, peace must be constructed on the basis of central human values: truth, justice, freedom, and love. In his encyclical *Pacem in Terris*, Pope John XXIII's leitmotif, occurring nine times, was: "Peace among all peoples requires truth as its foundation;

justice as its rule; love as its driving force; and liberty as its atmosphere."

Especially is peace an enterprise of justice (Is 32:17; see also Is 9:7; 60:17; Ps 72:7): "justice and peace shall kiss" (Ps 85:11). Pope Paul VI's statement that "if you want peace, work for justice," summarizes much, and is still on many bumper stickers. A letter bore a sticker that said, "Without concern, no justice. Without justice, no peace. Without peace, no future"; it had to be returned to the sender with a line added: "Without address, no delivery."

As a symbol of justice, we take for granted the figure that we often see: the blindfolded lady in long-flowing robes holding scales in one hand and a sword in the other. The blindfold allegedly prevents Lady Justice from seeing whether a petitioner is old or young, rich or poor, black or white. The sword is said to indicate the swiftness and decisiveness with which she can act and the punishment with which she can back up her decisions. Her equally-balanced scales are another reminder that justice is measured equally to all.

The prophet Amos had a different, and in some ways better, symbol. In a land where water was precious, his symbol for justice focused on a mighty mountain stream (Am 5:24) — a stream which could renew, refresh, give life, and bring to fruition. This torrent of justice, surging with thundering power, was to flow in the direction of the elimination of any kind of oppression that keeps people, especially the poor, from fully developing as human beings. Amos further spoke of social injustice as being blasphemy against God.

Cesar Chavez, the founder of the United Farm Workers who struggled to improve their lives until his death in 1993, was in this tradition. He said: "I am convinced that the truest act of courage, the strongest act of humanity is to sacrifice ourselves for others in a totally nonviolent struggle for justice."

But what is justice? The *classical* definition, which comes through Plato, Aristotle, Saint Ambrose, and Saint Augustine, is expressed in a single phrase: "to each his own" (*suum cuique*). That phrase affirms that all persons should receive the rewards which are appropriate to their work and duties.

The Jewish scriptures speak of an individual as being just if he is in "right relation" to God and others, with a special concern for those "others" who are powerless. In the Jewish decalogue, the first three commandments provide direct regulations about people's relations with their God. The last seven constitute essential elements of relations with other people — but with a very important difference: In the codes of the other Near Eastern peoples, violation constituted only a crime against one's fellow human beings; in the Jewish scriptures, it's a crime against God. This is an entirely new orientation, and one that has become part of Christian teaching.

The New Testament has that in mind when, in giving St. Joseph its only tribute, it called him a "just man." In the New Testament, while it's axiomatic that Jesus was not a social reformer, his teachings had strong social implications. The Gospel of Matthew and the Letter of James expressed to Jewish converts to Christianity concerns on behalf of powerless and poor people. St. Luke's gospel expresses the same concerns. In Luke's Acts of the Apostles, the early Christian community shares its goods in common and stresses almsgiving (10:2, 4, 31; 24:17). So in the specifically Christian concept, the word justice implies obligation to others, or to an Other.

If peace can only result from justice, consider the size of the task. Think of the number of homeless people; the amount of poverty that in many cases amounts to destitution; the illiteracy that prevents earning a living and participation in community affairs; the unfairness to our children from starvation, disease, poverty, lack of education, and military conflict; the number of people whose health is not properly cared for; the pornography that stimulates deviant sexual behavior and child molestation.

Consider, in addition, the amount spent world-wide on armaments rather than peaceful pursuits. The arms trade has been compared to the trade in illicit drugs: The commodities are lethal; the profits to be had are dazzling; corruption (kick-backs in the case of arms) is rife; the outcome is productive of much misery; it's no good just going for the dealers, for it is sources of supply and demand which power both trades. The main difference between the two is that the arms trade is legitimized and the drugs trade is not.

Consider also the inadequate generalization which terms have-not nations the "third world." That constitutes four-fifths of modern humankind, soon to be five-sixths, thus becoming the most important component of the world. Added to that is a growing ecological crisis which may alter the climatic zone, leading to shortages of fresh water and suitable land in places where they were once plentiful. All of this, in turn, may give rise to new and menacing conflicts — wars for survival.

Peace is especially important today to construct for all people everywhere a world more genuinely human. We Christians particularly have principles, theories, and examples that can bring it about. Our God is a God of peace. Bethlehem demonstrated *individual* peace, even in the face of difficulties: the cave, Joseph's suspicions, women's gossip, the trip from Nazareth, the flight to Egypt. Mary pondering these things in her heart was an example of an individual, interior, personal peace like the bottom of an ocean during a tempest.

The early Christians found some of Jesus' recommendations for peace as difficult as we do, recommendations that in two thousand years the world has proved itself not sufficiently able to grow into: offering no resistance to one who is evil, for example, and turning the other cheek, putting Christian generosity above legal rights, and going beyond the call of duty. Yet the human race grows in sensitivity. As Vatican Council II said, "The whole human race faces a moment of supreme crisis in its advance toward maturity."

In the Christian social vision, the *human person is central*. The human person is in the image of God (Gn 1:26f.), the clearest reflection of God's presence in the world. For each person not only reflects God, but is the expression of God's creative work and the meaning of Christ's redemptive ministry. These considerations prescribe that Christians approach the problem of war and peace with fear and reverence.

True peace calls for reverence for life. No society can live in peace with itself, or with the world, without a full awareness of the sacredness of all human life (Jm 4:1f.). When we accept violence in any form as commonplace, our sensitivities become dulled. Violence has many faces: oppression of the poor, deprivation of basic human rights, economic exploitation, sexual exploitation and pornography, neglect or abuse of the aged and the helpless, and innumerable other acts of inhumanity. Abortion in particular blunts a sense of the sacredness of human life. In a society where the innocent unborn are killed wantonly, how can we expect people to feel righteous revulsion at the act or threat of killing non-combatants in war?

As Bethlehem demonstrated *individual* peace, Nazareth exemplified peace in the *family*. Of all God's marvelous creations the family is His most tangible and enduring. A happy home, with free self-giving at its heart, is as sacred a place as a chapel or cathedral. A Chinese proverb has it: "If there is righteousness in the heart, there will be beauty in the character. If there is beauty in the character, there will be harmony in the home. If there is harmony in the home, there will be order in the nation. When there is order in the nation, there will be peace in the world."

Married couples can help promote *world peace* by keeping their marriage vows. This includes spending time together, thus building intimacy and increasing understanding; creating a relationship of mutual sharing; both parents spending time with their children; and all taking part together in simple acts of charity or community work such as helping in a soup-kitchen — deeds that "give life." All of this prevents moral chaos. *International* conflicts often reflect injustices that have their prime source within inharmonious families.

Because sin, human weakness, and failure are parts of history, the achievement of peace is never established finally and for ever. Christians are called to live the tension between the vision of the reign of God and its concrete realization in history. The tension is often described in terms of "already but not yet": that is, we already live in the grace of the kingdom, but it's not yet the completed kingdom.

For Christians especially, peacemaking is not an optional commitment. We're called to be peacemakers, not by some movement of the moment, but by our Lord Jesus. The virtue of patriotism means that our love and loyalty for our country make us examine carefully and regularly whether our country is living up to its full potential as an agent of peace with justice for all people.

At Mass, we give one another a sign of peace: a kiss, a handshake, a bow, an embrace. Let's make that an authentic sign of our doing all in our power to bring peace to the world.

COMMUNICATIONS

Jr 1:4-9   Ps 117   Ac 13:46-49   Lk 8:5-8, 11-15

The word "broadcast" comes from Jesus' story of the farmer casting his seed abroad (Mt 13:4-9, 18-23; Mk 4:3-20; Lk 8:5-15). You remember it: Jesus compared the seed to God's word. Some of the seed fell on the footpath and was taken from people's hearts by the devil; some on the rocky, rootless ground of people who are superficial; some among the briars of people with worldly cares that choked it; and some among the good fertile soil of wide-open people in which it grew and gave a tremendous yield. We're obliged today to be that farmer, casting God's word broadly.

On *an individual level*, we should develop communication skills for opening ourselves to friendship, expressing support and affirmation, and dealing with confrontation. That last, confrontation, virtually assures closeness with other people. If we're at times dissatisfied about our relationships with relatives, perhaps it's because we feel that they don't sprinkle enough incense to our pride, and we're unable to deal with confrontation. If we're unable to say "I love you" and deal in touching, openness, and relaxation with friends, there's something wrong with our skills of relating.

Much is simply everyday courtesy and civility. Behind that is our religion's notion of the dignity of persons. If there were ten commandments of human relations, they would contain material such as the following. First, *speak to people*: There's nothing so nice as a cheerful word of greeting. Second, *smile at people*: It takes 72 muscles to frown, only 14 to smile. Third, *call people by name*: The sweetest music to anyone's ears is the sound of his or her own name.

Fourth, *be friendly and helpful*: If you would have friends, be a friend. Fifth, *be cordial*: Speak and act as if everything you do is a genuine pleasure. Sixth, *be genuinely interested in people*: You can like almost everyone if you try. Seventh, *be generous with praise*, cautious with criticism. Eighth, *be considerate with the feelings of others*: There are usually three sides to a controversy: yours, the other person's, and the right one. Ninth, *be alert to give service*: What counts most in life is what we do for others. Tenth, *add to this a good sense of humor*: A big dose of this will reward you manyfold!

All that isn't as difficult as it may at first sound. If we envision how words influence people, we realize that the most influential messages often come in three-word phrases: Phrases that attract everyone are, for example, "I love you," and "There's no charge," and "And in conclusion."

There are others: "I'll be there," for instance. If you've ever been stranded on the road with car trouble and used your last coin to call a friend, you know what a balm these three words can create. Another such phrase is "Maybe you're right." If more people were to learn to say that phrase, maybe many marriage counselors would be out of business and, with a little luck, the gun shops.

To help when we're trying to *communicate in groups*, there are other helpful hints. Clarify and summarize the feelings of the group by asking questions, getting feedback, drawing them out. Harmonize when strong feelings or disagreements come out. Try to get opponents to see each other's point of view. Be aware of personality conflicts, moods, and relationships within the group. Encourage others, especially shy ones, to express opinions.

When groups get into potential arguments, think about the following. Keep the discussion on the issues at hand rather than on the people involved. Do *not* allow anyone to attack another with personal comments. Try negotiation using the following steps: Define and list the problems; list all the possible solutions to the problems; criticize the solutions objectively; and list advantages of the solutions. Above all keep an open mind, and remember the importance of prayer.

There's another obligation we Christians have to communications, and that's *the ministry of hospitality*. This goes toward the greatest commandment of all, to love one another as Jesus loves us. Against the complaint of coldness in parishes, some have instituted "parish greeters." They, observant to the interior needs of individuals, take the initiative to introduce people to each other and to direct them to areas of their interests.

The parish greeter should let it be known, by a particular manner of dress or a recognizable flower or button, that "I'm here to serve you." The greeter makes every effort to build a rapport in helping the sick and suffering, and their loved ones, and letting them know "I care about you." The greeter takes the responsibility of reaching out to the handicapped, being sure that they are placed comfortably. The greeter takes the needed time to listen, assist, guide, and direct those in need. The leaders of the ministry of hospitality meet regularly for prayer, open discussion, counseling, critiquing, and guidelines, drawing from the professional talents of the community.

We've too often neglected major opportunities that are all around us: the media. As the old saying has it: "If you're not sitting in the window, nobody knows you're home." Assumptions organized around the printed word are dissolving in favor of the rapid emergence of a speed-of-light electronic image. Film is *the* modern popular art form.

From the time since Thomas Edison cranked up his Kinetograph and recorded "Fred Ott's Sneeze" to the present, the possibilities of cinema as an art have rapidly increased, and are still increasing. No other art can so powerfully exploit the dimensions of time and space. No other art has so many ways of involving a human being: the eyes, ears, mind, heart, and appetites all at once. At one and the same time it's drama, music, poetry, novel, and painting. It spirits the person away into a dark cave; it envelops the person in silence, in night. The world is well on its way to a cinema culture: By the year

2010, the TV and film industry will multiply three times. New technology is already available which will involve the viewer more and more: for example, buttons installed on seats which the audience can push to determine the course of a film.

Film exerts a strong, deep, effective, powerful influence on education, knowledge, culture, and leisure. Wonderment about the influence of film violence on adolescent behavior is nothing new. As long ago as 1956, an investigative committee of the United States Senate concluded that "the impact of a single motion picture is many times that of a single presentation in a comic book." Of the many school system reports on the subject, one referred to film's "tremendous influence on the development of attitudes and the directing of emotions, and on the shaping of such other patterns of human conduct as behavior skills, styles of dress, modes of play, etc."

Some of the influences are negative. Suspicions are mounting that among these with children are increased hyperactivity, attention-deficit disorders, mental passivity, and decreased language skills. One of the most pressing concerns is the effect of media violence and aggression on children: Health and safety officials have begun citing media violence as a contributing factor in alarming juvenile crimes. Unfortunately for our impressionable youth, violence on film is easy to produce and generates high advertising revenues.

One reputable authority (Dr. Brandon Centerwall, *Journal of the American Medical Association* [June 10, 1992]) estimated that, if television had never been invented, there would be annually in the United States 10,000 fewer murders, 70,000 fewer rapes, and 700,000 fewer injurious assaults. Furthermore, educators have long suspected that television rapid-fire images hinder children's development of imagination. Fortunately, it's been found that when parents control television and explain things to their children, there are dramatic beneficial results over years of time.

The Church, too, has been aware of the influence of the communication industries. As long ago as 1936 Pope Pius XI devoted an entire encyclical to motion pictures in which he said, among other things, that "even the crudest and most primitive minds are captivated by the cinema." In 1945 Pope Pius XII spoke of "this tremendous power that films possess, and the wide influence they exert on people and on customs, moral habits included." In his 1957 encyclical *Miranda Prorsus*, he said that "motion pictures must today be numbered among the most important means by which the ideas and discoveries of our times can be made known."

And bishops all over the world have at various times issued instructions, norms, pastoral letters, decisions of provincial councils, and the like, on the importance of film. Some foreign bishops have laid special stress on the influence of United States motion pictures on their countries.

Many films that are considered classics reflect the human condition and deal with specifically religious themes. Yet for the most part the mass media have neglected this, and Christians don't seem sufficiently interested in getting into the film business. Reliable studies have shown that fifty percent of those in the media have no religious affiliation and only eight percent admit to going to church or synagogue weekly. They seem to want to redefine life values along their own lines: Absolutes are out and toleration is the ultimate and only virtue to be respected.

The media's neglect isn't necessarily caused by bias against religious institutions, but by ignorance. Some of the reasons for it are that contemporary journalism, both electronic and print, is oriented toward covering specific events rather than such expressions of people's lives as spirituality, many who are assigned to cover religious stories are often intellectually lazy about getting their facts straight, there are too few full-time religion reporters, and an unhealthy mistrust has grown between religious leaders and journalists. Despite the fact that many Americans are embarking on spiritual quests and groping with deep questions of value and meaning, and these could be seminal stories of our time, curiously we let the news media ignore values and searches for meaning.

While the media impart an air of reality to what they report, they diminish the popular estimation of whatever they pass over in silence. Ratings battles and marketplace economics seem at times to replace legitimate public interest standards, sometimes adversely affecting the free flow of information required in a democratic society.

There are many areas in which we have an obligation to take an interest. Broadcasters should air more educational and informational children's programs and curtail commercialization during children's television programming. We should advocate measures which will lead to the improvement of moral standards in the public media and an increase in values-based programming. We should publicly advocate reasonable and constitutionally acceptable regulations to limit the distribution of indecent, pornographic, or sexually explicit materials. And we should oppose advertisements of contraceptives, since such presentations infringe on the right of parents to teach their children about responsible sexuality.

Broadly, we should try to see to it that three principles are maintained: first, that broadcasters operate truly in the public interest; secondly, that citizens are able to participate effectively in licensing decisions; and thirdly, that fairness and diversity be assured in ownership, employment, and public access.

Vatican Council II, acknowledging that the medium of television "has access to the minds and hearts of everyone," urged that, on the level of our Church as well as on our personal level we give communications the attention they deserve. Catholics ought to be competitive in presenting their message, sponsoring not only dull television programs for the wee hours of Sunday morning when most people are asleep (to satisfy a network's "public service" requirements), but emotional, passionate, interesting, comic, sad, joyful, suspenseful, dramatic, attractive programs for prime time as well. The proclamation of the Good News should not be the production of solely amateurish renditions. It ought to be easier to sell religious values than underarm deodorants.

The media — press, radio, and television — are, for the most part, owned and controlled by those at the top of the economic and political structures. That they support the status quo is therefore not surprising. On film, the sacred becomes so deeply associated with the commercial and entertainment worlds that it's difficult to present it in a frame worthy of sacred events. Also, on film everything that makes religion an historic, profound, and sacred human activity is stripped away; there's little ritual, no dogma, scarcely any theology, and above all no sense of spiritual transcendence. As someone said, "You'd never know by looking at TV that religion is a source of joy for so many people. It's as if religion didn't even exist."

While every survey about United States citizens and religion indicates huge interest in God, spirituality, and the supernatural, television doesn't reflect this. Is the Good News destined to be heard by no one except those who go to church? Where are the personalities, entertainers, and characters of the Christian Church?

In her work, the Church simply must become aware that the language in which our faith is expressed is often too tied to ancient and obsolete formulae or too closely linked with Western culture. In this updating, the Church seems at times to be lacking in sophistication.

Television can't convert people, nor should it. That's the work of God's grace. But television can interest people in the idea of religion. It can only do this through personalities convinced of their own faith and willing to share it. This was the way it was done two thousand years ago. As Vatican Council II said: "Since the media are often the only channels of information that exist between the Church and the world, a failure to use them amounts to 'burying the talent given by God.'"

By the time youth reach age eighteen, they will have spent more time watching television than on any other activity except sleep, and twice the time spent in school. We must therefore encourage artistic taste so that children can use discrimination in choosing the publications, films, and broadcasts that are set before them. Film is a teacher of morality, so sophistication is necessary.

Everybody today must be film literate. This means we must know the subtleties of film: that, for example, a camera shot from below looking up exalts a film character, while one looking down from above denigrates the character. During the Communist days of the Soviet Union, their exhibits in their atheistic museum on the

Nevsky Prospekt in what was then Leningrad used this kind of knowledge to their advantage.

In our personal attitudes, in our communities, in our conduct toward the media, and in taking up careers in social communications, we ought to observe our Christian duty to broadcast the Good News.

ST. VALENTINE'S DAY

Jr 31:1-4   *Ps 33*   *Ep 3:14-19*   *Lk 10:29-37*

St. Valentine's Day as a lovers' festival and the modern tradition of sending valentine cards have no relation to the two early legendary martyrs named Valentine, both beheaded for their faith. Rather, the feast seems to be connected either with the Roman fertility festival of the Lupercalia (February 15) or with the mating season of birds.

It's probable that what we call the "valentine" was the first of all greeting cards. The paper valentine dates from the 16th century; by the year 1800, hand-painted copperplates were produced to meet large demands.

Our celebration of St. Valentine's Day and our general knowledge that love is "what makes the world go 'round" prompts us to ask again the very profitable question, "What is true love, anyhow?"

Love is so important that the ancient classical Greeks had at least three words for it in comparison with English's one. That didn't even include *romantic* love, as exemplified by Romeo and Juliet, Lancelot and Guinevere, and St. Valentine's Day. Those are a more modern invention, and often of a less permanent nature than what the Greeks meant by love. (Perhaps part of the reason why classical Greece had no romantic notions of love was that they considered women so inferior to men that they weren't worthy of serious affection: For a man to get emotional about a woman was for them a sign of illness, or insanity, or both.)

The Greeks' word for the least important form of love was

eros, which meant love in the sense of desire, a getting, a thing of life, an *elan vital*, and a *joie de vivre*, as opposed to *thanatos*, which meant death. The "erotic" does not, however, deal only with the sexual, as some people would have it. Eros is commemorated in Piccadilly Circus, the hub of London's entertainment world. In the center of the Circus, or Circle, is a memorial fountain topped by a winged archer which its sculptor in 1893 intended as the Angel of Christian Charity. But everyone knows it today as Eros. Radiating from the circle are smart shops, theaters, restaurants, and London's cinema world.

On our level of immediate experience — the human level, the superficial level — what comes to mind with *eros* is the physical. It's easily confused with lust. It's the world of *sense*, as one can see in perfumes and the names given to them.

It's the notion of Hollywood, where all actors are handsome, all actresses beautiful. It's tragic that so few and such irresponsible people should influence the world on this subject. Once, at a Hollywood party, a disconsolate man was noticed sitting on the floor in a corner. When asked why, he answered, "Just look at these people. They're acting as though they believe all their press notices!"

There are, however, two truths to this Hollywood notion of love. One is that love necessarily involves another person. The second is that in God's plan sex is a part of love, but of *married love*. Obviously, this is the lowest element, and it's not at all present in some forms of true love. What's dangerous is that from Hollywood presentations youth might get unwholesome ideas of *God's creation* of sex. The importance of right ideas here is shown by the devil's interest and success in degrading it. The devil has much knowledge — witness his recognition of the importance of this subject — but no love.

The highest form of love for the Greeks was *agapé*, which had overtones of the spiritual. Although eros had to do almost entirely with *getting, agapé* entailed *giving* much more than getting. It had to do mostly with person-God and God-person relationships, and frequently involved ecstasy (another word of Greek origin, meaning etymologically "to stand outside oneself").

This form of love should predominate over all others. In boy-girl love, it's the type the Church envisions in the exhortation before marriage, praying that the spouses' love grow stronger and stronger as the years go on. This form of love uses the faculties of one's soul. It uses the *intellect*, recognizing the good in another — sometimes a special something seen by no one else. It uses the *will*, wanting to be united with the beloved and to do all the things that will make the beloved in some way happy or well-off. Self-sacrifice is the language of this kind of love.

Children know how to love in that whole-hearted way. A distraught mother—a single parent who had been abandoned by her husband — brought her son to see a priest. She didn't want her son to grow up to be like his father, and she claimed that her son was stealing. As evidence she said that she'd gone through her son's trousers prior to washing them, and found a larger sum of money there than he should have had. He claimed that he hadn't stolen. She stated that she'd tried everything to get an admission out of her son, including beating him, but he wouldn't abandon his story that he had stolen nothing.

The priest took the boy into another office and assured him that whatever the boy told him would be in complete confidence. The boy, thus assured, reluctantly told the priest that the money came from his not having spent any of his allowance for many weeks, because his mother's birthday was coming up and he wanted to surprise her with a gift.

This kind of love is especially beautiful in old folks. In them love is often stronger than death; it's a frequent experience that one elderly lover will die soon after the other. They also prove the possibility of true human love without a physical expression. The love is present when he has become skinny and bald, she gray and frazzled. With one such couple, a woman in her elderly years had become close to a vegetative state, and yet her husband lovingly cared for her, feeding her, cleaning her, whispering terms of endearment to her. When she eventually died, he was completely broken up.

Such love — like all true love, really — admits of many questions. Is it better to love than to be loved? How much of loving is giving, really, and how much getting? How long can unrequited love last?

On the very highest level of love — the divine — love is more ineffable than on any other. The essence of this love can in no way be adequately expressed by any created image whatsoever. God the Father out of love created the world and keeps it in existence; Christ reduced the whole law to love; the word "love" synopsizes our religion; it will constitute the happiness of heaven and its absence the misery of hell — both here and hereafter. "He who does not love abides in death" (1 Jn 3:15).

That leaves us with the classical Greeks' middle word for love: *philia*, love of friendship. This is at times all affection, sentiment, heart, and no head. With a youthful boy-girl relationship, this means the butterflies-in-the-stomach feeling at the touch of the beloved, the reveries at the mere sight of the other, the ecstasy at only the mention of beloved's name, carrying the picture of the "beloved" and looking at it often. It's good, it's necessary, and it applies to more than boy-girl relationships. But it's obviously incomplete — when love goes only this far, "puppy love" or "crushes" can be the result.

As for true friendship, sociologists steer clear of attempting a definition, perhaps because it lends itself more easily to art than to numbers. Painters have rarely touched the subject: The dozen or so versions of "The Good Samaritan" deal more with charity than friendship. Even the New Testament generally ignores the idea of temporal individual friendship, perhaps in order to suggest that these, like other temporal relationships, should be subsumed in Christianity. (It is, of course, true that Jesus loved St. John, that St. Paul had friends, and that there were other friendships in the New Testament.)

Poets, too, have had quite a time with friendship. The probable reason that Shakespeare had Mark Antony address his audience as "friends" before "Romans" and "countrymen" is that he knew how the heart leaps at the slightest sign of brotherhood.

Philosophers, both popular and profound, have written about it more. Aristotle wrote that "without friends no one would choose to live, though he had all other goods." Emerson waxed so lyrical about it as to sound insecure. Montaigne, who wrote a beautiful essay on friendship, in it gave more of a personal tribute to his friend La Boetie than a definition. Bacon, who wrote "Of Friendship" as well as "of" many other things, was a very bad friend: he considered friendship a "hazard."

A distillate of the writings on friendship shows several things. There are friendships based on passion, on pity, on pleasure, on companionship, on professional advantage, on camaraderie-in-arms, on intellectual agreement, on mutual admiration, on spiritual conviction, on personal advancement, on hero worship, on protection, on fear, on need, on loyalty, and on many other things. Most friendships incorporate several of these elements at once.

But no matter how reasoned they may be, all friendships are and must be voluntary. Though all friendships are precarious, those between unequals are even more fragile. Whatever lofty purpose friendship may serve, it's always a reciprocal thing, a giving as well as a getting, and is something generous and expansive.

For us who are trying to find our way to God, it's good to remember what St. Theresa of Avila said:

> People will tell you that you do not need friends
> on this journey, that God is enough.
> But to be with God's friends is a good way
> to keep close to God in this life.
> You will always draw benefit from them.

Let's remember to love, not less, but more. More love, not more knowledge, is the answer to the world's ills. Knowledge is important for the part it has in loving, but it's love that's the most important thing in the world. Love has a power to transform. That power is for good and for ill, but loving the right people can change us fabulously for the good. The greatest tragedy in all this world is someone who is unable to love.

ST. PATRICK AND EVANGELIZATION

Jr 1:4-9   *Ac 13:46-49*   *Lk 10:1-9*

St. Patrick, who lived between the end of the fourth century and the middle of the fifth, was born in Roman Britain. At the age of 16, Irish raiders seized him from the villa of his father, Calpurnius, a deacon and minor local official, and sold him as a slave in Ireland. As with many another youth before and since, he had been worldly in his young days, even though a nominal Christian. His six bleak years of captivity became a means of spiritual conversion.

At the age of 22, he was encouraged by a voice in his sleep to escape. He found a ship to take him and he eventually reached Britain. There he came near to starvation and suffered a second brief captivity before he was finally reunited with his family.

He tells of a dream, after his return to Britain, in which one Victoricus delivered him a letter headed, "The Voice of the Irish." As he read it he seemed to hear a certain company of Irish beseeching him to preach the Christian faith to them.

Because of the shortcomings of his education he was reluctant for a long time to respond to the call. As with the prophet Jeremiah, Patrick wasn't at all sure that he was the right one to go on the Lord's mission. As also with Jeremiah, however, the idea to respond to the call took on a sense of urgency, an urgency which Jeremiah had compared to burning coals within him.

He went to the Continent to train for the priesthood. Even on the eve of re-embarkation for Ireland he was beset by doubts of his fitness for the work. Once in the field, however, his hesitations vanished. He became like St. Paul, the fearless Apostle to the Gentiles. As with Paul, he came to see that the Good News had to be proclaimed to the pagans.

Utterly confident in the Lord, he journeyed far and wide, baptizing and confirming with untiring zeal. In diplomatic fashion he brought gifts to a small ruler here and a lawgiver there but accepted nothing from any of them. Upon the death of Palladius, the first bishop of Ireland, Patrick was named his successor. His mission concentrated on the west and north of Ireland, where nobody had preached the gospel before.

In his missionary work he lived in constant danger of martyrdom. Probably his chief opponents were the Druids. Things came to a head when he demanded the excommunication of the British Prince Coroticus, who during a retaliatory raid on Ireland had killed some of Patrick's converts and sold others into slavery. To his critics Patrick replied with his *Confessio*, a short account of his spiritual development and a justification of his mission, set down in his old age. It was a kind of last will and testament, the writing through which he would like to be remembered. Central to it is his perception of the role of the Holy Spirit. It was, he said, the Holy Spirit within him who held him together during his Irish captivity, who brought him back to Ireland, who stood by him when a number of bishops opposed his appointment as bishop to the Irish, and who — most of all — held him together when a dearest friend of his youth circulated a defamatory document intended to discredit him.

His only other extant work is his *Epistola*, written in denunciation of the ill-treatment inflicted on some Irish Christian captives by the soldiers of Coroticus. His writings show a man of action rather than deep learning, and a man of courage and humility. No diarist has ever bared his inmost soul to the same degree as did the patron saint of Ireland.

One of his greatest griefs in what he called his "laborious episcopate" was a charge, endorsed by his ecclesiastical superiors in Britain, that he had originally sought office for the sake of office. In point of fact, he was a most humble-minded man, pouring forth a continuous paean of thanks to his Maker for having chosen him as the instrument whereby multitudes who had worshipped "idols and unclean things" had joined "the people of God." Patrick's was the last missionary enterprise of the British church before it sank under the impact of the Anglo-Saxon invasion.

Before the end of the seventh century, Patrick had become a legendary figure, and the legends have continued to grow. One of these is the beautiful "Breastplate of St. Patrick," which reads: "Christ be with me, Christ within me, Christ behind me, Christ before me, Christ beside me, Christ to win me, Christ to comfort and restore me, Christ beneath me, Christ above me, Christ in quiet, Christ in danger, Christ in hearts of all who love me, Christ in mouth of friend and stranger." Another legend would have it that he drove the snakes of Ireland into the sea to their destruction. Still another, probably the most popular, is that of the shamrock, which has him explain the concept of the Holy Trinity, three Persons in one God, to an unbeliever by showing him the three-leaved plant with one stalk. Today Irishmen wear shamrocks, the national flower of Ireland, in their lapels on St. Patrick's Day.

And St. Patrick has engendered great Irish pride, about which there are many stories. One story has it that an Irish tourist agent suggested to a matron in the United States seeking a place for a vacation that she try Ireland. Her reaction was, "No, I don't want to go there: it's cold, damp, and full of Catholics." His Irish-brogued response was, "Well, lady, you can go to hell, where it's hot, dry, and full of non-Catholics!"

What Patrick did in Ireland, other missioners did to other countries: St. Peter to Rome, for example, St. Paul to the entire Mediterranean, St. Boniface to Germany, Sts. Cyril and Methodius to the Slavic peoples, St. Casimir to Poland and Lithuania, and so forth. That's *evangelization* — a word which means to bring or to announce the Good News, to testify and proclaim God's salvation of humanity in Christ Jesus. Viewed from another perspective, evangelization is the means by which God places in human hands the power to change the universe.

We're called to do it every day. Since the Second Vatican Council (1962-65) the Catholic Church has shifted away from the view of evangelization which looks primarily for visible and quantitative results. The Church has replaced this with a view similar to that of Christ in the Gospels — a primary concern with individual, interior conversion and the depth of one's spiritual life.

As Pope Paul VI wrote (*On Evangelization in the Modern World*, 1975, #14), our Church "exists in order to evangelize, that is to say in order to preach and teach, to be the channel of the gift of grace, to reconcile sinners with God, and to perpetuate Christ's sacrifice in the Mass, which is the memorial of his death and glorious Resurrection."

The Holy Father continues that "evangelizing means bringing the Good News into all the strata of humanity, and through its influence transforming humanity from within and making it new." He emphasizes that the methods of evangelization ought to vary according to the time, place, and culture. Care must be taken to be sensitive to the needs, customs, and traditions of each person or group that is evangelized.

Essentially involved in evangelization is the goal of *conversion*, which is the change of our lives that comes about through the power of the Holy Spirit. All who accept the Gospel undergo change as we continually put on the mind of Christ by rejecting sin and becoming more faithful disciples in his Church. Conversion signals the occasion when the Gospel first takes root in response to a call from God. In our time this basic evangelization is equally necessary for innumerable people who have been baptized but who do not live a Christian life, for people who have an imperfect knowledge of the basic teachings of the faith, and for intellectuals seeking to know Jesus Christ more deeply.

People experience conversion in many ways. Some experience a sudden, shattering insight that brings rapid transformation. Others experience a gradual growth over many years. Still others undergo conversion as they take part in the Rite of Christian Initiation of Adults — the normal way adults become members of the Church today. Many experience conversion through the ordinary relationships of family and friends. Others have experienced it through the formation received from Catholic schools and religious education programs. Still others have experienced ongoing conversion in renewals, ecumenical encounters, retreats, parish missions, or through one or other great spiritual movements. However it comes about, it's crucial that we be converted — and that we continue to be converted!

Evangelization involves both *individuals* and *society*. Faith isn't something that only happens to each of us privately, within ourselves. The Gospel also speaks to society, with its values, goals, and systems. The Gospel must overflow from each heart until the presence of God transforms all human existence. Sometimes this means that, as believers, we must confront the world like prophets, pointing out the claims of God to those who are blind to God. More often, however, it means that we must let our faith radiate the love of Jesus to the world by the everyday way we speak, think, and act.

Inwardly, evangelization calls for our continued receiving of the Gospel of Jesus Christ, our ongoing conversion both individually and as Church. It nurtures us, makes us grow, and renews us in holiness as God's people. *Outwardly*, evangelization addresses those who haven't heard the Gospel or, having heard it, have stopped practicing their faith, and those who seek the fullness of faith. Evangelization, then, has different implications depending on our relationship to Jesus and his Church.

Why do we evangelize? Simply put, because the Lord Jesus commanded us to. Unless people know the grandeur for which they're made, they can't reach complete fulfillment. The Lord gave us yet another reason to evangelize: our love for every person, whatever his or her situation, language, physical, mental, or social condition. Because we've experienced the love of Christ, we want to share it. As Jesus wanted to gather all Jerusalem as a mother bird gathers her young (Mt 23:37), so also do we want to gather all people into God's kingdom, proclaiming the Gospel "even to the ends of the earth" (Ac 1:8).

The last question we ask is, *Who* should be an evangelizer. The task of the bishop, the chief evangelizer in the local diocese, is to teach, inspire, and guide his flock to Christ. Priests derive their ministry from Jesus through the bishop. Religious carry out their apostolates according to the command of Christ himself and thereby are called to inspire those whom they serve. Less obvious, perhaps, is the fact that, as the Second Vatican Council's *Decree on the*

Church's Missionary Activity states (#83): "The work of evangelization is a basic duty of [all] the People of God."

Lay people, whose particular vocation places them in the
midst of the world, exercise a very special form of evangelization.
Their primary and immediate task is to give Christian witness to the
people they encounter in their neighborhood, on the job, when
shopping, and at social functions. In daily life, family members
evangelize each other, men and women their spouses, and workers
their fellow employees by the simple lives of faith they lead.

In sum, evangelization's goal is simple. It's to bring about in
all Catholics such an enthusiasm for their faith that, in living their
faith in Jesus, they freely share it with others. In other words, what
Patrick did in Ireland we're called to do every day

WORK
[ST. JOSEPH THE WORKER; LABOR DAY; ETC.]
Gn 2:4-9, 15   Ps 127   Col 3:14f., 17, 23f.   Lk 16:1-13

When introduced for the first time, people often ask, "What do you
do for a living?" There's an implicit understanding that work is what
defines you. Work is a term most commonly applied to manual or
physical labor, but there's no satisfactory reason for excluding
intellectual effort from one's understanding of it.

The ancient Hebrews held physical work in some esteem, and
it penetrated the social fabric of God's First Testament. The pattern
of work and rest was taken from God's creative work and rest
recorded in Genesis (2:1-3). Work directed to God merited divine
blessing. Work had significant earthly values in discipline, security,
and the avoidance of evil.

Yet the wickedness of exploiting people was present even
then. The prophet Amos shows many of the Israelites as being so
greedy that, like Scrooge at Christmas, they couldn't wait for the
end of the holy days so that they could get back to work for business

profits (Am 8:5). Not only that: They would make their profit by cheating their customers.

Purely physical work, with some exception for agricultural pursuits, wasn't held in high esteem at the height of the Greek and Roman civilizations. The Roman attitude was that it made no sense for Rome to be ruler of the world if its citizens had to do their own physical work. For that, they had slaves. Christianity came into that kind of world with the good news that all persons are precious because all are so loved by God that he gave His only Son. The Gospel atmosphere is that of people at work: farmers, fishermen, harvesters, vinedressers. St. Joseph, the foster-father of Jesus, was a carpenter.

In the eyes of his compatriots, Joseph's humble position as carpenter had nothing degrading about it. The majority of famous rabbis had worked with their hands. The Rabbi Judah expressed one of the five principle duties of the father of a family: "He who does not teach his son a trade, teaches him to steal." When Jesus was strong enough, he joined Joseph in his workshop. After Joseph died, Jesus became a full-fledged working man, having to save for food and clothes, meet an occasional dissatisfied client, and handle customers who wouldn't, or couldn't, pay their bills. When Jesus returned to Nazareth to preach, though, the townspeople thought him not worthy of a hearing because he worked with his hands. That kind of thinking is still with us.

The carpenter's Son even spoke of his supreme mission in terms of work. His parable of the vineyard workers (Mt 20:1-6) shows the tender compassion of God for a man out of work, who is a tragic figure. Jesus understood the spiritual and psychological effects of being unemployed. In today's terms, being unemployed (and therefore poor) is to be a fish in a bowl. You look out with agonizing envy at the smiling, happy, socially accepted people strolling through life, getting into their grand cars, going to their middle-class homes and pleasures, having money, status, freedom, security, and admiration, all hardly aware of their good fortune.

Despite the Christian teaching on humility, no one thanks you for being a nobody. Although everybody wants to be wanted, the unemployed are branded as unwanted, and every rejection slip by an employer nails you afresh on the cross of unwantedness. Other people don't want to be tainted by the stifling dead-endedness of your existence. Your life implodes; you become isolated in a society where "networking" is a ladder to success. You're left alone with your torment, which is that you've failed self, family, and life.

Our society — unchristian enough to seem to favor the arrogant, proud, greedy, selfish, callous, and ruthless — has something to do with your sense of failure. You lack self-faith, and you pray for it daily. At the same time that you realize that self-pity is an ugly thing, you feel sorry for yourself. Your living on the edge gives you new insights denied to those insulated by security. You try to understand a society which aborts fit babies and lets good people live this death in life.

In the face of all that, Jesus taught justice and service; the worker was worthy of his wages; the Son of Man came to serve; and one who is greatest must serve his fellows. But his teaching was directly concerned rather with the intimate nature of salvation, and not with the economy.

As with Amos in God's First Testament, some of Jesus' stories showed the oppression caused by human greed. In his story of the rich man (Lk 12:13-21), among the man's wrong priorities was that his whole basis of security was wealth. The rich man believed in the modern axiom, "Money talks; learn its language." He never thought in terms of another proverb, "There are no pockets in a shroud." God called him a fool (v. 20).

The driving force today is, no less than in Jesus' time, to build bigger and bigger barns. Upper management receives obscenely high salaries, while workers are laid off by the thousands. For tax advantages, employers deliberately use temporary or part-time workers who often have no health or pension benefits, don't get paid if they're sick, have to take necessary time off without pay, have hours the employer can change at will, and often have no assurance that the job will be there next week. Big companies use bankruptcy laws to default on debts, which little persons have to pay. Corporations' dog-eat-dog philosophy encourages people to climb over the bodies of others to reach the top.

Another of Jesus' stories (Lk 16:1-13) is about a wily manager. Under the blow of his disgrace in having his sharp practices reported, he showed himself lazy, soft, and accustomed to deference from his master's workmen and customers: not strong enough to dig, and ashamed to beg (v. 3). A wheeler-dealer who was far from being repentant when he was caught, he turned to embezzlement, theft, and forgery to escape his predicament, with the definite impression that he'd practiced a whole career of it.

In that story the debtors, too, were scoundrels: They were ready to take advantage of every opportunity they could, moral or not. The master also was something of a knave. When he entered the picture, he wasn't shocked by what the manager had done and, rather than giving attention to his devious employee's dishonesty, he gave him credit for being enterprising (v. 8).

On one occasion (Lk 16:19-31), when Jesus addressed the Pharisees, who St. Luke tells us "loved money," Jesus told the story of Lazarus, a poor man, and Dives, a rich man — one of the "beautiful people" who went "first class" all the way: right out of the pages of Esquire or Gentleman's Quarterly. At a time when the common people worked six days a week just to keep body and soul together, Dives dressed expensively and dined sumptuously *every day*.

At the gate to his palace — right off the sidewalks of any modern city, where he lies in his cardboard shelter against the winds — lay Lazarus begging, almost a permanent fixture (v. 20). In abject poverty he longed to eat the scraps (v. 21) from Dives's table. Dives never gave him a tumble. Then death came to both. Lazarus was taken to the intimate fellowship of heaven, Dives to a place of torment (v. 23). Dives was condemned not because luxury is evil, but because he looked apathetically upon an unemployed worker's misery without feeling it, saw a fellow human being in pain without response, and had developed an anesthetized conscience.

In the teaching of the Apostles, work was propounded as a moral essential of the Christian life. For St. James, it was a grave wrong to deprive the worker of his just wage. St. Peter taught that the hardship of work in patient union with Christ guards a person from evil. According to St. John, even menial work is a task of love and the fulfillment of love's commandment (Jn 13:12-17).

But it's St. Paul who gave labor its Magna Carta. In the Christian life one has an obligation to work for his sustenance and for the avoidance of evil ways. Those who don't work shouldn't eat. Paul's own work in the apostolate gave him the right to support from the work of others, but for the sake of good example he supported himself by tentmaking. The precious linking of work with almsgiving and Christian discipline in right living is an essential element in Paul's theology of work (2 Th 3:8-15).

For the Fathers of the Church, work doesn't come to us as a curse or consequence of the fall of Adam and Eve — only the *hardship* of work comes through Original Sin. But work is for all a spiritual necessity: It molds our character, it develops strength and inner resources, and it gives to our soul a kind of beauty that can come from nowhere else. All work that meets these standards is noble, no matter what its nature.

In Christian monasticism, work was valued as a spiritual exercise and discipline which, particularly when burdensome, allays concupiscence, forestalls temptation, and promotes humility. Moreover, monastic work, especially in the form of agriculture, building, and copying manuscripts, contributed to the establishment of Christian culture. Medieval Christian thought contributed to a theology of work the development of the concept of an earthly common good, the assertion of the priority of the spiritual over the temporal, and the orientation to a supernatural final end.

With the Renaissance and the Reformation opening the way, the capitalistic spirit of unrestricted acquisition for its own sake gradually came to produce today's socioeconomic life. Modern people's total preoccupation with this world, the breaking of the moral bonds that had formerly acted as restraints, and the Church's lack of success in bringing forth its social and economic doctrine led to an unlimited exploitation of nature and people.

Since their first effective formulation by Pope Leo XIII, the Church's great social encyclicals have laid down the guidelines for a theology of work, but this theology is as yet not fully developed. The problems of work today have become more complex than at St. Joseph's workbench. Because all committed to work are human beings, there's enough blame for the faults involved to go to *management*, to *the labor force*, and to *the system*.

Among the faults of *management* is that it uses all manner of dirty tricks. Companies delay, undermine, disrespect, and generally avoid enforcement of labor laws, many of which have loopholes the size of Henry Frick's art collection for the bosses to prance through. Also, management practices "preventive labor relations," a euphemism for the art of keeping a company union-free. Some companies, thinking unions pose a threat to control of the company, hire spies, engage in disinformation campaigns by mail, use personal information gained through eavesdropping to spread rumors about pro-union employees, and fire workers sympathetic to the union idea. Employers sometimes hire permanent replacement workers when the original workers are engaged in a legitimate strike. They exploit such needy people as migrant and immigrant workers by establishing sweatshops.

Labor shares some of the blame. Workers often don't take seriously the obligation of doing a day's work for a day's pay, or of responsible union voting, so that the election process is often controlled by a court of princes instead of by the rank-and-file. Too frequent a phenomenon is mob-infestation that rapes unions' constituents. Leaders often use membership funds for their own uses, and defend indefensible workers for being lazy.

For still other faults, the *system* is to blame. The field isn't simple. Thanks to the trade unions, today's capitalism has introduced social safety nets, enacted good social policies, and is monitored by the state and the unions — but not everywhere: In some countries capitalism has remained in a savage state, almost as it was in the last century.

Automation roars ahead, putting great pressure on employment and wages and invading the lower-wage services. Bank tellers share work with automated teller machines. Insurance and credit card companies keep barns full of $5-an-hour clerks who type data from forms into computers. It can be hard and painful work. But it is work, and soon there will be less of it: Uncomplaining optical character readers are coming along to displace the typists.

Because of intensifying competition from Asia and Latin America, United States industry installs factories in Brazil or Malaysia, making goods abroad to sell to United States workers who in buying them put themselves out of jobs. The same is happening in services; data entry clerks can work just as efficiently in Jamaica or Ireland as they can in Wichita. Many people think that a mismatch between the United States school system and industry also impedes the creation of high-wage, high-skill jobs.

The solution to the problems? If you're in any way engaged on either side of labor-management relations, cooperate with the other side. Two moving men — a boss and his employee — were struggling with a big crate in a doorway. They pushed and tugged until they were exhausted, but it wouldn't move. Finally, the man on the outside said, "We'd better give up: We'll never get it in." The fellow on the inside said, "What do you men, 'get it in?' I thought we were trying to get it out!"

Even if you're not engaged directly, the field is sufficiently important for you to take an interest. Be involved. Be informed. We complain, but too few voices are raised urging government, business, and industry to cooperate in retraining workers for the future in high tech and service jobs. Good people will differ over practical implementation, but only by exercising our God-given responsibilities can we order our society toward the kingdom of God. With St. Joseph as our example and guide, may God help us to do the work he has asked and earn the rewards he has promised.

MOTHERS' DAY

Pr 6:20-23   *Ep 6:1-3*   *Lk 1:39-45*

In a lecture on the motherhood of Mary, the speaker began with a definition of motherhood. He defined a mother in these terms: "a woman who, having provided an ovum that is subsequently fertilized by an external agent, prepares it for the infusion of a soul and nurtures it from her own bodily substance till it can be physically separated from her." A girl in the audience whispered not too subtly: "Obviously, the poor fellow never had a mother."

A true definition of a mother or mothering is hard to come by. Certainly it must include notes of caring, tenderness, and affection. It would include not only Mother Hubbard and Mother Goose, but also many adults who aren't biological mothers but who provide nurturing and guidance for youngsters. These would include such "mothers of the heart" as adoptive and foster parents, teachers, nurses, religious sisters, and all others who give motherly love to countless children, especially those who are orphaned, handicapped, or neglected.

Here as elsewhere, to find what a thing *is*, we ask what it *does*. What, then, does a woman do as a mother? But even that's hard to pin down. If "all the world's a stage," as Shakespeare wrote, a mother's world is a stage where she plays many parts in one costume. Without benefit of double billing, she's cook and nurse, laundress and seamstress, and at times career woman and provider for her family. She's counselor, comforter, encourager. In her world there's no five-o'clock whistle. But what are the *essentials* of what she does?

First of all, she *loves*. No theme has stirred people to greater depths than a mother's love, yet centuries passed before artists could even suggest the height and breadth and depth of her devotion. The ancient Greek ideal of woman was Aphrodite, the goddess of sexual beauty. She was primarily a goddess of love and fertility, and occasionally presided over marriage.

Aphrodite's importance as a promoter of fertility was emphasized by the traditionally phallic nature of the objects borne by two maidens to her sanctuary during festivals, and also by her close association with Eros, the god of selfish getting. The Romans adapted the Greek ideal into their goddesses Juno and Venus. In Roman religion Juno was connected with all aspects of the life of women, most particularly married life. Venus was the Roman goddess whose name became associated with the idea of charm, winsomeness, and beauty. One of the planets came to be known as Venus because the planet was at first the star of the Babylonian goddess Ishtar, and thence of Aphrodite.

Early Christianity surpassed them all in presenting Mary as the ideal of womanhood. That ideal came to be synthesized in such physical representations as St. Francis of Assisi's Christmas crèche in the thirteenth century and Raphael's paintings of the Blessed Virgin Mary as Madonna in the sixteenth century; through such as these, the world was given its most beautiful ideal of womanhood. Venus had lovers, but Mary fussed over her child. Upon Mary's brow settled the holiness of beauty and the beauty of holiness. Mary's face was illuminated by an inner light unknown to Aphrodite or Venus, and Mary survives to the latest generation as the gentlest name in history for motherly love as the ideal of womanhood.

A mother's love is not only strong, unselfish, and undying, but it's a constant inspiration for a son or daughter to do always what's right and pure and noble and just — to rise to a higher life of virtue and nobility. A mother tries never to miss any opportunity to show her children what it means to be a loving human being. This world will never know how much of the heroism and success of men and women is traceable to the inspiration of a mother's love for them. Loving a child won't solve all problems, but unless a child is loved — and helped to accept and express love — nothing else will help enough: Such children will have difficulty developing relationships later in life.

A mother's love causes her to *nurture*. She delivers us obstetrically once, by car and bus ever after. She gives her very blood to our making, her milk to our nursing, her sweat to our rearing, her tears to our straying. She risks her life bearing us, and she spends her life bearing with us. Her concern for others, her words, attitudes, and judgments are powerful examples.

A mother also *accepts*. She realizes that she didn't select her children; they're entrusted to her care by God, in all their uniqueness and frailty. Her loving — and loving is the best way to know a person — makes her realize that her children's silence can cover quiet desperation, and their rebellion can be a plea for help. She instinctively knows that the most trying situations may be the very times when communication is most important.

She automatically knows, through her religion and her intuition as well as her love, the need to *forgive*. From minor irritations to major offenses, children need to be forgiven. A loving response doesn't exclude just punishment, but there's no place for resentment.

And the good mother *makes a home*. Gadgets and gimmicks can make a model house. But nobody ever learned to say his night prayers kneeling at the side of a deluxe refrigerator. Nobody ever came running home from his first day of school to throw his little arms around an electric juicer. Nobody who was all worried and mixed up over something ever looked for the answer in a brand-new VCR. It takes a *mother* to make a model *home*.

There's real work connected with making a home. It means providing an atmosphere of emotional comfort where children are able to work and play and invite their friends. Home is the place where children learn responsibility, discipline, and self-worth. The homemaking skill is an important ingredient in the mix of family happiness, and a homemaker who enlists every family member in housekeeping chores fosters cooperation and teaches useful skills.

None of this necessarily means the mother staying at home. Many mothers work full-time jobs these days by choice or necessity. Yet their commitment to their children still allows time for adequate nurturing and care.

Last but not least, the loving mother *teaches about God*. Children have an innate sense of the reality of God that must be encouraged. Psychiatrist Robert Cole spoke with children from every part of the world and found they could talk about God with openness, ease, and originality. Here as elsewhere, mothers teach most effectively by example.

Along with all the duties of motherhood, there are wonderful rewards. Seeing youngsters develop individuality and character as they grow into maturity gives great fulfillment.

But mothers aren't perfect. They're human beings with faults and failings. The mythology of perfect mothers only brings a sense of failure to women who realize they can't compete with an ideal model. Women who try to be super-moms are often exhausted, frazzled people who place unreasonable demands upon their children and themselves. Some mothers project their fears and lack of self-esteem upon their children, crippling them psychologically. Other mothers are so caught up with the daily workload that they forget to take care of themselves. Some believe they have to sacrifice themselves totally to the well-being of their children — a false and dangerous concept for all concerned.

Also, mothers need support. A father's involvement with his family is deeply important to the well-being of his wife and their children. And that involvement should be coordinated with the work of the mother. During a class discussion of mothers and fathers in Sunday School, a small child asserted: "Mommies are for telling you to ask Daddy; Daddies are for telling you to ask Mommy."

While it may be difficult for children to honor anyone, including a mother, who has abused or injured them, we're asked to love even the unloving. This can only be done with God's help, through prayer and the power of forgiveness.

Of course, the idea of honoring mother was in the commandments long before it ever got into the calendar as Mothers' Day. The celebration came into existence only in May, 1908, in the churches of Philadelphia through Miss Anna Jarvis in honor of her own mother; then, because those services were so widely acclaimed and because of Miss Jarvis's work, in 1914 President Woodrow Wilson declared it a national festival.

We often take our mothers for granted, and Mother's Day reminds us to say, "Thank you; I appreciate all that you do for me." Some of us, mindful that we came into this world through a mother as across a threshold, treat her like a door mat. Too many of us have never matured sufficiently to realize what we owe our mother. All of us should take heed, before it's too late, of the debt we owe our mothers. Be good to your mother: If your mother is no longer with you, pray for her; if you're lucky enough to have her still with you, pray for her and tell her often that you love her!

FATHERS' DAY
Sir 3:1-16 Rm 13:15   *Mk 7:10-13*

Today's celebration in honor of fathers began during a Mothers' Day sermon. That's fitting, because fathers and mothers are one. In the Spring of 1919, Mrs. John Bruce Dodd of Spokane, Washington, heard a Mothers' Day sermon which didn't even mention the word "father." Mrs. Dodd's mother had died when she was a small child, and her thoughts naturally turned to her father, who had been left with the responsibility of raising herself and her five siblings. To make a long story short, through her influence the first Fathers' Day was observed in Spokane on June 10, 1919, and on a national level in 1922.

Fathers are extremely important. That was recognized long before Christianity. History records, for example, a conversation between King Philip, powerful King of Macedon, and his young son Alexander, who was being instructed by Aristotle and who for a time in the fourth century B.C. was destined to become Alexander the Great, ruler of the entire Western world. King Philip asked the boy if his hero was Achilles, the legendary conquering hero. The answer was no: "Achilles was in subjection to others," Alexander replied, "and he went on a military expedition with a small force under the orders of a foreign general. I would in no case submit to the control of any king alive." Exasperated at this affront, Philip asked, "And aren't you, Alexander, under my control?" "In no way," answered his son, "for I don't obey you as a king, but as a father."

It's been shown that children who grow up without their fathers are worse off — economically, educationally, psychologically, and in every other way we can measure — than children who grow up with their fathers. Everyone deprived of a father because of early death or some similar reason feels the deep pain. While growing up alone can teach one to look to oneself for aid and comfort, it denies one an emotional haven, which young persons need if they're to grow up whole. Mothers, cops, and welfare reformers know that the lack of a "father figure" is one great cause of misdirected youth.

Among the symbols that Jesus chose to express God's relationship to humans — creator, king, judge, master — he tells us to address God by the name "Father." Even better, he calls the heavenly Father "Dad." The human father is a reflection of the Fatherhood of God, from whose heavenly Fatherhood the earthly father receives his dignity and authority. Of course, no one is father as God is Father.

That word "authority" is important for fathers. Mother-power is rooted in love and, whereas father-power must also contain love, it's also rooted in authority. The ultimate maternal sanction is, "This would break your Mom's heart." The ultimate paternal guilt-implanter is, "Dad will be disappointed in you."

The Bible presents God as a model for earthly fathers. It tells us, for example, that a good father has compassion: While the prodigal son was yet at a distance his father saw him and had compassion, and ran and embraced him and kissed him (Lk 15:20). The Scriptures tell fathers to bring their children up in the discipline and instruction of the Lord (Ep 6:4). And the Bible tells us that a father nurtures his children: Jesus asked, "What father among you, if his son asks for a fish, will instead of a fish give him a serpent?" (Lk 11:11).

Whereas any healthy male can biologically generate children, only a man who's at the loving center of caring guidance proves himself a true father — a "dad." Although a father should be friendly — ready to help and able to share a confidence — a true father isn't just a friend. He has an unspoken claim on his offspring's respect that no friend has. Fatherhood means helping with school work, museum time, involvement in sports with sons and daughters, family singing, dinner table discussions, and conveying the fact that parents are human and therefore fallible (saying "I'm sorry" when they're wrong). The job is full time, and isn't necessarily limited to natural parents: stepfathers, adoptive fathers, even strangers who care can enter the relationship. And many of the expectations of fathers apply to mothers as well.

A good father sets an example: "Words teach, but example compels." Even though in practice it's not easy to be a good father, here are some guidelines to be considered. They're offered, in no particular order of importance, with all the ignorance of one who is a spiritual father but not a physical one.

A father finds fulfillment by living up to his parental duties. When fathers abandon the upbringing of their children, a loss is suffered by everyone, but perhaps most by themselves. Among the things they lose is the possibility of human growth in themselves which is stimulated in the process of rearing their children.

A father should give his home top priority. For centuries now, fathers have had to go to their place of business to earn a living for their family. It wasn't always like that: There was a time when the father earned his livelihood right in his own home. What with computers and modems, we may see a return of that arrangement. Meanwhile, no matter how successful a father may be on the job, his life can be a failure if he neglects to give his family the time and personal attention they both deserve and need. Someone once asked, "How do you spell 'love' in connection with children?" The answer came back, "T-I-M-E."

What's more, *a father should make his home happy.* There's magic in laughter, and children especially love it. A father should develop each child's personality. A good father spurs each of his children's unique creativity. To do this, he listens to his children. To listen well, it's necessary to be active, involved, and interested. You have to listen with your whole self: your eyes, your ears, your heart.

A father was walking with his young son. The boy said, "Daddy, what's electricity?"

"Well now, I don't really know," said the father. "All I know about electricity is that it makes things run."

A little farther on, the boy said, "Daddy, how does gasoline make the automobiles go?"

The father replied, "Well, I don't know. I don't know much about motors."

Several more questions followed with much the same result, until at last the boy said, "Gee, dad, I hope you don't mind my asking so many questions!"

"Not at all, son," said his father, "you go right ahead and ask. How else will you ever learn anything?"

A father should understand the true meaning of discipline. Discipline means more than chastisement or punishment. To be comparable to the discipline of the Lord that should be its model, a father's discipline must be certain, consistent, commensurate with the wrong done, and loving. If he has to give orders, a father should take the trouble to do it in a friendly, reasoned manner. A teacher was giving a lesson on the weather idiosyncrasies of March. "What is it," she asked, "that comes in like a lion and goes out like a lamb?" And little Julia, in the back row, replied: "Father."

Discipline will include teaching the value of money. Henry Thoreau said, "Almost anyone knows how to earn money, but not one in a million knows how to spend it." A father should create opportunities for sharing resources generously with the less fortunate, and praise his children when they do something thoughtfully compassionate for another person. Children will thank their father later in life if he resists the temptation to hand them everything on a platter. Children need toughening and preparation for life.

A father should nourish his children's spiritual life. From their earliest years a father should instill in his children a sturdy sense of religion; add meaning and direction to their lives by keeping them aware of such basic questions as "Who am I? Where did I come from? Why am I here? Where am I going? How do I get there?"; accompany them to church; let them take turns in leading family prayers and saying grace at meals; and impress on them to try throughout their lives to bring spiritual values into public and private life.

Nourishing children's spiritual lives includes giving them a healthy attitude toward sex, especially before adolescence. The serious responsibility of giving adequate sex instructions belongs to parents and is one they can't delegate entirely to others. A father should set high personal standards of conduct with regard to dress, companions, dating, conversations, literature, and entertainment. There's the story of the daughter who said to her father, as the TV was grinding out the latest in youthful music: "Did you ever hear anything so wonderful?" To which her father replied: "Can't say I have — although I once heard a collision between a truckload of milk cans and a car filled with ducks!"

The respect and courtesy the good father extends to his wife and daughters lays the foundation for healthy boy-girl relationships. With that foundation, his sons will respect girls as friends, not just sex objects, and his daughters will accept nothing less than the respect and courtesy accorded them by their father.

A father should help his children acquire a liking for books. A teacher may take care of the mechanics of reading; a father can supply the fun. If he reads aloud to them at an early age and introduces them to the joys and inexhaustible treasures of the world of good books, his children will never be able to thank him enough.

A father should teach his children to be open-minded. It's been said that "every bigot was once a child free of prejudice." Hatred or dislike of people of a different religion, skin color, or nationality originates in the family. So do love and acceptance. Fathers should teach their children to see every person as a child of God.

All of this is the way St. Joseph saw it. The primary concern of his life was to obey God's law. He married Mary even though the child with whom she was pregnant wasn't his, because God told him to, and to protect his family he went into exile, because God told him to. When Jesus spoke publicly of God as *abba*, "daddy," a term of intimacy and endearment, on the human level it was from Joseph that he had learned what a daddy was.

We congratulate fathers every day, but especially today. We pray that our Father in heaven will help them to be good fathers on earth.

THE SACRED HEART

1 Jn 4:7-16   *Jn 15:9-17*

It's impossible to speak or to act as a human being without the use of signs and symbols: the wedding ring on the bride's finger, the words in a dictionary, a handshake between business associates, a kiss between lovers. The use of symbolic signs and actions is found among places and ages ranging from the regalia of the Egyptian pharaohs to the hammer and sickle of Marxists.

A "symbol" is a visible sign of something invisible — a lion is a symbol of courage, for instance. A symbol is a visible sign which suggests something else — perhaps an abstract idea — by reason of association or convention. The sensed image is never identical with the invisible being which it represents: It only gives a hint of the spiritual reality.

The early Christians made use of symbols to hide the mysteries of the new faith: the anchor symbolized hope, the ship the Church, the fish Christ. We still have Christian symbols: the dove, the lamb, Peter's barque, the grapes and wheat, Alpha and Omega, the Chi Rho.

The heart as a symbol of love goes back to Plato: he saw the head presiding over thought, the heart over affection, the abdomen over passions. It's a conventional symbol, not natural: Love is *not* in the heart alone. Interestingly, though, modern medicine shows a connection between heart diseases and disorders in love.

Although the essence of God's love can in no way be adequately expressed by any created image whatever, we adore the heart of Jesus in a special way, because his heart is the sign and symbol of his boundless love for the human race. The Sacred Heart is the symbol of that divine love which Jesus shares with the Father and the Holy Spirit, but which in Jesus alone is manifested to us through his human body, since in Christ the fullness of God resides in bodily form (Col 2:9).

He sees something special in us, even though we leave something to be desired. And he loved us *first* — even while we were in sin! His love *makes* a certain goodness in us. *We* love what's good; *his* love is what *makes* goodness. God's love is proclaimed both in the First and Second Testaments in vivid images.

To the people of Israel in God's First Testament, the weightiest reason for obeying God was not the fear of divine vengeance, which the thunder and lightning flashing from the peak of Mt. Sinai struck into their souls, but rather love for God. We're not surprised when Moses and the prophets described the dealings between God and His people in terms of the mutual love of a father and his children or of a husband and his wife, rather than in any stern terms of God's supreme dominion or of our own subjection in fear.

There are many examples of this among the prophets. Perhaps no prophet more than Hosea expresses clearly and forcefully the love which God always showed His people. In his writings, which are outstanding for the austere grandeur of his diction, God manifests a solicitous love for His people, a love like that of a merciful father or that of a husband whose honor is offended: "When Israel was a child I loved him, out of Egypt I called my son . . . it was I who . . . took them in my arms; . . . I fostered them like one who raises an infant to his cheeks; Yet, though I stooped to feed my child, they did not know that I was their healer . . . I will love them freely; . . . I will be like the dew for Israel" (Ho 11:1, 3-4; 14:5-6).

Isaiah is similar: he has God say, "Can a mother forget her infant, be without tenderness for the child of her womb? Even should she forget, I will never forget you" (Is 49:15). No less touching are the words of the Song of Songs (Canticle of Canticles) when describing graphically the bonds of mutual love which join God and His chosen people in terms of conjugal love: "As a lily among thorns, so is my beloved among women. . . . My lover belongs to me and I to him. . . . Set me as a seal on your heart, as a seal on your arm" (Sg 2:2; 6:3; 8:6).

That we may be able so far as it's possible for mortals to grasp fully the breadth and length and height and depth (Ep 3:18) of the love of the Incarnate Word for his heavenly Father and for people defiled by sin, we must understand that his love is spiritual, as becomes God, because God is Spirit (Jn 4:24). But it wasn't only spiritual. The love spoken of in the Gospel, in the letters of the Apostles, and in the pages of the Book of Revelation, all express not only divine love but also human sentiments of love.

The heart of Jesus Christ beyond doubt vibrated with love and the rest of the impulses of human affections. These impulses were in such perfect accord with his human will filled with divine love, and with the infinite love itself which the Son shares with the Father and the Holy Spirit, that there never was anything conflicting in his kinds of love.

Wherefore the heart of Jesus Incarnate is the chief symbol of the love with which he continuously loves the Father and the whole human race. It's the symbol of that divine love which he shares with the Father and the Holy Spirit, but which in him alone is it manifested to us through his mortal human body. It's the symbol of that most ardent love which sanctifies the human will of Christ.

Finally, in a more direct and natural manner, it's a symbol of *affectionate* love, since the body of Jesus has a most perfect capacity for feeling. So Jesus felt joy, sorrow, and other emotions much more than we. We can understand such an experience as Gethsemane only by poor analogy. In sunlight, people wear dark glasses to accustom themselves to the sun's brightness. It's the same with God's love. The truest, best, and most beautiful love in the world is God's.

Jesus' human will and divine love were present in the home at Nazareth. His love drove him on during his lengthy apostolic journeys. His love motivated the innumerable miracles which he wrought; the labors he endured; the sweat, hunger, and thirst he suffered; the nocturnal vigils in which he prayed to his heavenly Father; and his discourses and parables.

The heart of Jesus was moved by great charity when words full of love fell from his lips. That was true, for example, when he saw the crowds tired and hungry: "My heart is moved with pity for the crowd" (Mk 8:2). When he looked over Jerusalem, his most beloved city which was blinded by her sins and therefore destined for destruction, he grieved: "O Jerusalem, Jerusalem, murderess of prophets and stoner of those who were sent to you! How often have I yearned to gather your children, as a mother bird gathers her young under her wings, but you refused me" (Mt 23:37).

His heart was moved by a special love when he saw that the hour of his cruel sufferings was at hand. Hanging on the cross, he felt his heart on fire with varied and vehement affections — affections of the most ardent love, of dismay, of mercy, of a most intense longing, of serene calm: "Father, forgive them, for they do not know what they are doing" (Lk 23:34); "My God, my God, why have you forsaken me?" (Mt 27:46); "I assure you: this day you will be with me in Paradise" (Lk 23:43); "Father, into your hands I commend my spirit" (Lk 23:46).

A powerful manifestation of Our Savior's thoughts and desires about devotion to his Sacred Heart took place during the years 1673 to 1675 in the chapel of the Visitation Sisters in Paray-le-Monial in France. A series of visions was given to a nun, St. Margaret Mary Alacoque. The Lord made it clear that he was full of longing to share the treasures of his love in wonderful ways with any and all who would practice devotion to his Sacred Heart. He extended several promises to Margaret Mary, commissioning her to present them to the world.

Margaret Mary suffered rejection of her visions and ridicule by everybody for ten years — ten years! Finally, a Jesuit priest, Claude de la Colombière, entered her life as her confessor. Through him and the Jesuits in general the saint's visions at last reached the outside world. The promises made to Margaret Mary weren't radically new but were an affirmation of those given in the Gospels by our Lord himself (Mt 17:20; Mk 16:17; Jn 4:1-3). During the visions, Jesus asked that a special feast-day dedicated to the Sacred Heart be established, and that was eventually done.

When we adore the Sacred Heart of Jesus, we adore in it and through it the uncreated love of the Divine Word, his human love, and all his other affections and virtues. We don't maintain that the heart of Jesus is to be understood in such a way that in it we have and adore a perfect and absolute sign of his divine love, since — as we said — the essence of that love can in no way be adequately expressed by any created image whatsoever.

Jesus' unique command is that we love one another as he has loved us (Jn 15:12). He knew he had to remind us of this, because sometimes we act as though we were made for competition rather than love. Jesus has given us the example of a love than which there is no greater: he laid down his life for his friends (v. 13); he calls all of us for whom he died *friends* (v. 14).

The consequence of following his advice will be joy (Jn 15:11). That's *his* new and peerless joy that will come our way, more fulfilling than any other and with a new completeness. The ranting of joyless followers are, when you think about it, more harmful than good. A gloomy Christian is an oxymoron, a contradiction in terms.

Jesus' love extends, of course, to today. What he started by living and by dying on Calvary is extended through His Mystical Body, which is his way of living on earth now. Because Christ intended his love to extend to all people of every time, he invites us to show that love to the nations. His invitation is *not* "look me up." No, he said: "Come to me, all you who labor and are burdened, and I will give you rest" (Mt 11:28).

A result of all this is expressed in the First Letter of John (1 Jn 4:7-16). It tells Christians of all times and places that the centerpiece of Christianity isn't knowing inner secrets, or understanding science and technology. That doesn't seem to have contributed to a better world. No, the essence of Christianity is love's total dedication. If we spent as much time and energy trying to love as we spend on technology, the world would be a much better place. John tells us that love has its origin in God (v. 7). In fact, the person without love doesn't know God (v. 8). Paradoxically, it's only by knowing

God that we can truly love, and it's only by loving that we can truly come to know God (or anyone else).

INDEPENDENCE DAY

Is 57:15-19   *Ph 4:6-9*   *Ps 122*   *Jn 20:19-23*

It's good for us, and for our country, to give regular attention to our roots. That includes the historical documents and symbols which are part and parcel of our national heritage. These documents and images are a living part of us, individually and collectively. There are, believe it or not, at least fourteen such items which point to the identity of our country as being religious.

First is *The Mayflower Compact*. In 1620, 41 pilgrims on the deck of the Mayflower prepared the first written constitution of our land. It opened with these words: "In the name of God. Amen." It stated that the long and difficult voyage to the new world had been "undertaken for the glory of God," and was signed "solemnly and mutually in the presence of God." Second is the *Liberty Bell*. When the bell was cast in 1751, these words of Moses were inscribed on it: "Proclaim liberty throughout the land unto all the inhabitants thereof" (Lv 25:10).

Third is what we may call the *Declaration of Dependence*. On June 12, 1775, a year before the signing of the Declaration of Independence, the Continental Congress officially called on all citizens to set aside a day "that we may, with united hearts and voices, . . . offer up our joint supplications to the all-wise, omnipotent and merciful Disposer of all events." It was a declaration of *dependence* — on God.

Fourth is the *Declaration of Independence*. In 1776, this was a great risk: There had been nothing like it since the fall of Rome. It includes four specific references to the dependence of our nation on Almighty God. Thomas Jefferson, the author of the declaration, was justifiably proud of his words, the relevant part for us being:

"We hold these truths to be self-evident: that all men are created equal; that they are endowed by their Creator with certain inalienable rights; that among these are life, liberty, and the pursuit of happiness; that to secure these rights, governments are instituted among men, deriving their just powers from the consent of the governed. . . ."

Fifth is *The American Seal*, approved by Congress on June 20, 1782. On every dollar bill the seal is pictured: It has the "Eye of God" directly above a pyramid, and the words *Annuit Coeptis*, which mean "he [God] has favored our undertakings." Sixth is the *Oath of Office*. The oath of office originated by George Washington when he took his first oath as President of the United States on April 30, 1789 had the powerful petition: "So help me God."

Seventh is the *Northwest Ordinance*. The same Congress that adopted the First Amendment disestablishing churches and granting freedom of religion passed this document on July 13, 1787, establishing federal control of the territory west of the Allegheny mountains and north of the Ohio River. It included this stipulation: "Religion, morality, and knowledge, being necessary to good government and the happiness of mankind, schools and the means of education shall forever be encouraged." Eighth is *Thanksgiving Day*. Shortly after his inauguration, George Washington proclaimed an annual national Thanksgiving Day to render thanks to Almighty God.

Ninth is *Washington's Order Regarding Chaplains*. On July 9, 1776, General George Washington issued this order: "The honorable Continental Congress having been pleased to allow a chaplain to each regiment, the colonels or commanding officers of each regiment are directed to procure chaplains accordingly, persons of good character and exemplary lives, and to see that all inferior officers and soldiers pay them a suitable respect. The blessings and protection of Heaven are at all times necessary, but especially so in times of public distress and danger." All branches of the United States armed services are now officially staffed by thousands of chaplains.

Tenth is our *National Anthem*. Francis Scott Key scribbled on

an old envelope the "Star Spangled Banner" during the bombard-
ment of Fort McHenry by the British on the night of Sept. 13, 1814.
On March 3, 1931, Congress adopted it as our national anthem. It
closes with this reverent praise of God: "Praise the Power that hath
made and preserved us a nation. Then conquer we must, when our
cause it is just and is our motto — 'In God is our Trust.'"

Eleventh is the *Motto on our Coins*. On Dec. 9, 1863, Secre-
tary of the Treasury Salmon P. Chase instructed the director of the
United States Mint in Philadelphia to inscribe the words "In God
We Trust" on all coins. Twelfth is our *Pledge of Allegiance* to our
flag. On June 14, 1954, President Dwight D. Eisenhower made it the
law of the land to add the words "under God" to the pledge of
allegiance to the flag. Thirteenth are our *State Constitutions*, many
of which still specify that our rights and liberties stem from God.

Last, and greatest of all, is the *United States Constitution*.
James Madison's creation, it drew on notions of higher law and has
come to be a constellation of our deepest convictions as one people.
It had many sources: classical Greece, the ancient Roman Republic,
the Renaissance, the "Enlightenment," Montesquieu's notion of the
separation of powers. Best of all, from Christianity our Constitution
received the notion of the primacy of the individual.

Christianity came into the world with the good news that every
human being is created in God's image, that all persons are precious
because all are so loved by God that he gave His only Son. This
principle of the sacredness of persons resulted in new relationships
and conditions: for example, democracy itself.

The United States isn't Christian in any formal religious
sense: Its citizens transgress Christianity's precepts freely. But it's
Christian in the sense that the basic teachings of Christianity are in
its bloodstream. The central doctrine of its political system — the
inviolability of the individual — is inherited from two millennia of
Christian insistence upon the immortality of the soul. Christian
ideals are manifest in the arguments that politicians use in public,
in the popular ideas of good taste, in the laws and manners of our
people.

The United States Constitution presumes moral values.

Jefferson wrote that "human rights can only be assured among a virtuous people," and that "the foundation of our national policy will be laid in the pure and immutable principles of private morality." These positions were basically presumed by the other founders of our country. When George Washington bade Americans farewell as their president, and pondered what it would take to preserve democracy in these United States when so many other efforts had failed, his answer was: "Of all the dispositions and habits which lead to political prosperity, religion and morality are indispensible [sic] supports. . . . let us with caution indulge the supposition that morality can be maintained without religion."

In September of 1787 Benjamin Franklin warned the 39 men at the Convention who signed the Constitution for a nation of barely four million people that the new government would end in despotism if the people became corrupt. Outside the Convention, he elaborated this thought: "Only a virtuous people are capable of freedom." President John Adams said the same, writing that "our Constitution was made only for a moral and religious people."

One of our greatest Supreme Court Justices, Joseph Story, in the early Eighteenth Century wrote: "Piety, religion, and morality are intimately connected with the well-being of the state, and indispensable to the administration of civil justice." The noted French jurist Alexis de Tocqueville in 1835 admonished later generations that "America is great because she is good, and if America ever ceases to be good, America will cease to be great." After looking for the greatness of America in her rivers and harbors, in her fertile fields and boundless prairies, in her rich mines and vast commerce, he wrote: "Not until I went to the churches of America and heard her pulpits aflame with righteousness did I understand the secret of her genius and power."

It's noteworthy that de Tocqueville described our country's *individualism* with a mixture of admiration and anxiety. Although the biblical and republican traditions dating from the colonization of the United States stress individual freedom, they didn't mean the freedom to do whatever an individual wants, but rather the *moral* freedom to choose what is *right*.

Over time, especially since World War II, the traditions of *atomic* individualism have grown stronger, while the traditions of the individual *in society* have grown weaker. The negative side comes out in the images of our heroes — for example, the cowboy riding off alone into the sunset. The image contains no sense of community.

These observations have been backed up by impartial commentators right up to our time. Sociologist Robert Bellah has observed that our individualism may have now grown cancerous. Historians Will and Ariel Durant, no espousers of formal religion, concluded their multi-volume history of the Western world by writing that "[t]here is no significant example in history . . . of a society successfully maintaining moral life without the aid of religion." We're coming to recognize the extent to which many of our social problems require for their solution the nurture and improvement of character. And for that, religion plays an essential role.

One of the biggest bones in the throat of some in our country is the First Amendment of our Constitution's Bill of Rights. Its relevant part states: "Congress shall make no law respecting an establishment of religion, or prohibiting the free exercise thereof." Under the first part — the *establishment* clause — there can be no legal compulsion for anyone to accept any belief against one's will.

Particularly troublesome to some are the words "prohibiting the free exercise thereof." It seems to be lost sight of that both phrases of the Amendment were written to be taken together, and that they were written to protect religion from the government, and not the other way around; a government-sponsored orthodoxy would stifle healthy religious liberty. The way Justice Story put it was to say: "The real object of the amendment was . . . to prevent any national ecclesiastical establishment which would give to an hierarchy the exclusive patronage of the national government."

The establishment clause is the phrase under which most Church-State issues arise. And most of those pertain to aid to church-affiliated schools. In that connection, in the Senate debate on tuition tax credits in 1978, one senator wrote: "Every member of the Constitutional Convention came from a state that, prior to the adoption of the Constitution and after, levied taxes . . . collected those taxes, and gave the taxes to churches to run primary and secondary schools for the education of those children who chose to go to school."

With reference to Jefferson's metaphor about a "wall of separation" between Church and State, there's nothing wrong with the metaphor so long as the wall has a few doors and windows to make the Founders' vision compatible with the needs of society. The metaphor originally appeared in Jefferson's 1802 letter of assurance of freedom of religion to the Danbury Baptist Association. Secularists conveniently forget Jefferson's 1804 letter to the Ursuline Sisters of New Orleans who, upon the Louisiana Purchase in 1803, also wanted assurances. Jefferson wrote to assure them of both the *protection* and *patronage* of the government.

And now we use the phrase that's guaranteed to cheer an audience: "And in conclusion . . . ." We ask, "What can we do?" Our answer begins with the suggestion to be mindful of William Penn's observation almost 300 years ago: "Those people who are not governed by God shall be ruled by tyrants." Publicize all the facts connected with the spiritual origins of our nation. Stimulate organizations to help. Remind people that only three out of 100 United States citizens deny the existence of God. This tiny but vocal minority should not result in the imposition of an atheistic country on the other 97 percent. Let's play our part in having this nation adhere to the foundations that made it great.

MEMORIAL DAY

Ep 6:10-17   *Mt 8:5-13*

The very best Memorial Day speech was given a long time ago, on a battlefield that commemorated one of the bloodiest battles this nation ever fought. It was the War between the States, or the Civil

War, in which more of this nation's young men died than in all the other wars of our country combined. Comparable to today's population, the losses of soldiers in that war would mean the deaths of five million men. That's to say nothing of the many civilians who died because of malnutrition, disease, and chaos. The money cost was staggering, and — as it is with most wars — the moral devastation, with the North emboldened by victory and the South demoralized by defeat, was never totally renewed. The great memorial speech of that day was given at Gettysburg, Pennsylvania, by Abraham Lincoln. It comprised only 166 words, but it has been called "the only great modern English prose poem of classical perfection."

Today's Memorial Day is a successor to Decoration Day, which originated with the Southern States after that war. Widows and friends of the slain Southerners showed their love and gratitude to their fallen heroes by strewing flowers over the soldiers' graves. These fine women of the South also decorated the graves of the northern dead. The news of this touching tribute flashed across the North as a ray of new hope for brotherhood, and in 1868 General John A. Logan, then Commander in Chief of the Grand Army of the Republic, showed his deep admiration of this custom by issuing an order designating May 30th as the day on which the custom would be repeated for all the dead of the Civil War. State legislatures thereafter set aside May 30th for remembering all our honored war dead.

As we think of Gettysburg, and the Vietnam War Memorial, and the Tomb of the Unknowns, and the countless little crosses row on row on graves all over the world, we can't help but wonder what war accomplishes. Those who have sacrificed because of war may not have died in vain, but there has to be a better way. A poet has written: "Give me the money that has been spent in war, and I will clothe every man, woman and child in the attire of which kings and queens would be proud. I will build a schoolhouse in every valley over the earth. I will crown every hillside with a place of worship consecrated to the gospel of peace."

The diversity of views on war found in today's society are found even in our sacred Scriptures. In the Jewish scriptures, violence and war are very much present in the history of the people of God. God is often seen as the one who leads the Hebrews in battle, protects them from their enemies, and makes them victorious over other armies. But the image of the warrior God was not the only image, and it was gradually transformed, particularly after the Hebrews' experience of the Exile, when God was no longer identified with military victory and might.

In the New Testament, there's no notion of a warrior God. Military images appear in terms of the preparedness which one must have for coming trials (Lk 14:31; 22:35-38). Swords appear in the New Testament as an image of division (Mt 12:34; Heb 4:12); they're present at the arrest of Jesus, and he rejects their use; weapons are transformed in the letter to the Ephesians, when Christians are urged to put on the breastplate of righteousness, the helmet of salvation, the sword of the Spirit, and the equipment of the gospel of peace on one's feet (Ep 6:10-17). Soldiers, too, are present in the New Testament. They're at the crucifixion of Jesus, of course, but they're also recipients of the baptism of John, and one centurion receives the healing of his servant (Mt 8:5-13).

Jesus challenged everyone to recognize in him the presence of the reign of God and to give themselves over to that reign. Such a radical change of allegiance was difficult for many to accept and families found themselves divided, as if by a sword. It was in that sense that Jesus said he came not to bring peace but rather the sword (Mt 10:34). The division caused by the word of God, like a two-edged sword, "pierces to the division of soul and spirit, of joints and marrow, and discerns the thoughts and intentions of the heart" (Heb 4:12).

In Israel during the time of Jesus, there were revolutionary groups. Barabbas, for example, was among the rebels in prison who had committed murder in an insurrection (Mk 15:7). Although Jesus had come to proclaim and to bring about the true reign of God which often stood in opposition to the existing order, he makes no reference to nor does he join in any attempts such as those of the zealots to overthrow authority by violent means.

Counting on today's reservoir of integrity and good will among people, we propose remedies for war on the national level, and recourse for individuals on the personal level. In doing so, we're trying to live up to the call of Jesus to be peacemakers in our own time and situation.

To begin, the paradox we face as Christians living in the world is that we must continue to articulate our belief that love is possible and the only real hope for all human relations, and yet accept the idea that force, even deadly force, is sometimes justified and that nations must provide for their defense. It's the mandate of Christians, in the face of this paradox, to strive to resolve it through an ever greater commitment to Christ and his message.

This commitment begins with the presumptions which bind all Christians: We should do no harm to our neighbors; how we treat our enemy is the key test of whether we love our neighbor; and the possibility of taking even one human life is a prospect we should consider in fear and trembling.

In a nuclear age, many Christians and others say that war is never allowed, because nuclear arms — with all their horror — will inevitably be used by the losing side. Under certain circumstances, recourse to war might be permissible. Among them are the following. There must be a *just cause*: the confronting of "a real and certain danger." War must be declared by *competent authority*, not by private groups or individuals. There must be *comparative justice*, the basic question here being: Do the rights and values involved justify the violence, destruction, suffering, and death involved in war? There must, of course, be a *right intention*. For resort to war to be justified, war must be *the last resort*: all peaceful alternatives must have been exhausted. The war must have *a probability of success*. Lastly, there must be *proportionality*: The damage to be inflicted and the costs incurred by war must be proportionate to the good expected by taking up arms.

Even when the stringent conditions which justify resorting to war are met, the conduct of war remains subject to continuous scrutiny. Remembering the massive slaughter and destruction of past wars — of even civilian targets — and the kind of weapons now stockpiled in the arsenals of many nations causes a realization that war is the most barbarous and least effective way of resolving conflicts.

What about *deterrence*? May a nation attempt to deter another nation from initiating a conflict by storing weapons? In current conditions, "deterrence" based on balance, certainly not as an end in itself but as a step on the way toward a progressive disarmament, may be judged morally acceptable. But deterrence, if and when permissible, is a transitional strategy, justifiable only in conjunction with resolute determination to pursue disarmament.

There *is* a substitute for war. There is *negotiation* under the supervision of a global body realistically fashioned to do its job. The United Nations should be particularly considered in this effort.

All of that had to do on the level of *government*. Unfortunately, decisions in that area are often not made by the citizenry. What can we do on a *personal* level? For the individual, we must always take into account the role of *conscience*. There are, of course, legislative provisions to recognize *conscientious objectors*, deeply sincere individuals who, far from being indifferent or apathetic to world evils, refuse to carry arms because they object to all wars, and *selective conscientious objectors*, those who refuse because they object to this or that particular war.

No government, and certainly no Christian, may simply assume that such individuals are guilty of cowardice. And the Jesus-inspired cause of *pacifism* is not to be confused with *passivity*. We admire all who forego the use of violence to vindicate their rights and resort to other means of defense available, provided it can be done without harm to the rights and duties of others.

A citizen may not, however, casually disregard his country's decision to call its citizens to acts of "legitimate defense." Even conscientious objectors must accept some other form of community service. Moreover, the role of Christian citizens in the armed forces can be a service to the common good and an exercise of the virtue of patriotism.

On the value of *non-violence*, some have understood the gospel of Jesus to prohibit all killing. One of the great non-violent figures of all times was St. Francis of Assisi. Besides making personal efforts on behalf of reconciliation and peace, Francis stipulated that lay persons who became members of his Third Order were not "to take up lethal weapons, or bear them about, against anybody." In the twentieth century, the non-Christian non-violent witness of Mahatma Gandhi and the Christian non-violent witness of such figures as Dorothy Day and Martin Luther King have had a worldwide impact.

What about *war tax resistance* as a means of preventing war? This involves the refusal to pay a percentage or the total of one's federal income tax because of opposition to the military spending of the government. Is it ever right for a person to act against the law in that way? The Church passes no judgment, either positive or negative, on people who have decided to refuse to pay their federal income tax. For a person to practice it, one has three areas to consider.

First, *the individual has a right and a duty to follow through on decisions of conscience* in striving to discharge one's earthly duties conscientiously and in response to the gospel spirit. The second consideration involves *the moral principles for evaluating war and the preparation for war*, provided that one doesn't injure the rights and duties of others or of the community itself. The third consideration involves *law and morality*. Specifically, can the protest of those in opposition to war take the form of an action that is against the law, like hammering dents in a warplane? To answer that question, we must consider the relationship between law and morality.

To begin, there is to be no individualistic morality here. And one's moral decision should contribute to the common good. But the law of the land doesn't *always* conform to the demands of the common good. Jesus alluded to this in some of his confrontations with the Pharisees — for example, his comment that the Sabbath is made for people, not people for the Sabbath (Mk 1:26). Law, then, is not the final word on human behavior; it's always answerable to morality. No law by its very existence automatically binds us in conscience. We must ascertain whether it is just.

But even though we reach a judgment that a particular law isn't just, two further factors must be taken into account. First, we must assess the seriousness of the issue under consideration; a decision to disturb the public order cannot be taken lightly. Secondly, the underlying rationale guiding an individual making a decision about obedience to a law must be the same as that which guides the legislators in framing the law: concern for the common good. Any rationale of a lesser nature, such as purely personal advantage, is inadequate.

Civil disobedience has a long history in Christianity. Christians, from the time of the Apostles and Martyrs right up to the present, have confronted situations where laws have made demands which they judged immoral, and have refused to comply. They paid the legal consequences, as must all who are guilty of civil disobedience.

If ridding the world of the weapons of war could be done easily, the whole human race would do it gladly tomorrow. Shall we shrink from the task because it's hard? Let's have the courage to believe in a bright future and in a God who wills it for us — not a perfect world, but a better one. The *perfect* world, we Christians believe, is beyond the horizon, in an endless eternity where God will be all in all. But a *better* world is here for human hands and hearts and minds to make. With regard to our war dead, the best way to honor and remember them — and at the same time to make a better world — is the work to end war.

CELEBRATING DIFFERENCES
Dt 10:17-19   *Ac 2:1-11*   *Lk 10:25-37*

Our Church today probably embraces as many different peoples as were present at the first Pentecost. Today we're European, American, African, Asian, Indian, Oceanic, and more. Yet there's evidence that, instead of accepting all persons as our Lord instructed, we discriminate, based particularly on racial/ethnic differences.

Even though it's not approvable, perhaps it's understandable. Thomas Jefferson, one of our founding fathers and a most intelligent man, embodied the most powerful contradiction of the American legacy. His declarations on individual liberty, which remain a moral and political compass, showed the brilliance of a transcendent mind. But he also believed in the inferiority of black people, demonstrating how even a great thinker can remain captive of the racist stereotypes of his time.

Then, too, to what extent can Christians be expected to transcend the opinions of their times and arrive at God's own vision of things (which constitutes the true reality)? As Christians, we must be mindful of our responsibility to discuss the signs of the times and interpret them in light of the Gospels; to be resolute in our continuing commitment to the eternal truths embodied in the Gospels, and in the social doctrines and traditions of the Church; and to proclaim the Good News to the poor and the oppressed.

Racism is an insidious cancer that invades the structures of our institutions. Like a pervasive smelly sulfur from the sky, it's rooted in the hearts and minds of people who profess to know God. It's in our families, our churches, our schools, and our places of work.

Racism is not merely one sin among many. It's an evil at our very root that divides the human family, blots out the image of God among specific members of that family, denies the new creation of a redeemed world, and violates the fundamental dignity of those called to be children of the same heavenly Father. To struggle against it demands an equally radical transformation in ourselves and in our society.

Our inherited prejudices apply particularly to Blacks, Jews, refugees, immigrants, those who request asylum, the disabled, and those who espouse different religions. With all these subjects, there are stereotypes, and there is the reality.

With *Blacks*, among the stereotypes are that they have a disagreeable smell; their color and facial features make them less beautiful than whites; they're sexually more physical and active; although they're equal to whites in memory, in reasoning powers they're much inferior; they have a predisposition to theft; in music they're more gifted than whites, but not in other arts like painting or sculpture. They're more addicted to alcohol and drugs, and grabbing bags from the arms of unsuspecting women.

Among the *facts* are the following. Blacks are intelligent, decent, attractive citizens. They pray, they have children, they have spouses. Some of their moral problems result from an inheritance of 300 years of slavery in which there was a cruel breakup of families and the lack of educational opportunities. Whites who oppose antidiscrimination measures often argue sincerely that they're not responsible for a past that's long gone. What they don't acknowledge is that while legal slavery and legal segregation have ended, many attitudes that drove those practices remain, although muted and concealed beneath the surface of propriety.

For *Jews*, false stereotypes have ancient roots. Anti-Jewish feelings were present even before the Christian era. In a "trip through the sewers" of Christian history, we see how Christians oppressed Jews in their pursuit of an image of the hated outsider. Hatred of Jews was reflected in the early symbol Christians used for them — the scorpion — and in the burning down of the Jewish quarters by angry crowds, especially after services on Good Friday. From the eleventh century onwards, laws were passed all over Europe forbidding Jews to inherit property — thus driving them into such alternative sources of income as money-lending and dealing in things they could take with them in a hurry, like jewelry.

Beginning in the twelfth century and persisting up until the 1920s in Poland and Germany, the implausible myth circulated that Jews murdered children to drain off their blood for their rituals; this led to the execution of innumerable Jews whose "confessions" had been obtained under torture. Even saints were tainted. St. Bernadine of Sienna said it was probably a mortal sin to eat with Jews. Peter the Venerable suggested that Jews might not be truly human — an excuse which human beings have often used to persecute others. A passage from St. Augustine attributing guilt to the Jewish race for the death of Christ was read in the Good Friday Tenebrae service up until Vatican Council II.

In the period of the Reformation, the Catholic Counter-Reform was no better than the Protestant Reformation in its conduct toward Jews. In the beginning of the modern era in Poland, merchants and artisans gradually drove Jews out of business; this in turn forced the Jews to work as tenant farmers on the estates of the nobility; and this aroused the hatred of the peasantry, who at times broke into frustrated bloody attacks. Is it any wonder that Jews feel animosity toward the crucifix?

To the disgrace of Christianity, Jewish emancipation began largely as a result of nonchristian liberal ideas in the eighteenth-century "Enlightenment" and of the French Revolution. The Revolution was the first civic emancipation of Jews; in all the countries occupied by Napoleon, the Jews were given full human rights, which changed completely the Jewish way of life and education.

In the 19th century Jews burst out of the ghetto in a great sweep of intellectual and artistic achievement. Even today, they're over-represented in science and the arts. Centuries in which they had been barred from owning land and from many occupations had turned them inward, and had thus developed the skills of the mind. But because many Jews won leading positions in economic life, the myth arose that all Jews are wealthy. A new force mis-named "anti-Semitism" tried to oust them from their positions and to prevent them from making further progress in social life. As a consequence of the resulting pogroms, starting around 1880 a great wave of Jewish emigrants came to the United States.

European Jews felt the brunt of World War I more than others, especially in Russia, and not too long after that came the persecution in Germany that resulted in the Holocaust before and during World War II. The 300-year migration of Jews to the United States presented a new experience. Today, the largest Jewish communities are in the United States, the Soviet Union, and Israel, the very largest — about six million — being in the United States. Their charities exceed on a per-capita basis the generosity of other groups.

Christians have forgotten — often — that the religious heritage of the Western world is *Judeo*-Christian. Judaism is at the base of Christianity, and both Christians and Muslims derive their monotheism from Judaism. Judaism remains a living legacy.

The problem of *refugees* has become a crisis that's getting worse. The world population of refugees from one country into another is now 18 million. An authority estimates that 24 million others have been displaced within their own countries. Additionally, a transitory population of nearly 40 million who are not recognized as refugees are compelled to cross borders. They have little access to humanitarian help. To simply continue aid at the grassroots level without addressing causes could easily lead to "compassion fatigue." One of the major root causes of current problems of refugees and migrants is poverty.

With those who become *immigrants*, there are many *stereotypes* and *allegations*. One *stereotype* is that immigrants take jobs that would otherwise go to other locals. The *fact* is that some studies show that the loss of jobs to immigrants is minimal to nonexistent. And other studies show that jobs are created and taxes paid by immigrant-owned or -supported businesses.

Immigrants help expand the demand for labor and increase the number of jobs, which tends to outweigh any negative effects they may have. Immigrants are more likely than the rest of the population to be self-employed and start their own businesses. Immigrant restaurants and businesses pay taxes, and their workers buy clothes and food and homes in neighborhoods that were formerly dead.

The *allegation* is that immigrants crawl or float or walk into the United States and use up a lot more public money — for education, medical care, welfare, and other social benefits — than they pay in taxes. The *fact* is that Naturalization Service surveys of immigrants legalized during "amnesty" programs indicate that only one percent or less had requested or received any public assistance. Additionally, most were found to have been working in low-paying jobs and, on the average, for longer hours than the general population. The Service's conclusion was that it's clear that undocumented immigrants are not the burden on our country they're portrayed to be. These people for the most part are migrating for labor, and when the jobs are not forthcoming to enable them to earn a living and become productive tax-paying citizens, there is a strong tendency for return migration.

The *allegation* is that immigrants have the audacity to come to this country, speak their own language, and bring their third-world lifestyle, causing a cultural war. The *fact* is that most citizens of this country came from immigrant forebears. Their cultures and lifestyle have contributed to the mosaic that this country is.

The Judeo-Christian view on immigrants predates the sovereign states. The Book of Leviticus (19:34) made it a law for the Jews that the strangers who sojourned with them shall be as the natives among them and they should love them as themselves. Abraham welcomed the stranger in the desert and found he was entertaining angels with a message from God.

The specifically Christian viewpoint on immigration begins, of course, with Jesus. Zacchaeus shared a meal with the Lord and he and his household were transformed. The two disciples on the road to Emmaus talked and walked with a stranger, who turned out to be Jesus. The Christian viewpoint is that even though a country has the right to control its own borders, the human right of persons to save their family transcends it. So in a way Christianity has a view of the future that is transcultural, transnational, and global, and in many ways postdates sovereign states. Emma Lazarus summarized it well in her inscription on the Statue of Liberty that welcomes "your tired, your poor, your huddled masses yearning to breathe free."

Another group we look down upon because they're different from us is *the disabled*. Jesus often sought out their company: the paralyzed, the blind, and the lame, all of whom had the gospel preached to them — no mean feat in those days. We have the duty to enable many to resurrect their disabled bodies into worthy vessels full of the loving decency of human life.

That we treat unfairly persons with disabilities is one of our society's sorrier sins. Deaf, blind, misshapen, or inflicted with other physical or mental impairment, they sometimes exist by the charity of the so-called "normal" community and are expected to wait submissively for equal treatment. Every individual deserves equal opportunity with everyone else to develop him- or herself to the fullest extent possible, regardless of how limited their natural capacities.

Perhaps one group of the disabled suffering more greatly than others today is those with *AIDS*. Some have contacted the disease because of a basic insecurity that resulted in their going from one partner to another to prove to themselves that they were lovable. Others, like nurses and physicians, have contacted it during an accident while serving people. Still others have innocently acquired it through birth, or injections, or guiltless contact.

In dealing with people with AIDS, what matters most is that they have the disease and that we deal with them with love. God calls us to love unconditionally. Love heals, and is never wasted. We were placed on earth not to force others to agree with us in exchange for our help, but to be an example of how life might be lived, actively, with love and compassion. Quite simply, we should treat them, as we should treat all persons, with respect and dignity because they're the image of God.

The challenge of having AIDS isn't dying of it, but living with it. Those with the disease are human; they want to be loved, and have a lot of love to give. No one wants to leave this earth alone; if during their trial someone would just hold them, at least they know they're loved and aren't alone. They, like everyone else, discover unconditional love not by hearing about it but by receiving it. In the final analysis, we rely on faith. We believe in the Father of mercies, who comforts us in *all* our afflictions (2 Cor 1:3f.).

Lastly, it seems a shame to remind believers in the gospel of love what a scandal it is to behave poorly to those who have other religious beliefs. Our Savior traveled outside Jewish territory, dealt amiably with such non-Jews as the Syro-Phoenician woman and the Roman centurion, and spoke kindly of all. Yet wars have raged in the name of religion, even though religion has in very few cases been the primary cause of the conflicts. But Thomas Jefferson knew from history and human nature how easy it is to arouse murderous passion when religious demagogues cry that God wills it; in 1786 he drafted the Statute of Virginia for Religious Freedom, which decreed that "no man shall be compelled to frequent or support any religious worship, place, or ministry whatsoever . . . nor shall otherwise suffer on account of his religious opinions or beliefs."

So entrenched is religious obstinacy that it took nine years for that statute to be enacted into law — Jefferson calling the effort his "severest contest." The idea was so important that among the three accomplishments that Jefferson wanted engraved on his tombstone, he gave handwritten instructions that this was to be one of them. (The other two were that he was the founder of the University of Virginia and author of the Declaration of Independence.) The concept came to be enshrined in the First Amendment of our Constitution, and is called our "First Freedom." We must come to appreciate it and practice it.

We conclude with the observation that in a world torn with bigotry and racial strife, isolation, mobility, and stress on family life, there's an intense need to belong, to be accepted, to be welcomed, to be treated with care and respect. We Catholics have two levels on which we can deal with that.

First, we can thank God for the continued existence of parish life: It's the one thing that can recover that sense of neighborliness, of community, of belonging, of care. As a parish we're called to welcome the stranger — those who look, act, and think in ways which are different from us. Believing that each person is made in the image of our Creator and gifted for the building of God's reign, we greet and welcome them, inviting them to belong to our community. Our motivation should be the realization that we're all part of God's family.

Secondly, as individuals we should expressly reject stereotypes, slurs, and jokes at the expense of those who are different. We should urge scrupulous attention at every level to ensure that minority representation and employment go beyond mere tokenism. We should make a personal commitment to join in efforts to bring about justice for those who are victims of deprivation. And all of us should pray for equal treatment for all.

ELECTION DAY

Is 6:11-3   Ep 4:11-16   Jn 15:9-17

It's always easy to give in to rationalization, especially one that says that "what little talent I have will never be missed." But just think for a moment. If each note of music were to say "one note doesn't make a symphony," there would be no symphony; if each word were to say, "one word doesn't make a book," there would be no book; if each brick were to say, "one brick doesn't make a wall," there would be no house; if each of us were to say, "one act of love can't help humankind," there would never be justice and peace on earth.

Our faith calls us to work for justice; to serve those in need; to pursue peace; and to defend the life, dignity, and rights of all people. This is the challenge of the prophets, the call of Jesus, and the living tradition of our Church.

Across this country and around the world, Christianity's social teachings constitute a story of remarkable compassion, courage, and creativity. Yet in United States elections, only a small percentage of people eligible to vote turn out — ironically, when people in other parts of the world are struggling to participate in public life. This alienation threatens to undermine the heart of our democratic traditions.

Lutheran Pastor Martin Niemoller wrote a valuable lesson about his experience with the Nazis: "In Germany they first came for the Communists, and I didn't speak up because I wasn't a Communist. Then they came for the Jews, and I didn't speak out because I wasn't a Jew. Then they came for the trade unionists, and I didn't speak out because I wasn't a trade unionist. Then they came for the Catholics, and I didn't speak out because I am a Protestant. And then they came for me — but by that time there was no one left to speak."

As campaigns focus more and more on symbols and soundbites, citizens seem to focus less and less on candidates and issues. The news media sometimes seem more interested in the *tactics* of campaigns than in issues and character. And citizens seem too often preoccupied by narrow self-interest, indifferent to public life or unconvinced that politics makes any difference. We give in to public cynicism which too often ridicules public officials in sometimes understandable but often misguided frustration with all politics.

Our society has many issues, challenges, and problems. Can our nation bring together the strength of a powerful market economy and the pervasiveness of poverty? How can our society best combat continuing prejudice and discrimination, and heal the open wounds of racism and sexism? How can our society support families in their irreplaceable moral role and social duties? How can our nation pursue the values of justice and peace in a world still too often marked by violent conflict and denial of human rights? How can we find fair ways to invest in our human needs, deal with our global responsibilities, and meet our fiscal and moral obligations to future generations without mortgaging our economic future?

In all of these problems, we have a religious call to civic responsibility. Every proposal, policy, and political platform should be measured by how it touches the human person: whether it enhances or diminishes human life, human dignity, and human rights; and how it advances the common good. While it is increasingly acknowledged that major public issues have clear moral dimensions and that religious values have significant public consequences, there is often confusion and controversy over religious motives in public life.

The Christian community is remarkably diverse, all across the political spectrum. But we're all called to a common commitment to ensure that political life serves the common good and the human person. Our call, neither partisan nor sectarian, is a call to reinvigorate the democratic process as a place for debate about what kind of society we want to have, about what values and priorities should guide our nation.

This kind of political responsibility doesn't involve religious leaders telling people how to vote or religious tests for candidates. But American Christians, as both believers *and* citizens, should use the opportunities of this democracy to help shape a society more respectful of the life, dignity, and rights of the human person, especially the poor and vulnerable. Jesus came to bring glad tidings to the poor, to proclaim liberty to captives, and to free the oppressed (Lk 4:18). He called us to feed the hungry, clothe the naked, care for the sick and afflicted, and comfort the victims of injustice (cf. Mt 25:35-41).

It's our role as members of a community of faith to call attention to the moral and religious dimension of secular issues, to keep alive the values of the Gospel as a norm for social and political life, and to point out the demands of the Christian faith for a just transformation of society.

Pope John Paul II wrote (*Centesimus Annus*): "The social message of the Gospel must not be considered a theory, but above all else a basis and motivation for action." We must speak out with courage, skill, and concern on the entire spectrum of public issues, a consistent ethic of life being the moral framework from which we address them.

Overriding this spectrum of issues are six basic principles. First is *the life and dignity of the human person*. In the Christian social vision, the human person is central, the clearest reflection of God among us. Second are *human rights and responsibilities*. Our dignity is protected when human rights are respected — the right to life and those things which make life truly human: religious liberty, decent work, housing, health care, education, raising and providing for a family with dignity.

Third is *the call to family and community*. The human person is not only sacred, but also social. No community is more central than the family, the basic unit of society. Fourth is *the dignity of work and the rights of workers*. Workers have basic rights — to decent employment, to just wages, and to form and join unions, among others. Fifth is *the preferential option for the poor*. The Scriptures tell us we will be judged by our response to the "least of these." Sixth and last is *solidarity*. We're one human family despite differences of nationality or race. Today, loving our neighbor has global dimensions.

There are some issues to be plumbed in looking at candidates for election which, despite some opinions to the contrary, are not confined to Christians. Among them is *abortion*. The right to life is the most basic human right, and it demands the protection of law. We support public funding policies that encourage childbirth over abortion, and we urge society to provide programs that assist pregnant women and children, especially those who are poor.

Another issue not confined to Christians is *arms control and disarmament*. We should look for opportunities to restrict the proliferation of arms, especially weapons of mass destruction; and to redirect resources from excessive military spending toward programs that meet the basic human needs of the poor at home and abroad.

Controversial throughout our society, in view of our commitment to the value and dignity of human life, is *capital punishment*. Return to the use of the death penalty seems to be leading to further erosion of respect for life in our society. There are better approaches to protecting our people from violent crimes which are more consistent with the Gospel vision of respect for life.

There are basic moral principles that should guide *economic life*. Among them is at least the principle that every economic decision should be judged in light of whether it protects or undermines the dignity of the human person. All people have a right to life, food, clothing, shelter, rest, medical care, and employment.

Education is an inalienable right. There should be sufficient funding for quality education; moral education integrated into the total curriculum; improving the opportunities available to the economically disadvantaged; equitable tax support for the education of pupils in government and non-government schools to implement the vital principle of parental freedom of choice in the education of their children; salaries and benefits of teachers and administrators that reflect justice; and the right of non-government school students and professional staff to equal participation in all government programs to improve education.

A growing problem is *euthanasia*, the killing of the elderly and those who are no longer useful. We must remember the dignity of those who are dying. We should provide legal safeguards against direct killing, and abolish suicide and assisted suicide. We must favor those who provide properly for *family life*, this being the most basic unit of social organization and essential in humanizing society.

Food, agriculture, and the environment are also basic issues upon which we decide our vote. Our agricultural policies should enable farmers to produce good quality food; increase the opportunities for the widespread distribution of farmland; renew a viable family farming system; ensure fair compensation; negotiate fair international trade practices; and establish food security. Our respect for the creation of our environment is a demonstration of our reverence for God and respect for life itself.

Health is another basic human right. Access to appropriate health care must be guaranteed for all. *Housing* is not a commodity, but another basic human right; shelters cannot substitute. On *immigration*, family unification must be maintained and fair treatment given to the emigrants of all nations. And voters should put themselves behind full rights for all *workers* to be permanently employed and not receive only temporary allocations.

Closely allied to that is the issue of *refugees*. The Catholic community operates the largest refugee resettlement system in the United States. We must offer resettlement to refugees out of genuine humanitarian concern. United States policy should make provisions for international refugee assistance at levels that ensure the dignity and human rights of all uprooted peoples. The world community needs to increase its protection of, and assistance to, the estimated 20 million persons internally displaced within their homelands because of civil strife, repression, or natural disasters.

There are many other issues which common sense tells us must be considered at least at election time. Among them are *welfare reform, the civil and political rights of the elderly and disabled, and reform of the criminal justice system.* At election time, we can help decide them.

As Winston Churchill said: "At the bottom of all the tributes paid to democracy is the little man walking into the little booth with a little pencil, making a little cross on a little bit of paper. No amount of rhetoric or voluminous discussion can possibly diminish the overwhelming importance of that point."

THANKSGIVING DAY

Dt 8:7-18   *Col 3:15-17*   *Lk 17:11-19*

There's an old European story about a traveler who came upon a barn where the devil had stored seeds which he planned to sow in the hearts of people. There were bags of seeds variously marked "Hatred," "Fear," "Doubt," "Despair," "Unforgiveness," "Pride," "Greed," and the like.

The devil appeared and struck up a conversation with the traveler. He gleefully told the traveler how easily the seeds he sowed sprouted in the hearts of men and women.

"Are there any hearts in which these seeds will not sprout?" the traveler asked.

A melancholy look appeared on the devil's face. "These seeds will not sprout in the heart of a thankful and joyful person," he confessed.

Thankful and joyful people go back to the very beginnings of our traditions. Moses reminded the children of Israel that they were nothing but what God had made them. Through no merit of theirs, God brought them out of slavery to freedom and gave them a land flowing with milk and honey. So they should never arrogantly think that their success was due to their own efforts. In response to the Lord's goodness to them, they must gratefully keep to His holy Law.

In the Gospels, there are many examples of gratitude and ingratitude. Jesus told the man who was cured to go home; contrary to this instruction, he began to broadcast his cure. The rich man built bigger barns instead of showing his gratitude by sharing with others. Nine of the ten cured lepers didn't come back to thank Jesus; the only one who did was a Samaritan.

A good case can be made for our nation's success on the basis of the accident of God making it replete with every kind of resource. If other nations had the same resources and circumstances as we, they would have been as great. Perhaps we should be reminded that we who have more wealth and resources than any other nation on earth are *tenth* down the list in per capita giving to charity and hunger relief for the nations of the world!

We're here today to encourage thanksgiving and joy on this beautiful day in our history. The history of Thanksgiving Day, as every school child learns, began with a feast in the autumn of 1621 at the settlement of Plymouth, Mass., a festivity that brought together Pilgrims and Massasoit Indians heralding a good harvest. Although today's custom dictates turkey for this day, there's no evidence that it was present on the first Thanksgiving.

Although never intended to be an annual holiday, Thanksgiving eventually became recognized as an annual celebration by the 1640s because of a scarcity of holidays. Strict Puritanism had banished Christmas, Easter, and All Saints' Day from the calendar as both too Roman Catholic and laden with pagan practices. Well into the 18th century, New England's only holiday excitement was Muster Day, Election Day, and the Harvard commencement.

Even the Puritans battled over Thanksgivings. In 1685, "extream sharp words" were spoken in Boston in the Massachusetts General Court when the legislative body could not agree what to give thanks for. On other occasions Puritans united in calling a special day for giving thanks, but could not agree whether to have a feast or a fast. Other Puritan controversies followed on whether Thanksgiving should be reserved for extraordinary occasions or should become a regular holiday. In 1697, Judge Samuel Sewall (later a judge in the Salem witchcraft trials) recommended Thursday, the regular day of religious lectures in Ipswich and Boston, as suitable for Thanksgiving Day.

Thursdays were fitting. Puritans observed the Sabbath as a biblical ordinance and refused to intrude on it with a holiday. Saturdays were for preparing for the Sabbath. (Boston is "Bean Town" because the Puritans weren't allowed to cook on the Sabbath; so they cooked beans on Saturday, ate them on Sunday.) Mondays were apparently for recuperating. Fridays were overruled because they were the fasting days of the Roman Catholics and automatically carried unacceptable papal overtones. Thursdays were the favorite days for fasts and weekday religious meetings.

From the Christian point of view, it was providential that our national Thanksgiving was placed on a Thursday, for it was on a Thursday that the Lord himself gave us the real Thanksgiving — the Eucharist. *Eucharist* means "thanksgiving," and the Eucharist is our thanksgiving to God.

But which Thursday? By 1708, Massachusetts and New Hampshire had come to favor the third or fourth Thursday in November, but individual towns stubbornly kept their own other customs. The Puritan hamlet of Easthampton on Long Island observed Thanksgiving on the first Thursday after the cows came home from Montauk Point.

Shortly after his inauguration, at the request of the first Congress, George Washington proclaimed an annual national Thanksgiving Day to render thanks to Almighty God. It was the first Thanksgiving proclamation by a president of the United States.

More than any other individual, a New Hampshire widow named Sarah Josepha Hale is credited with making Thanksgiving truly a national holiday as a family festival. As editor of *The Lady's Book*, a predecessor of such magazines as *Redbook* and *Good Housekeeping*, she started her state-by-state campaign in 1846. She wrote the governors of all 32 states, asking that the last Thursday in November be proclaimed a day of Thanksgiving throughout the nation. By 1858, largely due to her efforts, every northern state had adopted the custom.

Mrs. Hale had less success in the South. Virginia's Governor, Henry Wise, wanted no part of a Yankee day. But Southern ladies, too, read *The Lady's Book*, and by 1860 an annual Thanksgiving was observed in many households throughout the South. Early in the Civil War, Union regiments observed Thanksgiving in the field. So did some Confederate soldiers, but on different days.

In 1863, after the Union victories at Vicksburg and Gettysburg,

Mrs. Hale wrote Abraham Lincoln in her official capacity as "editress of *The Lady's Book*," urging the President to "have the day of our annual Thanksgiving made a National and fixed *Union* Festival."

Lincoln agreed. On Oct. 3, 1863, after a season of Union victories, he proclaimed the last Thursday of November to be a day of "Thanksgiving and Praise to our beneficent father who dwelleth in the Heavens." This was controversial because until then individual states saw the setting of holidays as a *local* prerogative. During Reconstruction, the Yankee Thanksgiving spread throughout the South.

In the mid-1880s, Thanksgiving became the day of the greatest gridiron contests, notably the Yale-Harvard game at the Polo Grounds in New York City. By the late 1800s Thanksgiving Day had become a day of parades, rising commercialism, and general debauchery. Expressing a desire to instill immigrants with the values of our forefathers, the Daughters of the American Revolution rediscovered the Pilgrims.

In Eastern cities, the new immigration of the late 19th century ignited another round of Thanksgiving controversy. Some Roman Catholic priests forbade their parishioners to celebrate what seemed to them a Protestant festival; they were overruled by James Cardinal Gibbons of Baltimore. By 1909, Catholic priests were celebrating a Thanksgiving Mass in Washington. The ceremony was attended by Woodrow Wilson in 1913, igniting such a storm of protest by Protestants that the President stayed home the next year.

By the 20th century Thanksgiving was so popular that Florida and Virginia claimed to have invented it. Texans, not to be outdone, erected a defiant highway marker declaring that the first Thanksgiving was held by Conquistadors in the panhandle.

When President Franklin Delano Roosevelt bent to pressures from national retailers in the Depression year of 1939 to move up the date of Thanksgiving from the last Thursday in November to the third Thursday to create an extra week of Christmas shopping, it threw the holiday into chaos. Businessmen were delighted, for once, with a New Deal reform, but moralists and sports fans were outraged. In 1941, Congress restored the holiday to the fourth Thursday in November.

As often in our history, Thanksgiving is again a time of controversy. Multiculturalists and secularists have demanded that Pilgrim pageants be banished from elementary schools. Even while Americans unite in varying degrees of recollection, thanks, and prayer, they do it in remarkably many ways. For Christians, Washington's "beneficent Author" is God the Father, Son, and Spirit; for Jews, the Holy One who led Israel from bondage; for Muslims, Allah, the all-gracious, the all-merciful; for Hindus, the ultimate reality of Brahman or the deities Vishnu, Siva, and others; and for agnostics, plain good fortune.

In the face of all the controversies, we give thanks for laughing children wherever the sound rings out; for free elections, during which those who exercise their rights can either vote the rascals out, or back in, as they wish; for trees; for a free press, even if it means we sometimes have to read headlines we don't like; for public libraries with good books; for the teachers who taught us how to read; for the land that's still rich in natural resources and opportunity; for computers that correct our spelling, balance our checkbooks, and help the kids with their homework.

Thanks for everyone with a sense of humor to help us laugh our way over the rough spots; for volunteers, who help the helpless; for the energy of the younger generation and the wisdom of the older generation — and the chance to tap the best of both when we need to; for love, at any age.

Thanks for every day that something happens to make us more tolerant of one another; for the wonders of Niagara Falls, the Grand Canyon, the snowcapped Rockies, the rolling Mississippi, and all the other scenic delights this country has to offer.

Thanks for people who care about other people; for warm kitchens on chilly mornings; for weekends with nothing to do and somebody special to do it with; and for working men and women, who carry their briefcases or lunch pails to office and factory day in and day out, and make the country hum.

An old clichè says that thanksgiving should be thanks-living.

The meaning is that we show our gratitude by how we act daily more than by what we sing or say on this day. Gratitude means that we recognize the giver, that we express our appreciation, and that we have a desire somehow to pay back for the gift, even though it's a gift.

To give thanks to God is to restore order to a disordered world, for it restores humility where pride reigned. Let's use this Thanksgiving day to renew our spirit of humility and our generosity each day in spreading the good things of heaven and earth.

MISSION SUNDAY — A

Jon 3:10-4:11   Ps 117:1f.   Rm 10:9-18   Mt 28:16-20

In Your Place

Religion deals with all the basic aspects of life that give meaning — God, the nature of persons, life, death, nature, self. Are there any such things as good and bad religions? True and false religions? Worthy and unworthy religions? To answer, one would have to look at the religion in question. If, for example, a religion's god is a perversion, as with satanic cults or voodoo, the religion is bad. As for a religion's worthiness, if a religion elevates people it's worthy, and if it denigrates them it's unworthy.

Another way to categorize religions is by the degree to which they engage in efforts to gain new members. In Japan, because you can legitimately practice many religions simultaneously, that doesn't make much difference. Jews don't proselytize much, because of the possibility of engendering anti-Semitism. Muslims definitely do, and other religions working in Muslim countries find it difficult to maintain themselves.

Despite the United States tradition that religion is a purely private matter, Christians also proselytize. Why can't they leave other people alone? Why missions, anyway? Is mission work among non-Christians still relevant? Hasn't missionary work been replaced by interreligious dialogue? Doesn't respect for conscience and for freedom exclude all efforts at conversion? Isn't it possible to achieve salvation in any religion?

The Christian religion puts many examples before us of sacrificing for the faith. Tradition has it that right from the beginning, in New Testament times, all of the Apostles but John were martyred for their faith. About twelve years after Jesus' death James, the first of the Apostles to suffer martyrdom, was beheaded at Jerusalem. Andrew was tied to a cross, where he preached to his persecutors until he died. Bartholomew was skinned alive. Peter was crucified at Rome with his head downward. James son of Alphaeus ("James the Less") was thrown from a high pinnacle of the temple, and then beaten to death with a club. Thomas was run through with a lance. Matthias was stoned and then beheaded. Jude Thaddeus was shot to death with arrows. Philip was hanged at Heiropolis in Phrygia. Barnabas was stoned to death by the Jews at Salonica.

Although John the Evangelist was the only Apostle to die a natural death, he was put into a cauldron of boiling oil but miraculously escaped, was scourged, and afterwards exiled to Patmos. The other three evangelists suffered martyrdom: Matthew was run through with a sword at a distant city of Ethiopia, Mark was cruelly dragged through the streets of Alexandria, and Luke was hanged on an olive tree in the classic land of Greece.

St. Paul, after various tortures and persecutions, was at length beheaded at Rome by the Emperor Nero. St. Ignatius of Antioch, on his way to martyrdom in 107 A.D., wrote: "Let me be food for the wild beasts, for they are my way to God. I am God's wheat and shall be ground by their teeth so that I may become Christ's pure bread. . . . The time for my birth [to real life] is near at hand." For most of the early Christians, sacrifices for their faith were a way of life. In social gatherings, they were shunned. When they sought work, they were excluded. Today that condition still exists in some parts of the world.

But the prime reason for mission is our belief about Jesus: he is the way, the truth, and the life for *all* people. Jesus Christ is God's *definitive revelation*. As St. Peter said in one of his discourses after Pentecost: "There is no salvation through anyone else, nor is there any other name under heaven given to the human race by which we are to be saved" (Ac 4:12). There's nothing, absolutely nothing, more central for the Christian than the person of Jesus Christ. This is clear from the New Testament, from our oldest creeds, from our liturgical tradition, and from nearly 2,000 years of Church history. The Church and every aspect of her life are based on the person and life of Jesus Christ. As Lord of all, Jesus is absolutely unique. He's the one person sent by God as his Son to be the Savior of the whole human race.

Jesus isn't merely one savior and mediator among others — although there are other mediators. We may consider the outstanding figures in the world's great religions as mediators, but their mediation is derived from the unique mediation of Jesus Christ. So mission isn't only a matter of salvation for others, but also the criterion for our own salvation. Mission is an issue of faith, an accurate indicator of our faith in Christ.

To further the work of mission, Jesus founded his Church as the universal sacrament of salvation. Her mission flows from Christ's work as Redeemer or Savior. So the Church's missionary mandate has permanent validity. Missionary activity renews the Church, revitalizes faith and Christian identity, and offers fresh enthusiasm and new incentive. Faith is strengthened when it's given to others! Missionary drive has always been a sign of vitality, just as its lessening is a sign of a crisis of faith.

And common sense tells us the truth of the ancient philosophical axiom that the good is diffusive of itself (*bonum est diffusivum sui*). On the level of daily living, if we've experienced something good — a brilliant book, a new friend, a delightful film — we find extra joy in sharing it. If we truly value our faith, we take great pleasure in sharing it with others.

Our country has sent not only priests and religious, but lay nurses, physicians, social workers, and others who have generously contributed their lives to Jesus' cause. And now many mission countries, like Nigeria and India, appreciating the generosity of those through whom they've received the faith, have begun contributing their share to other places in need of ministers of the faith.

Often Catholics see missionaries as almost an addendum to our Church. The truth is that all Christians share responsibility for missionary activity. This responsibility comes from baptism, through which sacrament we're consecrated and "sent." Everyone, in accord with Jesus' command to go forth and teach all nations, has an obligation to do *something*.

Sometimes, like the rich young aristocrat in the gospels, we try to excuse ourselves. The young man must have made quite an impression on the apostolic band: His story occurs in all three synoptic gospels (Mt 19:16-30; Mk 10:17-31; Lk 18:18-30). His eagerness is shown by his running to kneel at the feet of Jesus. The conversation showed that the young man had interpreted Jesus' words as a command to be *respectable* — one thing he had been for his entire life. He was satisfied with the commandments' negatives — avoiding evil — but he hadn't gotten very far with the positive: *doing good* for people. But for the follower of Christ respectability isn't enough: One must *do* things for others. This young man didn't understand that.

It was touching that "Jesus, looking at him, loved him" (Mk 10:21). It was a look that was sad that this loved one might refuse to be all that he could be. There must have been many things in Jesus' look. It was an appeal, essentially, with no anger, and here it included a challenge to the rich young man to get out of his comfortable and respectable life.

Did the young man make the right choice? Heartbreakingly, no: Impetuosity isn't always equaled by strength of character. His face fell, and "he went away sad, for he had many possessions" (Mk 10:22). This young man was the only person recorded in the entire New Testament to have left the presence of Jesus "sad"! Challenged to return love for love, he couldn't, because he couldn't remove the obstacle of his wealth. Wealth can be a prize to share with others or a prison, and for him it was a prison.

The missions ask you for a contribution. Best of all to

contribute, of course, is yourself. The patron of the missions is, understandably, St. Francis Xavier, most of whose adult life was spent on missions in the Orient. To go personally to the missions means not only leaving all the familiar behind, but also trying to find new ways to convey Jesus' message to new cultures.

But not all can go on missions personally. So most of us fulfill our duty of mission by witnessing in our homes, neighborhoods, and places of business, and have others go to far-away places in our stead. For them, we contribute our prayers and whatever money we can afford.

Surprisingly, perhaps, the patroness of the missions is St. Thérèse of Lisieux, the "Little Flower," who never left her convent. She contributed mightily to the missions what she could: her prayers, her sacrifice, and her witness.

You're asked to contribute whatever you can: your self and your money to the extent possible, and your prayers and witness always.

MISSION SUNDAY — B

Zc 8:20-23   *Ps 19:2f.,4f.*   *Ac 13:46-49*   *Jn 11:45-52*

God's Kingdom Come!

As early as the year 50 A.D., the Church in the Apostolic Council of Jerusalem, confronted with problems stirred up by overzealous Judaizers, officially proclaimed the supra-national character of Christianity (Ac 15:10-30). From that day to this, many Church usages, such as incense, candles, priestly vestments, certain liturgical symbols, holy water, some aspects of art and music, processions, holydays, and liturgical seasons have been contributed to the Church mostly by the give-and-take of missions in lands other than our own.

As the Church brings her missionary activity to the nations of the world, she meets different cultures and embarks on the long process of inserting herself in those cultures. The process is called inculturation. It requires the transformation of authentic cultural values through their integration in Christianity and the insertion of Christianity in the various cultures. While doing this, Christianity has to avoid compromising the distinctiveness of the faith.

This has always been, both for the missioner and the missions, a difficult process. That's why in 1659 the Congregation for the Propagation of the Faith in Rome wrote: "Can anyone think of anything more absurd than to transport France, Italy or Spain or some other European country to China? Bring them your faith, not your country." On the mission side, in northern Tanzania, when a missioner had explained that Jesus is the savior of all humankind, an elder stood up and said, in terms of his own culture, "I want to know more about this Jesus. Did he ever kill a lion? How many cows did he have? How many wives did he have?"

In our times the Church has laid great stress upon missionary adaptation. Recent popes leave no doubt about the supranational character of the Church and of the role indigenous people play in making Christianity truly "at home" wherever it may be. And one of the basic goals of Vatican Council II, continuing today, is "unity in diversity." The door must be kept as wide open as possible to the emerging exigencies of accommodation.

Papal decisions have indicated that the older churches must have a spirit of sacrifice and generosity, as well as a sympathetic understanding of new ways of life. Inter-religious dialogue is not in opposition to our mission to the peoples of the world, but one of its expressions. Dialogue should be conducted and implemented with the conviction that the Church is the ordinary means of salvation.

But for the missioner there are many practical difficulties: the loneliness, the strange food, the harsh living conditions, the new language, the alien customs. Especially difficult are countries, like India, which by law allow missioners only to contribute their services, without notice of any denominational attachment. There, missioners can teach in schools all their lives long without their students ever having any real idea of what they stand for. Also difficult are those countries, like Thailand, where the climate and other factors result in happy-go-lucky dispositions of people who feel no need for what the Christian missioner stands for.

For the missioners, it's truly a labor of love: a lifetime of constant selfless giving. They continuously remind themselves that religion affects the whole of life, and our religion has much to offer. They meditate on the fact that the purpose of Jesus' whole life and teaching was to announce the Kingdom of God and bring it about. Their mission is along the lines of the summary in St. Mark's Gospel of Jesus' proclamation of the gospel of God: "This is the time of fulfillment. The kingdom of God is at hand. Repent, and believe in the gospel" (Mk 1:14f.).

The Kingdom of which we read in the Gospels is the Kingdom of God, not a purely human kingdom. It can't be reduced to one more version of a purely earthly plan for progress. The Kingdom is before all else a person with the face and name of Jesus of Nazareth, the image of the invisible God.

The Kingdom of God is the fulfillment of the commandment of love. It consists in communion among all human beings — with one another and with God. That Kingdom makes demands on all of us. From beginning to end, the Gospels and the entire New Testament show us what the Kingdom of God is. We see that it calls for a commitment to liberation and salvation, and addresses human beings in their spiritual as well as their physical dimensions.

Although the Kingdom has something to do with the Church, they're not identical. The Church is surely at the service of the Kingdom, first of all by preaching and then by establishing communities and particular churches and guiding them to mature faith and charity. Although the Church is at the service of the Kingdom, the Church isn't a body independent of it. The Church is distinct from Christ and the Kingdom, but at the same time she is indissolubly united to both.

Christ endowed the Church, his Body, with the fullness of the benefits and means of salvation. The Church is the sacrament of salvation for all human beings, and her activity isn't limited only to those who accept her message. The kingdom is the wider community of salvation, to which belong all people of good will. The mission of the Church is to help build the kingdom. Missionary evangelization is the primary service which the Church can render to every individual and to all humanity in the modern world.

The missionary mandate given the Apostles after meeting the Risen Christ is extremely important. This mandate, which appears in every Gospel (Mt 28:18-20; Mk 16:15-18; Lk 24:46-49; Jn 20:21-23), is a sending forth in the Spirit, as we see most especially in John's Gospel. The Gospels complement one another in their presentation of the mandate. Each one is different, but at the same time all have two elements in common: the universal dimension of the mission given, and the assurance that the Apostles will receive the strength and the means to carry it out.

The whole Church is missionary because of the work of the Holy Spirit, its principal agent. From the New Testament, and especially from the Acts of the Apostles, we see how the Holy Spirit was active in the Apostles, in the whole apostolic community, and in those who heard their proclamation of the Kingdom and benefited from their ministry. Without the Holy Spirit, the proclamation of the Church would be but a human word and her efforts in behalf of the kingdom fruitless.

In gratitude to God for the gift of faith, let's contribute our part to our treasured religion by contributing to our missions our prayers, our services, and our finances. Please consider a sacrifice equal to the cost of some other legitimate expense in your life: a family outing, the purchase of a home, a gift for a friend, a day's wage. The cost of a medium-priced television set represents one year's educational support for a religious sister or brother in the missions. A moderately-priced pair of shoes can support two catechists in the Missions, each for one month. The cost of a modestly-priced car can build several chapels. The expenditure for a family of four to enjoy a day at the ballpark translates into one month's help for a mission seminarian.

No matter what financial contribution you may be able to make, the missions ask in addition for your participation in their work to the degree possible. Perhaps you may even find it possible to visit a mission on a vacation or at another time. After all, in the dwindling numbers of clergy, lay missioners have grown in numbers. Their journey's strong sense of direction is to go wherever the poor are going. And the missions ask for your prayers always.

MISSION SUNDAY — C

Is 2:1-5   Ps 98:1, 2f., 3f., 5f.   1 Tm 2:1-8   Jn 17:11, 17-23

Contributions from the Missions to the World

Mark Twain once attended a church service where a missionary appealed for funds to evangelize the heathen in a foreign land. "After 10 minutes of a description about their unhappy plight, I wanted to give $50," Twain wrote. "The preacher kept on another 15 minutes and that gave me time to realize that $50 was an extravagance, so I cut it in half. At the end of another 10 minutes, I had reduced it to $5. When at the end of an hour of speaking the plates were finally passed, I was so annoyed that I reached in and helped myself to a quarter."

Inasmuch as I want you to give the missions your self — your prayers, your participation, and your money — I shall be brief. People need religion for the best in their personal development, and the contributions of Christianity to that end have always been vital. Many people throughout the world have been waiting for almost 2,000 years for the message of Christ. And missionaries go out with but one purpose: to serve people by revealing to them the love of God made manifest in Jesus Christ, and all the consequences of that.

Consider some of Christianity's worldwide contributions to the betterment of humankind. Those contributions began with Jesus himself, who taught us a different God from all others, a God completely new. We're lucky to have had Jesus teach us about the true God as a loving Father. Our God has chosen to rule the world only with the cooperation of us human beings.

In Jesus' name, Filipinos have confronted and toppled an oppressive dictator. By living Christ's principles, an Albanian nun received the Nobel Peace Prize for ministering to the poor, diseased, and dying people of Calcutta. Under Jesus' teachings, workers in Poland overcame a Communist government. With Jesus' joy, Latins celebrate his feasts. In many parts of the world, his churches provide sanctuary to immigrants, and dedicated Christian laity and religious help the poor to escape barbaric living conditions. In Egypt, some of his followers stay with the people on the outskirts of Cairo who try to eke out a living from the garbage dumps. In many countries of the world, such as Ethiopia and Haiti, Christians contribute money and labor to keep starving people alive. In India, missioners serve the poorest of the tribal peoples.

Lowly people in Pakistan weren't for most of their history allowed to settle down near those of so-called "noble" origin. There was no place in their system for the poor and lowly, no room in their schools or workshops. From generation to generation, these people had to work like slaves from birth to death: not allowed to draw water from the village well, not able to touch the food of others.

The real good news that these people who for ages hadn't even been considered human beings were wanting to hear was that all men and women are sons and daughters of the same Father and brothers and sisters in Christ. They began to experience this newness of life in Christ about 100 years ago when Christian missionaries came. These missionaries strongly believed that to live in fraternal communion means "to be of one heart and one soul" (Ac 4:32), establishing fellowship from every point of view: human, spiritual, and material. Indeed, a true Christian community is also committed to distributing earthly goods, so no one is in want and all can receive such goods as they need (Ac 2:45).

The basic and decisive step toward this liberation was taken when the people began to receive religious and academic education. The early missionaries went from door to door to collect children and bring them to school. They went into fields and forests to gather people together. Slowly the children came to elementary schools; people learned technical skills. Within years, small communities were formed where people could live with dignity and could work for the well-being of their families. The transformation was slow but steady.

But the work is long, arduous, and difficult. Among the poor people in Pakistan and elsewhere even today there are those who are extremely marginalized, who are born, live, and die in sub-human conditions. They have no possibility of receiving education or health care, of having a decent job or house. They and their children have no hope, at all, of getting out of this deep pit of helplessness. They are like Lazarus in the grave. They await the messengers of Christ who will go to them and will call out: "In the name of Jesus, the Redeemer, come out of the grave of your misery. Jesus gives new life, come and share it, because you too are human beings and children of one heavenly Father."

Their liberation can come only through Jesus Christ. Hence, the priests, catechists, sisters, and lay workers are trying their best to continue to reach these people, to be with them, to start small schools in their communities, to help them morally, legally, and even financially. Christian mobile health teams go and reach out to these people in their mud huts, wherever they are. The Church is starting small workshops where people have had no opportunities to learn trades and skills.

In Bolivia, the Sisters of Charity give themselves to people with leprosy, tuberculosis, and other illnesses. In Korea, the Good Shepherd Sisters take care of hundreds of unwed mothers and their babies; their witness of true Christian love brings many to the faith. The Brothers of St. John of God care for 100 mentally retarded patients and about 20 persons with tuberculosis. The Columban Sisters continue their efforts for the sick poor in three clinics.

In South America and other lands with contrasting enormous wealth and widespread poverty, the Christian Church reaches out to work with the poor in the base church communities they have established in the *favellas* (slums), encourage the poor to help in a *mutirao* (a community project in which members contribute whatever they can in whatever way they can), and represent the poor in thousands of land conflicts brought about by drought-ridden farmers and landless peasants. In Caracas, Venezuela, lay missioners go to mountainside barrios on slum terraces gradually being eroded by torrential rains.

In Mabiri, Bouganville, the Kristen Famas Asosiesen tries to give the young a useful trade to keep them busy, safe, and happy, a means of stopping the exodus to town and a reprobate's life. In the slums of an ever-expanding section of Mexico City, prayer groups, courses to fathers of families, pre-marriage courses, and instructions to community workers develop a caring community spirit. In the poorest sections of the slums of Dakar, Senegal, missioners distribute clothing, provide food, and repair the shacks of the elderly.

Jesus' caring people sacrifice to feed the hungry of the world, clothe the earth's poor, raise the condition of women through Mary the paradigm, and bring medicines to the sick — even in remote snake-infested islands. In totalitarian countries, Jesus' followers defy imprisonment and death to preach human rights. In refugee camps all over the globe, his ministers share the pain of separated families. In the planet's dark corners, Jesus' ministers bring meaning to life, guidance to the perplexed, and solace to the disheartened.

We in the United States can be grateful for the Christian missionaries who first came to these shores. As we've passed the 500-year mark of the coming of the Gospel to the Americas, we reach across the earth to share our good fortune. Despite some current criticisms that the "discovery" of America by Christopher Columbus and his fellow voyagers was the *invasion* and *conquest* of America, we're grateful for its *evangelization*. The Christian religion even in Columbus's day fiercely denounced the military atrocities and mitigated them. Bartolomé de las Casas, a Dominican friar who accompanied the adventurers and whose account is the prime source of the richest historical materials about the subject, included forthright denunciations of the brutalities inflicted upon the Indians. No other imperial system, anywhere or at any time, ever tolerated such open and conscientious debate over the moral consequences of its expansion.

There are many so-called "scholarly" myths about some of the American natives who were overcome by the colonizers. Many of these myths pertain to the Maya, a highly-developed Indian tribe who built massive pyramids all over Central America. Among the myths that scholars formerly taught about this population is that they were a peaceful race, living in a kind of new Garden of Eden.

Experts now generally agree that warfare played a key role in Maya civilization. The Maya used torture and human sacrifice throughout their culture. The gruesome ritual of bloodletting accompanied every major political and religious event in ancient Maya society. In their ball games, for example, which were both ritual and recreation, human sacrifice frequently provided the grisly finale: Either the defeated players were decapitated and their heads used as balls, or the winners trussed up their bodies into human spheres and bounced them to their death down high pyramid steps.

So whereas we celebrate all spreading of the Gospel, we celebrate in particular the evangelization of the Americas. That was one of the great events in history.

Despite the contributions to world civilization of our Christian religion, though, we've not done our jobs sufficiently. "God is love," the Apostle John tells us (1 Jn 4:8): love that calls and love that sends. The mission of evangelizing God's love for human beings — for *each* individual person — is still so far from being completed that it can be considered as only just begun.

Of the world's roughly six billion people, only about two billion are Christian, only about half of that number Catholic. Current demographics indicate that the percentage of Christians relative to the world population is decreasing. And a scholar a short time ago put Jesus as only third in a list of the most influential people in history, the first being Mohammed and the second Isaac Newton (Michael Hart, *The One Hundred: A Ranking of History's Most Influential Persons* [New York: Citadel Press, 1978; paper, Coral Publishing, 1987]). He did this regretfully, saying that if Jesus' flock were truly following his precepts, Jesus would be first. We who have received are challenged to give, to share our gift of faith. No Christian community is faithful to its duty unless it's missionary: either it's a missionary community or it's not even a Christian community.

Please don't imitate Mark Twain in taking any quarters out of the collection basket! And please go further in giving the missions your resources and your service where possible, and your prayers always. Thank you!

MASS FOR THE ANOINTING OF THE SICK

Jm 5:13-16   *2 Cor 4:13-5:1*   *Mk 2:1-12*

Many of us enjoy good health and accept it as a matter of course. In times of sickness we discover that health is a great gift. God allows us to experience sickness in order to test our strength and our faith. If, further, we see our suffering as a share in Christ's suffering, it can be of even greater value: Our sickness is a time of grace. Today's celebration is meant to help us in that direction.

When you ask sick people if they would like to have a priest come to anoint them, they often say something like, "Am I really that sick?" or "Am I dying?"

That dismay is understandable, considering the fact that not long ago anointing of the sick was performed only for those close to death. Calling for a priest to administer "last rites" or "extreme unction," ("last anointing") as it was called then, indicated that the physician did not give the patient long to live. How did a sacrament originally intended for healing come to be performed only for those who were dying?

In ancient times, there was no sharp distinction drawn between one's physical well-being and spiritual well-being. Those suffering a physical ailment suffered mentally and emotionally as well; those depressed or guilt-ridden often showed physical symptoms of their spiritual ailment. This reflects the wholistic attitude people had regarding the relationship between soul and body.

Because Jesus had a wholistic attitude toward life, he was concerned about people's physical as well as their spiritual health. In fact, the word *salvation* is from the Latin *salus*, which means "health." In announcing the Good News of salvation, Jesus was declaring that God cares for not only our soul but for our entire being as persons.

In a few places, Jesus shows that the two dimensions of human life — the physical and the spiritual — are connected, and that God has the power to heal both. When, for example, a paralyzed man on a mat was brought to Jesus, Jesus, with calm reassurance, told the man to have courage, because his sins were forgiven (Mk 2:1-12; Mt 9:1-8). Everybody understood what Jesus was saying, including the scribes, who said that Jesus was blaspheming, because only God can forgive sins. Jesus, aware of what was going on, told the paralyzed man to roll up his mat and go home. A feeling of awe came over the crowd present, and they understood that God's concern for people extends to us as whole persons.

At another time, some disciples of John the Baptist came to ask Jesus whether he was the Messiah. Jesus answered that they were to report to John what they had seen and heard: that the blind were recovering their sight, cripples walking, lepers being cured, and the poor having the Good News preached to them (Lk 7:22). Again salvation entailed the well-being of the whole person. Jesus' ministry to people was, then, a healing ministry to people's spiritual lives as well as to physical ailments.

Jesus' followers continued his wholistic ministry. They preached the Good News of God's forgiveness of sin, and they demonstrated that God's power was real by curing people in Jesus' name. The Apostles often performed the same kinds of miracles that Jesus had performed. One time, when a crippled beggar asked St. Peter for some money, Peter answered that he had neither silver nor gold, but what he had he would give. Then he dramatically said: "In the name of Jesus Christ the Nazorean, walk!" (Ac 3:6).

There is evidence in the New Testament that in some communities there was even an organized ministry of healing. James wrote to the Christians in Jerusalem, to ask if anyone among them was sick. Those whose answer was positive he advised to ask the priests to pray over them, anointing them with oil (Jm 5:14f.). Because olive oil (like salve or ointment today) was one of the few medicines in ancient times, this anointing action combined the healing power of nature with the healing power of prayer.

Thus, for a number of centuries, anointing of the sick was an informal sacramental practice performed by Christians for members of their family, neighbors, and themselves. Some bishops blessed oil specifically intended for this purpose. It was not until the ninth century that some reform-minded bishops in France composed a ritual similar to one already being used by monks in monasteries. Later, this French sacramentary was carried back to Rome.

As it happened, the rite for anointing the sick was in the same section of the book as the rites for the dying — making one's last confession and receiving one's last Communion. This, combined with the fact that without modern medical care people often died after they were anointed, caused the prayers in the rite to be changed from asking for physical healing to asking for spiritual well-being. It seemed that the purpose of this anointing was not recovery in this life but preparation for entry into the afterlife.

If people who were dying confessed their sins and received absolution before being anointed, one might ask what additional benefit could be derived from this sacrament. Various theories were proposed. One said that this healing rite forgives people their unconfessed venial sins, another that it shortened people's time in purgatory, still another that it prepared souls for judgment. The Church also agreed that in addition to the forgiving of sins the sacrament might even bring physical recovery in some cases.

At that time, leaders were unaware of the early history of the sacrament, which showed that anointing had originally been more for the sick than for the dying, and that its purpose had been for physical as well as spiritual well-being. When they made the discovery, they felt that something should be done about it. Accordingly, Vatican Council II declared that this sacrament isn't only for those who are at the point of death, and that a better name for this sacrament than "extreme unction" would be "anointing of the sick."

Catholics can be anointed as soon as they learn they have any illness that might lead to death. We can even request the sacrament if we're going to undergo an operation, because sometimes even simple operations lead to complications. The Church also recognizes that those advanced in years have a right to be anointed, because older people are susceptible to more illnesses than the young.

In all cases, of course, a patient can't begin to come to terms with the spiritual aspect of dying until physical pain is dealt with. The control of pain can help people to deal with whatever "unfinished business" faces them at a time of illness, especially serious illness, and most especially if the illness is terminal.

So the revised rite of this sacrament is flexible. It can be performed for an individual, a group, or at a special Mass of anointing in a parish, hospital, or home for the aged. Besides being flexible, the new rite is also communal as well as individual. That means the sacrament is supposed to be performed in the presence of people who know and care about the sick person. The Church has come to recognize the importance of family, friends, and healthcare professionals for the well-being of people who are ill.

The essence of this sacrament takes place when the priest takes the oil and anoints the patient on the forehead and hands, saying while doing so, "Through this holy anointing may the Lord in his love and mercy help you with the grace of the Holy Spirit. May the Lord who frees you from sin save you and raise you up." Remembering our wholistic composition of body and soul, the priest concludes with the prayer, "Lord Jesus Christ, our Redeemer, by the power of the Holy Spirit, ease the sufferings of our sick brother/sister and make him/her well again in mind and body. In your living kindness forgive his/her sins and grant him/her full health so that he/she may be restored to your service. You are Lord forever and ever. Amen."

There is, of course, a sense in which the term "last rites" is proper. People may be anointed in conjunction with a person's last confession and last Communion. These three sacraments (reconciliation, anointing of the sick, and the Eucharist), administered together for a dying person, are properly called the last rites of the Church.

The sacrament of the anointing of the sick takes care of many spiritual needs. Primary, of course, is the forgiveness of sins. There is also the care of all the emotional and psychological needs that must be met for people to feel good about themselves: the need to know that they're cared for, that they're loved despite any handicaps or deformities, that they will be materially supported, and that they won't be abandoned in their final hours. Other spiritual needs include the need to come to terms with debilitating physical conditions, to forgive oneself and others for any carelessness or malice, to reestablish communication with estranged loved ones, and to be reconciled with God before death.

Because we — all Christians — are expected to live the spiritual and corporal works of mercy, we must all, not just healthcare professionals and clergy, do everything we can to reach out to those who are eligible for the anointing of the sick. This is a sacrament of *faith*, because it reminds us to trust in God no matter what happens to us. It is a sacrament of *hope*, because it enables us to believe that, with God's help, healing is possible. And it is a sacrament of *love*, because through it God's love touches us in a special way.

FUNERAL:
WITNESS TO THE RESURRECTION — A

Ws 3:1-9   1 Jn 3:1-2   Ps 27 Jn 6:37-40

Liturgical documents mandate a homily on this occasion. A homily is, of course, a message usually based on the scriptural readings. On today's occasion, this means it should concentrate on the Christian mystery of the death and resurrection of

Jesus, from which we all seek purpose and find hope. The
current ritual provides for the possibility of a more personal
eulogy on the life of the deceased by a friend or family member
at the end of the Eucharist, before the final blessing. Is the
celebrant's talk to be a homily or a eulogy? This presents a
dilemma, but surely coldly impersonal reflections, sometimes
simply used from "homily services," are insufficient at this
sensitive moment.

Death in the Judeo-Christian Tradition

Some say that the Neanderthals were the first human species to
entomb their dead. Their skeletons have been found arranged into
death-postures; pollen analysis has shown that they were strewn
with flowers. If that's all true, the Neanderthals made a discovery
more momentous than the discovery of the hand ax, the wheel, or
fire — for they pondered an ultimate meaning of death. They came
to think of things more profound than the mere succession of life's
daily events. Thereby, in some likelihood, they also discovered
religion, which deals with all ultimates.

Like the human race, we, too, discover death little by little:
Life is full of its little deaths. Every time we say "good-bye," every
time we have to stop doing something we like, and every time we
pass from one phase of life to another, we die a little. These little
deaths, and of course our final death, are usually unpleasant — so
much so that many say that, if they were God, they would extinguish
all death. Cooler heads ask if that would be wise. What would we
do on this planet with all the people who were ever born, if they were
still living?

Of equal importance, how would we unite together around our
friends, relatives, and loved ones, in times of real need? What
opportunities could we substitute for this invitation to exercise such
wonderful virtues as unity, fellowship, compassion, love, mercy,
kindness, and sympathy as are shown by your presence here today?
In times of trial and distress, those members of the community who
demonstrate the compassion, understanding, and love of Jesus
show how all the more precious they are. No, death isn't a bad idea.

It's full of misery and despair only for those who don't understand it properly, or for whom this present life is all.

Those in the Judeo-Christian tradition already see, in God's First Testament foreshadowing of his fuller teaching, a different perspective. The Book of Wisdom, for example, from which today's first reading is taken, tells us much about the little deaths of everyday living and the final death. Today's passage, expressly on suffering, tells us that the just, who seem to have died, are really alive in God. Though the little deaths which are called sufferings in this life appear to be punishments, they aren't necessarily punishments at all, but are at some times a discipline, at other times a correction, and at still other times a testing of fidelity in which God recognizes those worthy of Him.

So the Book of Wisdom confirms daily observations that so-called "deaths" can also be full of little births. Every time we make a new friend, every time we successfully meet a new opportunity, and every time we grow into someone greater than we were before, we experience a new birth. Final death is a farewell to what we have known, and also a birth to a whole new phase of existence. And so there are many ways in which we should be grateful for it.

The Church frequently applies Wisdom's words to those who lived these beliefs in a pre-eminent way: the martyrs. They, and all with a degree of their faith and courage, live "in the hand of God" — that is, under His special protection, in hope during their earthly life, and with no torment about that time after death which is so full of mystery. In the times of God's coming to such as these, especially in His definitive intervention at the last Judgment, the Book of Wisdom's powerful and expressive images of triumph come forward: "They shall shine, and shall dart about as sparks."

Jesus made these ideas more definite. In the words just before those in today's gospel of St. John, Jesus had said that he is the bread of life. To ask "What is life?" in this context takes us beyond the merely physical into the eternal life of which Jesus speaks in today's gospel. That life is the new relationship with God which he made possible. The hunger and thirst of the human situation come to an end when we know Christ, and when through him we come to know God.

We have the opportunity to see Jesus in many ways: in the Bible, in Church teachings, and through the experiences of life. Those who are of sufficient good will come to accept him not as some distant hero, but as a close, life-giving friend. The invitation is to everybody, but we all have to overcome whatever it is in us which prevents us from making any move in Jesus' direction, beginning with the first.

St. John's first letter reminds us that those who show their potential by taking the first step are rewarded by God's gift of enabling them to become His children in a special way. God's parenthood isn't a mere paternity, responsible for the physical existence of His children, but a true fatherhood that's an intimate, loving, continuous relationship in which father and child grow closer every day. Again this idea was foreshadowed in the Jewish scriptures — in the idea of covenant, whereby God was uniquely the God of the Jews and the Jews were uniquely His people. The concept came to fruition in the Newer Covenant notion of adoption, whereby through the grace and example of Jesus Christ we can become God's children in a special and intimate way.

All these thoughts come together in the deceased John Doe. He received God's invitations to know Jesus as a friend through many graces. This led to closer contact with his Lord. He suffered many little deaths before his final one. He liked his work and had an obvious love for people, and these qualities in turn attracted people to him and provided many little births.

John Doe was a second-mile person. You remember that, when Jesus spoke of the old commandment about "an eye for an eye and a tooth for a tooth," he countered with the injunction: "Should anyone press you into service for one mile, go with him two miles." In any occupied country at that time, such as Palestine under Rome, the occupying soldiers could force citizens into service. Under military law, therefore, a Roman soldier could compel a Jew to carry his burden for a mile. That's what happened to Simon of Cyrene when he was compelled to carry Jesus' cross to Calvary.

John Doe realized that we, too, are pressed into service — not by military law, but by social life and responsibility. He realized that we, like citizens of an occupied country, can resentfully trudge the absolute minimum in grudging silence. Or, as per Jesus' invitation, we can go beyond the requirements of one mile and smilingly go two. The crown of all relationships is voluntary two-mile persons.

To everyone with whom he came in contact, he showed a graciousness that came of his being a true child of God. It's the quality that God has with us, and the oft-forgotten quality that we should have with Him and each other. One example of Jesus' graciousness was his conduct with the woman taken in adultery. Another is when after his resurrection he appeared first to Peter — Peter who had just shortly before denied him three times when Jesus needed him most. Jesus' graciousness had the qualities of all graciousness: thoughtfulness, realizing that Peter had also cried his heart out, and love, thinking more of comforting the heartbreak of one who hurt than of the hurt that the other has caused. Graciousness is warm and accepting instead of the cold and objective way in which we sometimes conduct our morality. And with us, graciousness is what makes the difference between a housewife and a mother, between a breadwinner and a father, between progeny and children.

Like the others who have passed away before him, John Doe only seems to have died, but in reality is alive in God. The faith he had in answering God's invitations in this life has passed into knowledge, and the hope he continually showed in his acceptance of many little deaths has blossomed into possession. Only his love hasn't changed substantially. It has increased: The love he showed for God through his love for so many people has ripened from bud into flower.

His becoming more and more like God as His child has resulted in his seeing God as he is. John Doe's record on this earth being now ended, we see him more completely in some senses than we can see ourselves, who are still being tested by many little deaths before our final one. We reckon him to have been a faithful and true child of his heavenly Father. Sad at his departure, we're nevertheless glad to have had him with us. The very qualities that endeared him to us make his departure no small death for us but, knowing it to be God's will, and realizing John Doe's reward, we're happy for him. We therefore join in prayer, not only for John Doe in awareness of his human shortcomings, but to the praise of God who gave him to us for a while and now gives him eternal life.

FUNERAL:
WITNESS TO THE RESURRECTION — B

Ws 4:7-14   Rm 8:14-23   Ps 23   Lk 24:13-35

See notice at Funeral "A," above.

The Truths of Faith about Death

From the very beginning, humankind has been intrigued and often mystified by death. The concept fascinates people. We realize that by thinking about death we can come to appreciate life. It's our idea of death that orders life's priorities and determines its values. It's the knowledge of death that puts much of life into perspective.

The story in today's gospel, told by that expert story-teller St. Luke, confirms this. The story is probably the greatest of the post-Easter accounts of meetings with the risen Jesus. Cleopas and his companion were disciples of Jesus — not apostles or intimate friends, but disciples, which means simply that they were followers of Jesus. This may help to explain why they didn't recognize him. They'd left Jerusalem downcast because of their disappointment that Jesus their hope had been crucified — the end of their dream, they thought.

What went wrong, they wondered. They'd stayed in Jerusalem long enough to hear some of the women's tales of an empty grave and of angels, but they didn't put much stock in that: Perhaps the women were a bit emotionally overwrought. The atmosphere in

Jerusalem was gloomy, sad, and heavy. So they took to the road, and on the way a stranger joined them. Jesus — for the stranger was he — started up a conversation with them. The stranger understood that people who are caught in their own little world of discouragement and depression don't bother to look up and out. He understood their anger, frustration, and pent-up feelings.

Jesus' inquiry into their discussion (v. 17) drew the ironical, yet exasperated, response, "Are you the only visitor to Jerusalem who does not know of the things that have taken place there in these days?" (v. 18). "What sort of things?" inquired the remarkable stranger disingenuously; the disciples revealed the false expectations they had of the Messiah. They, like us, easily became disillusioned at setbacks like death; at times like these, God Himself may seem dead.

Very soon Jesus had their full attention as he assured them that nothing had gone wrong; rather, they had been unable to see the saving hand of God in Jesus' sufferings and death, as shown in all the scriptures beginning with Moses (v. 27). An educated guess tells us that what Jesus spoke of then was the constant scriptural theme: that God reveals Himself unceasingly as the One whose characteristic work is to bring life out of death. The first scriptural note of this theme is in God's promise to Abraham that he and his wife Sarah, whose hope of bearing children had, because of old age, long since died, would receive life through a son whose descendants all peoples were to find a blessing. Because Sarah laughed at the idea, their son when he was born was named Isaac, a word play on the Hebrew verb "to laugh."

The Hebrew Scriptures continue to present the idea of God raising up the lowly, of bringing joy out of sorrow, of the vocation of Israel being a "Suffering Servant" constantly defeated and yet always raised up again by the Lord. The escape of the captive Jews from Egypt through the desert to the Holy Land contains a death-resurrection motif. The Psalms speak of the stone rejected by the builders which becomes the cornerstone, and of one who is beaten down being vindicated.

These and other stories of God bringing life out of death show common patterns: In every case, God does the unexpected, the unimaginable, and the seemingly impossible. Applied to Jesus' Resurrection, who could imagine that his tomb was empty Easter morning because the Lord had gone to a new and higher life, beyond death? Too hard to believe? Impossible? Exactly! Such deeds are characteristic of God!

When Jesus pretended he was leaving them, their now-responsive hearts begged him to stay, which he was — and is — only too willing to do. Then, as he had nourished them on the word of God in Scripture, he nourished them on the bread of life, which he is; that's how they recognized him.

Thus he left them. The disciples, renewed and invigorated, without even finishing their meal hurried back to the city. They wanted to tell their good news to the others. There, though, they found the eleven and a few companions all so strongly emotional that, before the two from Emmaus had time to speak, the Apostles insisted upon explaining their own experiences and why they were there so late. But meeting Jesus had changed the Emmaus disciples: They were willing to listen. When they got their chance, without any frustration at the delay they told their story of how Jesus appeared to them and made himself known to them in the breaking of the bread (v. 35).

Among the things the Jerusalem group told *them* was one of the greatest untold stories of the ages: that Jesus had appeared to Peter! *There* was a man brought from death to life! Peter had during Jesus' lifetime shown his participation in spiritual death on many occasions — right up to his threefold denial at the end. Now Jesus, with divine compassion, gave Peter, as he does with all repentant sinners, the chance to redeem himself in God's eyes and regain his self-respect. Peter now had the chance to know the complete Jesus — not only Jesus of the suffering and death, but of the risen life and the mystical body; not only the pain, but also the joy, the unspeakable joy, which Jesus had said should be present among his followers. That joy is a proper consequence of meeting Jesus; if joy is absent then, there's something amiss: A joyless Christian is a contradiction in terms.

Like Jesus at Emmaus, today's reading from St. Paul's major theological treatise, his letter to the Romans, one of the most beautiful passages in the Bible, also reminds us that there's a much wider vision of life and the world than comprehended at first sight. His joyful message is that all who are baptized enjoy a new relationship to God: adopted children of the heavenly Father and heirs through Christ, with a destiny of glory.

While Jesus is God's *natural* son and heir, we're God's children and heirs *through adoption*, this gift of God giving new rights, unearned love, and inherited glory. Therefore, we don't look for God only "up in heaven." One of the areas where we may expect to meet God is in the depths of our being. God told St. Catherine of Siena, "I call the soul 'heaven' because I make heaven wherever I dwell by grace." And we're privileged to call upon God with the same affectionate and intimate term that Jesus used in his moment of supreme earthly confidence in God (Mk 14:36): "Abba," "Dad!" Paul sees all of us as God's representatives in His marvelous creation, and human destiny is intricately interwoven with the world in which we live. Despite the suffering of humanity, we've received help: redemption by Jesus, and the Holy Spirit as the principle of our new life.

All these thoughts come together in the deceased Diane Smith. She, like the rest of us, was intrigued by death. In its shadow, she came to appreciate life and order its priorities. As with us, her pondering the scriptural themes of death and resurrection gave her joy. What the deceased Diane Smith now possesses, we still hope for. What the deceased Diane Smith now knows, we have only by faith. Her love hasn't changed but grown.

But the concept of death has more facets than today's Scripture readings. Even in the Church, where we would naturally go for answers to the ultimate questions of life and death, there are varying emphases. Not too long ago, at funerals the priest wore black vestments as a sign of sadness over the loss of a loved one, the choir roared "Dies irae, dies illa" — "Day of Wrath" — to remind everyone of the terrors of the last judgment, and the entire liturgy centered around the misery connected with death. And these ideas are all correct and true.

Today, we've grown somewhat from that rather self-centered approach into other emphases which are equally true. The priest wears white vestments as a sign of joy over our having had the opportunity to appreciate the life of the deceased and the blessing of having had the chance to love her unique goodness, which God also loves. We place the resurrection candle at the coffin to remind us that death isn't the end of life, but only a change in the manner of life, and that we too shall rise again — just as Jesus did in the ultimate triumph of his resurrection over sin and death. We light that candle also to remind us that Jesus is the light of our life. And we reflect on the many selections from the Bible that remind us of these optimistic aspects of death. No matter what the selection, we're reminded that God loves us, and rooted in that love is His mercy.

On that mercy all of us, as well as the deceased, Diane Smith, rely. We live in the shadow of what the deceased Diane Smith has gone through. Like her, we won't find true immortality in the ways in which the world seeks it. We may find it in this world only indirectly, inasmuch as one who first seeks God's justice may have all these things added besides. But true immortality comes only from hearing the word of God and keeping it, and relying on God's mercy to enable us to live with Him in heaven forever.

FUNERAL:
WITNESS TO THE RESURRECTION — C

Ws 2:23-3:9 or Is 25:6a, 7-9	*Rm 14:7-9, 10b-12*
Responsorial Psalm	*27:1, 4, 7, 9, 13-14*
Verse before the Gospel: *Jn 3:16*	*Jn 14:1-6*
See notice at Funeral "A," above	

For the Christian, the End Is but the Beginning

Many have died, and many still live, on this tiny planet at the edge of the universe, not knowing where they came from, why they're here, or whence they might go forth. And still they laugh, and cry, and feel, and love. We Christians are different: We too laugh, and cry, and feel, and love, but we have a firm belief in certain answers to the ultimate questions. Our belief doesn't only involve our head, the way some moderns mean it, but goes to the language of the Bible.

That means that belief for us involves an alignment of the heart, a commitment of loyalty and trust. The Latin *credo*, "I believe," is from *cor*, "heart," as in the English "cordial"; from the closely parallel Greek *kardia* comes such English derivatives as "cardiac." The root meaning of the words is "I set my heart on," "I give my heart to." So belief is an action word. To say "I believe" means "I commit myself, I rest my heart upon, I pledge allegiance to." It means that I do what Jesus and his Church expect of me.

With regard to death, we believe that in it life is changed, not ended (Preface on Christian Death, I). Even in the darkest times, we believe that there is a purpose in life, and that that purpose has to do somehow with love. We believe that God is as Jesus taught him to be, and that in Jesus we see God; in the face of God's love we find even the unbearable becoming bearable, and it then becomes, not easy, but possible, to live through the storms of life, to accept what we can't understand. A philosopher (Kierkegaard) has said that life can only be understood backwards, but it must be lived forwards. We agree.

Those beliefs increase our laughter, diminish the anguish of our cries, heighten our feelings, and deepen our loving. The highest tribute we can pay to the dead is not grief over our loss, but gratitude for their having been, and joy that the sadness of death gives way to the bright promise of immortality (Preface on Christian Death, I).

For the disciples, the Last Supper was a time when in a short while their world was going to collapse and the roof of their life was going to fall in. At such a time, there's only one thing to do: cling to trust in God (Ps 27:13; Responsorial Psalm). That's what Jesus said in the beginning of one of his most profound discourses in St. John's gospel: "You have faith in God; have faith also in me" (v. 1). (Jesus never hesitated to put himself on the same level with the Father in the work of salvation.) Faith in both is the condition of Christians in this world.

Jesus reminds us that in his Father's house there are many dwelling places (v. 2). The Father's house is wherever God is. It is, for example, the heavenly Kingdom to which Jesus was now returning. The house of God is also one of St. Paul's favorite metaphors for the Church. In the present context, the "many dwelling places" of the Father's house may therefore refer to the many members of the Church on earth, in whom also Christ is present.

As for heaven, Jesus says, "I go and prepare a place for you" (v. 3) — his final reassurance that his departure is in order that we may be together forever. Jesus, here and always, goes on in front for us to follow: he chose to die that he might free all men from dying (Preface on Christian Death, II), and in him the world is saved, humanity is reborn, and the dead rise again to life (Preface on Christian Death, III). He shall return in a second coming to each of us, an invisible return through the Spirit, so that, as he said, where he is we also may be.

For the Christian, heaven is where Jesus is. There is no need to speculate about what heaven will be like: It's enough to know that we shall be forever with him. When we love anyone with all our hearts, life begins when we're together with the other; as the poet says, "I love you, not only for what you are, but for what I am when

I am with you." It's only in the company of those we love and who love us that we become our complete selves, and fully alive. That dance of creation of self implies a moving toward, not necessarily an arrival. It's a continual becoming, not a final accomplishment.

Jesus continues that where he's going we know the way (v. 4). The way is his sacrificial death, the model that all must copy who would follow him. Again and again Jesus told his disciples where he was going, but for a long time they didn't get the point. Thomas, reflecting the other disciples, shows how little they even yet understand. They show themselves to be as obtuse as Jesus' opponents; what saves them, though, is their good will — their love. Thomas, for instance, was too honest ever to say he understood what he didn't understand. Neither Thomas, nor anyone else, need ever be ashamed of their searchings. It's literally true that he who seeks will in the end find.

The deceased Mary Jones was, like the apostles, a practical person. She was a woman with a broom or a dustpan or a washrag in her hand in place of an apostle's fishing net. When she was able, she went through the house with a vacuum cleaner or soap, making things as spic and span as she could. In her day she also washed ceilings, walls, curtains, windows, and children. She pounded nails and repaired furniture. She kept a watchful inventory over the home and shopped for the best bargains. Though her joy in life was measurably lessened in her widowhood, she took pride in her children and liked to learn from them. She was attracted to down-to-earth homilies and those who gave them, and would probably have her doubts about this one.

Thomas' question gave Jesus the opportunity to utter one of his supreme statements, which puts into one sentence the most fundamental ideas of the entire New Testament: "I am the way and the truth and the life" (v. 6). This is a great saying, especially when Jesus spoke it for the first time. The Jews had often spoken about the *way*: God to Moses (Dt 5:32f.), Moses to the people (Dt 31:29), the Lord alone as Israel's and Judah's salvation (Is 30:21), the Psalmists (Ps 27:11 — today's Responsorial Psalm), and so on. Like the sheepgate to which Jesus had compared himself, he's the only way.

He's the mediator between God and people. Unlike the person on the street who only gives us directions, he *takes* us there.

Jesus is the *truth*, because he's the revelation of truth in both word and person. The character of one who teaches academic or scientific truth doesn't make much difference to his subject. But the character of one who teaches *moral* truth makes a big difference. He can't convey it only in words: His example is most important. Jesus is the exemplar *par excellence*: the model, the avatar. And Jesus is the *life*. In the final analysis, what people are seeking is always life. Only, they don't always know where to find it. Jesus is the *source* of life: spiritual life, *true* life. Life with him is life worth living.

In his letter to the Romans, St. Paul tells us that, as a result of Jesus' life and teachings, "None of us lives for oneself" (v. 7). It is, in fact, utterly impossible for anyone to live a completely isolated life, even with the confinement of increased age. None of us is completely self-contained; everyone is a link in a chain. Everyone is, for example, the inheritor of a tradition. Mary Jones, for instance, was the product of what her forebears made her. She made something of that, it's true, but she didn't start with nothing. Her mother and her father, for whom she had a great affection, had a profound influence that stayed with her even into her old age.

And Mary Jones, like all of us, is an influence upon, and is influenced by, others — especially in this ever smaller and smaller world. For Mary, this was mainly through the only place where in her older life she met people: at church. And everyone hands life on — to one's children, to one's grandchildren, and to an entire younger generation.

All of this is still more true of the faithful individual with Jesus. Jesus is forever a living presence which isn't broken even by death: "whether we live or die, we are the Lord's" (v. 8). We belong to and must acknowledge our relationship to the Risen Christ as *Kyrios*, "Lord." He is "Lord of both the dead and the living" (v. 9). Sovereignty over the dead and the living became his with Jesus' redemptive passion and exaltation, and with finality at his Resurrection. The Christian who through baptism shares in the redemption of Christ will eventually enjoy the glory of the Risen Lord.

Because Jesus underwent his passion, death, and resurrection for all people, to enable us to live for God, no one can judge others, whether they appear weak or strong: "We shall all stand before the judgment seat of God" (v. 10). That's the situation in which every person is most isolated: when he stands in judgment before God. Naked we came into the world, and naked we leave it (Jb 1:21). But we stand with Jesus. If we have lived with him in life, we shall be with him in death. And he will plead our cause.

DEATH OF A CHILD
Is 25:7-9   *Ep 1:3-6*   *Mk 10:13-16*

> In this talk, one is going to have to use imagination, creativity, and resourcefulness more than with the others. Children die in the womb, at birth, and at all ages. They die from many causes: miscarriage, stillbirth, sudden infant death syndrome, accident, cancer, leukemia, and a host of other diseases. No one talk can cover all of them.

In the face of death, all human wisdom fails. The death of a child is perhaps the ultimate shock. One of the most disturbing issues to deal with is the *wrongness* of the child's death, because the natural order is for parents to precede their child in death. Nothing and no one can remedy the loss.

One thing that should never be said when someone dies is, "It's the will of God." Never do we know enough to say that. The consolation of mourners lies in knowing that it was *not* the will of God that Joan died, that when the end came in whatever way, God's was the first of all hearts to break. I as God's minister don't have to answer for or defend God. Platitudes and "God talk" are unnecessary. God is big enough to withstand feelings of anger and frustration, and still love the people expressing those feelings.

Those who loved Joan are seriously affected by the absence of what she represented to us. To you, her parents, especially, she represented many things. She was *part of your self, part of your physical body*. You consider Joan's physical characteristics and focus particularly on those which bear resemblance to you. She was *your connection to the future*. Your personal continuity was embodied in Joan. You were bound together and moving forward into the upcoming years. She was your *love source*. No other source of love is the same as your child's love for you. She loved you with naivetè, tenderness, determination, joy, and perhaps even humor.

She had *some of your own treasured qualities and talents*. These attributes may even have seemed to be magnified and more highly developed in Joan. In your loss, you have *missed expectations*. The promised years of Joan's daily life and activities are thrown away. It's as if these years had been allotted to you and Joan, and then were suddenly retrieved.

You feel impotent. There doesn't seem to be any "fight" left in you, no strength for the most ordinary of tasks, and no mental capacity for, nor interest in, complex thinking. And you may have guilt feelings: You may have felt that Joan's death was an indirect punishment to you for some past behavior for which you feel ashamed or guilty. But you must consider that what you perceive may not necessarily be accurate. Be aware that you're not only punishing yourself for what you couldn't do, you're punishing yourself for what no one on this earth could do. Be aware that the grieving process is an emotional roller-coaster.

You of Joan's family must remember that you have sources of support in friends, relatives, and understanding neighbors. While everyone understands your grief, realize that *complete* withdrawal from others during this time often retards the grieving process. Your friends, relatives, and understanding neighbors, like parents with each other, should be attentive listeners who listen beyond words. Don't mask your feelings with one another or with them.

Then, too, the Lord teaches us, by his rising from the three days he spent in the tomb, that death has no hold over us. Trusting in Jesus, the loving savior, who gathered children into his arms and blessed the little ones, even in our sorrow for the loss of Joan we believe that, one short sleep past, she shall wake eternally.

And let's never forget that God understands. Remember the love he had for children: People were bringing children to Jesus that he might touch them and, when the Apostles objected, he rebuked them. And always, we have Our Lady of Sorrows who grieved the loss of her son, too. When an offspring dies after having been around long enough to be known and loved, and to be loving in return, it's that much harder.

Imagine, if you will, Joan being here now, to witness what's going on. Children die with softness. Their little hearts open wide. There's the letting go of the past that helps in not being so afraid and knowing that the present is the only time there is. There's the joy, release, and excitement of sharing moments together. There's the ability to be open in the midst of uncontrollable unknowns — open to the moment of death. The death of a child is often a teacher of unconditional love.

Let's never forget Joan. Commemorate her at special times. Plan a small private celebration for her birthday, show her picture, and share memories. Positive activity can turn a dreaded day into an observance of her worth, and can be a "thank-you" for her having lived.

May the God of all consolation bring us comfort and peace. We may find some support in the lines that the unknown poet put into the mouth of God upon the death of a child:

"I'll lend you, for a little while, a child of mine," he said,
"For you to love while he lives, and mourn when he is dead.
It may be six or seven years, or twenty-two, or three.
But will you, 'til I call him back, take care of him for me?
He'll bring his charms to gladden you, and shall his stay be brief,
You'll have his lovely memories as solace for your grief.
I cannot promise he will stay, as all from earth return,
But there are lessons taught down there I want this child to learn.
I've looked the wide world over in my search for teachers true,
And from the throngs that crowd life's lanes, I have selected you.
Now will you give him all your love — not think the labor vain,

Nor hate me when I come to call to take him back again."
I fancied that I heard them say, "Dear Lord, thy will be done.
For all the joy this child shall bring, the risk of grief we'll run.
We'll shower him with tenderness and love him while we may,
And for the happiness we've known, forever grateful stay.
And should the angels call for him much sooner than we planned,
We'll brave the bitter grief that comes, and try to understand."